Sex Rights

Nicholas Bamforth is a University Lecturer in Law at Oxford University and a Fellow of The Queen's College. He is the author of *Sexuality, Morals and Justice* (1997) and editor of *Public Law in a Multi-layered Constitution* (2003).

Sex Rights

The Oxford Amnesty Lectures 2002

Edited by

Nicholas Bamforth

OXFORD
UNIVERSITY PRESS

OXFORD

UNIVERSITY PRESS

Great Clarendon Street, Oxford OX2 6DP

Oxford University Press is a department of the University of Oxford.
It furthers the University's objective of excellence in research, scholarship,
and education by publishing worldwide in

Oxford New York

Auckland Cape Town Dar es Salaam Hong Kong Karachi
Kuala Lumpur Madrid Melbourne Mexico City Nairobi
New Delhi Shanghai Taipei Toronto

With offices in

Argentina Austria Brazil Chile Czech Republic France Greece
Guatemala Hungary Italy Japan South Korea Poland Portugal
Singapore Switzerland Thailand Turkey Ukraine Vietnam

Oxford is a registered trade mark of Oxford University Press
in the UK and in certain other countries

Published in the United States
by Oxford University Press Inc., New York

British Library Cataloguing in Publication Data

Data available

Library of Congress Cataloging in Publication Data

Data available

ISBN 0–19–280561–4

1

Typeset in Bembo and Univers
by RefineCatch Limited, Bungay, Suffolk
Printed in Great Britain by
Clays Ltd., St. Ives plc

Contents

Contributors

NICHOLAS BAMFORTH is a University Lecturer in Law at Oxford University and a Fellow of The Queen's College. He is the author of *Sexuality, Morals and Justice* (1997) and editor of *Public Law in a Multi-layered Constitution* (2003).

MALCOLM BOWIE is Master of Christ's College, Cambridge. He was previously Marshal Foch Professor of French Literature at Oxford University and a Fellow of All Souls College. His books include *Mallarme and the Art of being Difficult* (1978), *Freud, Proust and Lacan: Theory as Fiction* (1987), *Lacan* (1991), *Psychoanalysis and the Future of Theory* (1993) and *Proust among the Stars* (1998), together with the jointly written *A Short History of French Literature* (2003).

JUDITH BUTLER is Maxine Elliot Professor in the Departments of Rhetoric, Comparative Literature and Women's Studies at the University of California at Berkeley. She is the author of *Subjects of Desire* (1987), *Gender Trouble* (1990), *Bodies that Matter* (1993), *Excitable Speech* (1997), *The Psychic Life of Power* (1997), *Antigone's Claim* (2000), *Precarious Life: The Powers of Violence and Mourning* (2004) and *Undoing Gender* (2004).

ROY FOSTER is Carroll Professor of Irish History at Oxford University and a Fellow of Hertford College. He is the author of *Modern Ireland, 1600–1972* (1990), *Paddy and Mr. Punch: Connections in Irish and English History* (1996), *The Irish Story: Telling Tales and Making It Up in Ireland* (2001) and the two-volume biography *W.B. Yeats: A Life* (1997 and 2003).

ROSE GEORGE is a writer based in London. Her work has appeared in the *Independent on Sunday*, *Guardian*, *Sunday Telegraph* and other publications. She is the author of *A Life Removed: Hunting for Refuge in a Modern World* (2004).

MICHÈLE LE DOEUFF is Director of Research at the National Centre for Scientific Research in Paris. Her books include *Hipparchia's Choice* (trans. 1991), *The Philosophical Imaginary* (trans. 2002) and *The Sex of Knowing* (trans. 2003).

CHRISTOPHER McCRUDDEN is Professor of Human Rights Law at Oxford University and a Fellow of Lincoln College. He is the editor of *Regulation and Public Law* (1987), *Anti-discrimination Law* (1991), *Individual Rights and the Law in Britain* (1994) and *Regulation and Deregulation* (1999).

DAVID MILLER is Professor of Political Theory at Oxford University and a Fellow of Nuffield College. He is the author of *Social Justice* (1976), *Market, State, and Community* (1989), *On Nationality* (1995), *Principles of Social Justice* (1999) and *Citizenship and National Identity* (2000), and editor of *Liberty* (1991) and *Pluralism, Justice, and Equality* (1995).

SUSAN MOLLER OKIN was, until her death in 2004, Marta Sutton Weeks Professor of Ethics in Society at Stanford University. She was the author of *Women in Western Political Thought* (1979), *Justice, Gender and the Family* (1991) and *Is Multiculturalism Bad for Women?* (1999), and was editor of *Feminism* (1994).

CHRISTOPHER ROBINSON is Emeritus Professor of European Literature at Oxford University and an Emeritus Student of Christ Church. His books include *Lucian and his Influence in Europe* (1979), *C.P. Cavafy* (1988) and *Scandal in the Ink:*

Male and Female Homosexuality in Twentieth Century French Literature (1995).

ALAN SINFIELD is Professor of English at Sussex University. His books include *Faultlines: Cultural Materialism and the Politics of Dissident Reading* (1992), *The Wilde Century* (1994), *Cultural Politics—Queer Reading* (1994), *Gay and After* (1998), *Out on Stage* (1999) and *On Sexuality and Power* (2004).

RAJESWARI SUNDER RAJAN is Reader in English at Oxford University and a Fellow of Wolfson College. She is the author of *Real and Imagined Women* (1993) and *The Scandal of the State* (2003).

MARINA WARNER is a writer. Her books include *Alone of All Her Sex* (1976), *Joan of Arc* (1981), *Monuments and Maidens* (1985), *From the Beast to the Blonde* (1994), *Managing Monsters* (1994, based on her Reith Lectures), *No Go the Bogeyman* (1998), and *Fantastic Metamorphoses, Other Worlds* (2002). She has also published fiction, including *Indigo* (1994) and *The Leto Bundle* (2002).

ROBERT WINTEMUTE is Professor of Human Rights Law at King's College London. He is the author of *Sexual Orientation and Human Rights* (1997) and editor of *Legal Recognition of Same-sex Partnerships* (2001).

Acknowledgements

This volume contains revised versions of five of the six lectures given as part of the 2002 Oxford Amnesty Lectures series. In addition, two chapters—those by Rose George and Rajeswari Sunder Rajan—were specially commissioned for this volume. Jeanette Winterson, who delivered the sixth lecture, did not submit a written version. I should like to thank each lecturer (or chapter writer) for their contribution. Perhaps the most heartening aspect of the Oxford Amnesty Lectures is the extent to which distinguished and busy people are willing to take the time to prepare, deliver (often after a lengthy journey) and revise a lecture—or to prepare and revise a chapter—in the cause of human rights. Each lecture was kindly introduced by a faculty member from Oxford University, and a revised version of each introduction appears here (apart from Dr Carolyne Larrington's introduction to Winterson's lecture). For the present volume, Michèle Le Doeuff has kindly prepared an extended introduction to Rose George's chapter. I should like to thank each introduction writer (or giver) for their excellent contribution.

Various other people and institutions have played an immensely helpful role in the organization of the lecture series and in the production of this volume. The staff of Oxford's Sheldonian Theatre (where the Amnesty Lectures are delivered) lived up to their usual high standards of efficiency. Many students and Amnesty volunteers were good enough to act as marshals at the lectures. The Governing Body of The Queen's College, Oxford, kindly gave financial and administrative support. During the editing process, helpful comments, references or suggestions were provided by John Davies, Alison Fell, Brian MacDonnell, Maleiha Malik, David Richards, Zvi Triger, Nicholas Turner and Daniel Wakelin. Marsha Filion at Oxford University Press has been an outstanding in-house editor, ever-ready with helpful advice. The Committee of the Oxford Amnesty Lectures put in countless hours of work in order to make the lectures happen, and has served as a very useful sounding-board during the production of this volume. At the time of the 2002 series, the Committee consisted of: Tim Chesters, John Gardner, Chris Miller, Nicholas Owen, Fabienne Pagnier, Deana Rankin, Richard Scholar, Stephen Shute, Kate Tunstall and Wes Williams. Special thanks are also owed, dating to the time of the lecture series, to Ely Gutierrez Athron.

An element of real sadness has accompanied the final stages of work on this volume, given the tragic death of Susan Moller Okin—author of Chapter 2—in March 2004. Susan was one of the most distinguished philosophers of her time and a brilliant pioneer in the development of feminist approaches to political philosophy. On a personal level, she was also someone whose grace and concern for others made an important difference to everyone around her. She is and will continue to be greatly missed.

The bulk of the editorial work has been carried out while I have been on sabbatical leave at New York University. It is perhaps fitting that this should have been so: for I write these comments while sitting a few blocks from Christopher Street, Greenwich Village—the birthplace, in modern times, of gay resistance to homophobic oppression.

Nicholas Bamforth

New York City, 15 June 2004

Introduction

Nicholas Bamforth

The subject matter of this volume of essays—based on the 2002 series of Oxford Amnesty Lectures—is gender, sexuality and human rights. That issues of gender and sexuality fall squarely within the concern of international and national human rights law cannot be doubted. Discrimination on the basis of sexual orientation is, like sex discrimination, now recognized as being prohibited under the prevailing human rights instruments in Western Europe and Canada, as well as under the International Covenant on Civil and Political Rights.[1] In the USA, measures which discriminate on the basis of sex are open to judicial review under the Fourteenth Amendment's 'heightened scrutiny' standard.[2] US law has lagged behind somewhat in relation to sexual orientation, but a major breakthrough has been achieved in the Supreme Court's rulings that it is contrary to the Fourteenth Amendment to criminalize consensual sex acts between two persons of the same sex, and that laws which are motivated by 'animus' towards members of sexual minority groups cannot withstand scrutiny.[3] At a deeper level, however, it is less readily apparent how we should understand and categorize human rights violations based on sex and sexual orientation. Are they, for example, two separate types of discriminatory social practice, or should we see them as examples of a common phenomenon? Does their inclusion within the remit of human rights abuses require us to refine what we mean by human rights?

And what weight should we attach to the dictates of general human rights norms *by contrast with* demands made in the name of particular religious and cultural traditions which appear to restrict the rights of women and sexual minority groups?

Amnesty International has thought seriously about these questions in three major Reports: *Crimes of Hate, Conspiracy of Silence: Torture and Ill-treatment Based on Sexual Identity* (2001)[4] concerned lesbians, gay men, bisexuals, transsexuals and trans-gendered individuals (referred to hereafter as 'sexual minor-ities' or 'LGBT people'), while *Broken Bodies, Shattered Minds: Torture and Ill-treatment of Women* (2001)[5] and *It's In Our Hands: Stop Violence Against Women* (2004)[6] considered the position of women. The Reports cite a seemingly endless array of examples of horrific violence and ill-treatment. *Crimes of Hate* begins with the story of five people who were detained by the Ugandan police after forming a lesbian and gay human rights group. They were variously beaten and raped. Christine, one of the five, was asked repeatedly why she was not married, and told that homosexuality was taboo in Africa. On learning that her friend Rodney was gay, soldiers tortured him by repeat-edly kicking him in the stomach and slapping him in the face, after which he was made to sleep in a toilet which he was forced on a daily basis to clean using his hands.[7] In Romania (where homosexual acts have since been decriminalized) two 17-year-old males were arrested in a park and severely beaten in order to force them to confess to having sex with one another. The interrogators appeared intrigued to find out which of the two was the 'girl' and which was the 'boy'.[8] In the Bahamas, two 17-year-old males arrested on suspicion of having sex were forced to strip and were then beaten with an iron bar. They were subjected to homophobic insults, forced to stand naked at the police station, and refused access to a lawyer or to their families.[9] *Broken Bodies* and *It's In Our Hands* contain many similar stories. Zeynep Avci, detained by the Turkish police, was subjected to electric shocks, anally raped using a truncheon, and vaginally raped by a policeman.[10] Kajal Khidr was detained by her husband's relatives in Iraqi Kurdistan. Having accused her of engaging in extramarital sex, they cut off her nose and threatened to kill her.[11] 'K', a woman from the Democratic Republic of the Congo, was married to an army officer who regularly beat and kicked her. He also raped her—infecting her with sexually transmitted diseases—and threatened to kill her. One beating involved the knocking out of a tooth, the dislocation of the jaw, and a punch in the eye which was so hard that it gave rise to continual problems with her nose, neck, head, spinal column, hip and foot.[12] After a fire began in a school in Mecca in March 2002, fifteen female students were burned to death and dozens of others were injured after religious police prevented them from leaving the burning building because they were not wearing headscarves and had no male relatives present to receive them.[13]

These stories are only a small cross-section of the examples presented in the three Reports. Apart from the sheer intensity of the violence described, what is striking is that a number of closely analogous factors—five in total—emerge from the analyses articulated in the Reports. First, and most importantly, the three Reports are clear that the acts of violence which they highlight are intimately related to social conceptions of gender and of appropriate gender roles. There are two interconnected aspects to this point. First, many acts of violence committed against women appear to be committed because the victims—as women—are perceived to be 'rightfully' subject to the command of men. *Broken Bodies* thus identifies 'discrimination against women, the denial of basic human rights to individuals simply because they are women' as the 'common thread' running through the examples it presents of physical violence, rape and other sexual violence, forced marriage, and enforced female circumcision.[14] As *It's In Our Hands* goes on to suggest, 'Violence against women is an expression of historically and culturally specific values and standards.'[15] Second, women and sexual minorities are beaten, raped, imprisoned and murdered when their behaviour is perceived to defy socially enforced gender roles. *Broken Bodies* highlights examples of women who are abused because they are assertive or refuse to act in the way which is deemed 'appropriate' for their sex: a classic instance being because a woman has acted in a way that defies socially imposed codes of 'honour' which reflect the 'treatment of women as commodities—the property of male relatives'.[16] *It's In Our Hands* talks of 'society's fear of independent women, the false presumption that women who have acquired a degree of economic independence are sexually autonomous', and notes 'how easily such fears can erupt in violence'.[17] Meanwhile, *Crimes of Hate* is clear that 'Defiance of the "heterosexual norm" can provoke moral condemnation, exclusion and violence, including torture. In this sense, violence against LGBT people is gender-based violence, inflicted on those who challenge or fail to conform to traditionally defined gender roles.'[18] Indeed, it might be said that LGBT people *by definition* violate socially prescribed gender norms by failing to engage in sexual practices which are viewed as 'appropriate' to their sex. What the Reports would seem to be suggesting is that we are in fact dealing with different instances of a common phenomenon—the social enforcement of gender-related

norms and the 'punishment' of those who violate them—
rather than readily distinguishable social practices.[19] This is
clearly implicit in an observation—cited in *Crimes of Hate*—
by the UN Special Rapporteur on violence against women:

A woman who is perceived to be acting in a manner deemed to be
sexually inappropriate by communal standards is liable to be punished. . . . Women who choose options which are disapproved of by
the community, whether to have a sexual relationship with a man in
a non-marital relationship, to have such a relationship outside of
ethnic, religious or class communities, or to live out their sexuality
in ways other than heterosexuality, are often subjected to violence
and degrading treatment.[20]

This conclusion is reinforced by the second analogous factor
in the three Reports, which is that the violence inflicted on
women and sexual minorities often has a strongly sexual
dimension. The Reports make clear that '[m]ost abuses committed against women in armed conflicts involve the use of
sexual violence',[21] that a 'significant amount of violence
against women takes a sexualised form',[22] that in many countries 'acts of sexual violence by government agents are a
common method of torture or inhuman treatment inflicted
on women',[23] that 'Lesbians and other women who are seen
to transgress gender boundaries are often at heightened risk of
torture and ill-treatment',[24] and that 'Lesbian and gay
prisoners are at heightened risk of sexual violence in custody.
Many are subjected to persistent sexual harassment. Some are
victims of sexual assault, including rape.'[25] The fact that the
Reports identify rape as a common element of torture
inflicted on women, gay men, and transgendered and transsexual persons is surely no coincidence: for rape might be seen
as the ultimate acting out of the 'dominant' sexual role of

the heterosexual man, and thus as a classic weapon for the enforcement of gender norms against all women (and especially 'rebellious' women, whether straight or lesbian) and for putting men who depart from 'normal' sex roles in their place.

This is not just a theoretical argument. In fact, it is reflected in many of the horrific examples of rape or sexual molestation which are discussed in the Reports. *Crimes of Hate*, for example, tells the story of Irina, a Russian lesbian, who complained to the police about attempts to blackmail her because of her sexual orientation. The investigators responded by taking her at knife-point to an apartment where she was raped (by more than one man) to 'teach her a lesson' and to 'reorientate' her sexual orientation.[26] In the USA, Timothy Tucker, a gay and HIV positive prison inmate, was raped by another inmate; the guards responded by asking him whether he had learned his lesson, and by suggesting that since he was gay he ought to have enjoyed the experience.[27] In the (former) Federal Republic of Yugoslavia, Bojan Aleksov, a gay man, was detained by the state security service. Having been severely beaten and abused because he was 'queer', the interrogators threatened to ram a large car key up his anus.[28] After Katya Ivanova, another Russian lesbian, complained to the police about homophobic harassment by her neighbours, she was repeatedly raped by the police officer who was allegedly investigating her case.[29] In Chicago, USA, Frederick Mason was arrested after arguing with his landlord. At the police station, the arresting officer reportedly pulled down his trousers before ramming a baton covered in cleaning liquid into his rectum.[30] In Uganda, Norah, one of the five people detained by police after forming a gay and lesbian human rights group, was stripped by her interrogators and told that she should be punished for denying men what was 'rightfully theirs'. The interrogators then suggested that they would show her 'what she was missing' as a lesbian by taking turns to rape her.[31] *It's In Our Hands* documents the story of a young Zimbabwean lesbian whose family locked her up and forced her to submit to repeated rapes by an older man in order to 'correct' her sexual orientation. According to the victim, 'They locked me in a room and brought him every day to rape me so I would fall pregnant and be forced to marry him. They did this to me until I was pregnant.'[32] What stands out from all of these examples is that sexualised violence is seen to be an 'appropriate' response to those who defy socially dominant gender norms.

It is with this in mind that we must consider one distinction which *does* appear to be drawn in *Broken Bodies* between the ill-treatment of women and of sexual minorities. The Report points out that 'Violence against women is *compounded by* discrimination on grounds of race, ethnicity, sexual orientation, social status, class and age. Such multiple discrimination *further* restricts women's choices, increases their vulnerability to violence and makes it even harder for them to gain redress.'[33] Read literally, this statement must be correct: women (for example, lesbians) who violate social norms by adopting unconventional gender roles can be subject to violent attack, discrimination in the workplace and so on, not only because they are women but also because they are women who defy such norms. As some of the examples listed in the preceding paragraph might be felt to illustrate, each of the two interrelated aspects discussed above—that is, the devaluation of women as women, and ill-treatment for norm-defiance—is in play. It would therefore be an over-simplification—and one which disadvantaged those who are subject to multiple grounds of discrimination—to fail to acknowledge this point. But this, in turn, is no reason for failing to acknowledge that a common phenomenon—the enforcement of gender-based social norms—is the crucial underpinning factor. Indeed, we would lose sight of the important analogies drawn in the three Reports if we failed to do this.

A third analogous factor is that many countries seek to justify violence against women and sexual minorities *by reference to* local gender norms allegedly deriving from religions or cultural practices.[34] As *Broken Bodies* notes, the 'subordination of women to men is still widely accepted in all cultures, even by women, and presumed to be authorised by [the] "natural order", religion or tradition'.[35] In similar vein, *Crimes of Hate* observes that 'the repression that LGBT people face is often openly and passionately defended in the name of culture, religion, morality or public health'.[36] More strongly, *It's In Our Hands* notes that while women's groups have made 'enormous strides in the fight for equality and freedom from discrimination and violence' in the past twenty years,

cultural, religious and ethnic movements in many parts of the world have made organized efforts to reverse this progress and to reassert apparently traditional roles. These movements often justify or excuse violence against women in the name of religion, culture, custom and tradition. . . . Those advocating an extreme interpretation [of the religion, culture, etc., concerned] often justify or excuse violence against women in the name of maintaining social or religious values.[37]

The extent to which human rights considerations should pay deference to local cultural mores proclaimed by national governments is thus a constantly recurring theme when considering human rights abuses based on sex and sexual orientation.

The fourth analogous factor is that the laws of many countries appear to play a role in justifying violence against sexual minorities and women, while state agents—particularly the police—play an active part in inflicting it. *Crimes of Hate* draws our attention to the large number of countries in which same-sex sexual acts (especially between men) remain illegal, and suggests that there is a clear connection between the existence of such laws and the ill-treatment of sexual minority groups.[38] For the basic criminalization of same-sex sexual acts is often seen as lending a justification—culturally and some-times even legally—to those who would inflict violence on sexual minority groups. *Crimes of Hate* bluntly states that by 'institutionalizing discrimination', such laws 'can act as an official incitement to violence against LGBT people in the community as a whole, whether in custody, in prison, on the street or in the home'.[39] Relevant laws appear to be 'seen by law enforcement officials as a licence to ill-treat people believed to be homosexual'.[40] Furthermore, *Broken Bodies* highlights the inadequacy of laws concerning rape, forced marriage and trafficking in women in many societies—a fail-ure of concern on the part of the state which might be felt to underline the second-class status of women in the societies concerned.[41] As *It's In Our Hands* puts it, there are 'flaws in the legal framework of some countries which contribute to impunity' for acts of violence and discrimination against women.[42] This is compounded by the fact that, in their enforcement of the law, the police and courts frequently fail to take seriously complaints concerning violence against women (or sexual minorities).[43]

A final analogy is that all three Reports suggest that while the traditional concern of human rights law has been with the behaviour of the state, it is clear—presumably due to the connection between the violence we have discussed and local norms concerning 'appropriate' gender roles—that violence inflicted by agents of the state is just part of a broader continuum: for much of the violence inflicted against women and sexual minorities is inflicted by private actors, often within the home.[44] *It's In Our Hands* also draws attention to the role played by socially powerful 'private' mechanisms, such as religious courts and clan structures, in reinforcing a discriminatory social order.[45] *Broken Bodies* therefore suggests that the women's movement, by calling attention to the role of private actors, has helped to facilitate the acceptance of a wider view of the ambit of human rights in the sense that the state—by failing to intervene to protect women—can now be held accountable in some circumstances for human rights violations by private individuals, instead of being liable only for acts of violence which it has itself inflicted.[46] *Crimes of Hate* makes a similar point about state accountability, implying (without explicitly stating) that an equivalent view now applies when considering violence against sexual minorities.[47]

Despite Amnesty International's commitment—expressed in its Reports—to fighting human rights abuses based on sex and sexual orientation, it was only comparatively recently that the organization decided to categorize such abuses as *human rights* abuses (rather than examples of ordinary criminal or other wrongdoing). Some people might oppose this development on the basis that the term 'human rights' should be taken to mean the type of liberal political rights—to vote, to express oneself, to engage in public protest, not to be tortured into divulging information to state authorities, and so on— that are traditionally associated with the public sphere. On this view, abuses related to sex and sexual orientation ought not to be seen as abuses of a person's *human* rights.

In order to explain why Amnesty International's current position is correct, three arguments may be used. The first relates to the legal protections against discrimination (discussed above) which are now offered by national and international human rights codes. This argument is straightforward. Given that so much of international human rights campaigning work is focused on securing legal protection for people who would otherwise be disadvantaged or persecuted, it seems curiously short-sighted to say that we must ignore the drafting and case law of the many significant human rights instruments which say that the right not to be unjustly discriminated against is an important human right, and that acts of sex and sexual orientation discrimination violate that right. However, this is precisely what we would have to do if we were to say that we are not concerned with human rights abuses in this area. In fact, we would have to say that the courts which interpret the relevant human rights instruments have all been making a serious mistake when dealing with sex and sexual orientation, and that their definition of human rights should be less generous in scope: a heavy argument for anyone who would call themselves a defender of human rights to have to develop.

The second argument is of a more theoretical nature, and focuses on why we believe human rights are important. At a quite fundamental level, the things we think about as human rights might generally be said to reflect the basic components of what we regard as a dignified and autonomous life. It is unlikely that in practice most people will actually be forced to call into play all of their human rights: for example, only a small minority of people choose to stand for election or to attend political demonstrations, or seek to write newspaper articles or books. Whether or not we actually do (or try to do) such things, however, our dignity would be adversely and unjustly affected if we were forcibly stopped from doing (or trying to do) any of them. In consequence, the right to freedom of expression is generally deemed to be an important human right. In similar vein, in a generally law-abiding state, most people will not be arrested, questioned by the police or put on trial. But this does not diminish the importance for *anyone* of the existence of human rights-based protection against arbitrary arrest, 'confessions' extracted through torture or unfair trials: for our basic dignity again demands that we should not be subjected to such things. An analogous point may be made about discrimination due to sex and sexual orientation. Having the right to say no to unwanted sexual and/or romantic overtures, and the liberty to form a sexual and/or emotional relationship (however fleeting or long-lasting) with a willing partner are utterly central ingredients to our ability to live dignified and meaningful lives. The same may be said on a broader basis about our ability to live our lives free from discrimination and violence due to our sex or sexual orientation. Furthermore, by contrast with freedom of expression or protection against arbitrary arrest and unfair trials, this is one aspect of personal dignity which touches *just about everyone's life* in a uniquely central and personal way, and on a day-by-day basis. This is partly captured in the observation, in *Crimes of Hate*, that

Because it relates to the deepest affairs of the heart, the innermost desires of the mind and the most intimate expression of the body, sexual orientation goes to the core of a person's right to physical and mental integrity. That right must include the freedom to determine and express one's sexual orientation and to do so on the basis of equality—free of fear and discrimination.[48]

This being so, freedom from discrimination and ill-treatment due to one's sex or sexual orientation, together with appropriate accompanying rights, cannot—at least without artificiality—be denied the status of human rights, even if some people use such rights in ways that we would not ourselves wish to, or in ways of which we do not approve. In practice, of course, we would need to develop this argument at far greater length in order to justify the existence of a human right—or rights of a particular width or scope—to be free from discrimination, but we need not do this here.[49] The purpose of this second argument is simply to demonstrate the existence of a relatively deep-level analogy between claims to be free from ill-treatment based on a person's sex or sexual orientation and the types of rights claim which fall within the list of traditional liberal political rights. Restricting human rights claims to the traditional list can, in consequence, be seen as artificial.

This is reinforced by an argument developed in *Crimes of Hate*. As the examples gathered in the three Reports demonstrate, people are, on a day-by-day basis, being persecuted by state agencies (and private parties) on account of their deviation from socially approved gender norms. In basic form, this might be seen as a violation of the human rights to be free from torture, arbitrary arrest, unfair trials and so on, but to see such activities *only* in those terms is to miss their most crucial ingredient: namely, that the victim has been singled out *because* of their defiance of socially imposed norms concerning gender. As *Crimes of Hate* states, 'in countries all over the world, lesbians, gay men and bisexual and transgender people are being tortured or ill-treated by state officials, or with their acquiescence, because of their sexual identity'.[50] The Report's explanation of why this is a human rights issue is instructive. 'In the past,' the Report notes, Amnesty's 'work against torture has highlighted the plight of those subjected to torture in a political context, such as opposition activists or journalists'—in other words, it has been concerned with the traditional list of human rights discussed above.[51] The Report then refers to the case of the five Ugandans (discussed earlier), who are characterized as

dissidents of a different kind, targeted not only because of their opinions or activism, but on account of their very identities. The victims of torture . . . include lesbian, gay, bisexual and transgender rights activists seen as threatening the social order; women seeking to exercise autonomy over their bodies; men seen as traitors to masculine privilege because they are perceived as adopting 'feminine' roles; and transgender people calling into question the traditional assumption that all humankind must fall irrevocably into one of two gender categories. Defiance of the 'heterosexual norm' can provoke moral condemnation, exclusion and violence, including torture.[52]

As these comments powerfully demonstrate, we would be failing to provide a suitably full account of the *nature* of the violation of the victim's dignity if we choose to screen out the centrality to that violation of socially imposed gender norms; our invocation of human rights principles would, in consequence, be somewhat hollow.

The third argument concerns the gender of human rights claims. Susan Moller Okin argues (in Chapter 2) that—at least if one believes that human rights concern a person's ability to lead a valuable life free from oppression—to restrict the effective scope of human rights to the public sphere may be seen as not only artificial (the essence of our second argument), but also as reflecting existing patterns of gender discrimination which confine so many women to the realm of home and family. For if—as is still the case—the clear majority of politicians, senior civil servants, judges, company chiefs, senior journalists, university professors and so on are *men*, a rigid insistence that human rights concern only public activities such as voting, expression, protest and the conduct of trials (or activities—for example, questioning a prisoner—which, while carried out in private, are of a public character since they are officially entrusted *only* to state agents acting for the public good) could be said to make the label *human* seem somewhat hollow. We would be talking about rights which, in practice, are exercised rather more by men than by women. To give adequate weight to issues which offend in practice against the dignity of women, we are obliged to include gender and sexuality within the realm of human rights.

Analytically speaking, each of these arguments is capable of working on its own, although it is fair to say that the third argument presupposes an approach to human rights which is akin to that adopted in the second. Clearly, if all three arguments are plausible, then the case in favour of Amnesty International's current position will have maximum force. However, even if one does not support the second and third arguments, the fact that so many human rights instruments do now guard against discrimination for gender-related reasons must, in and of itself, be sufficient to place a heavy burden on those who do not regard this area as involving human rights issues.

If Amnesty International's current position is—as has been argued here—correct, then it becomes important to determine what, exactly, constitutes a human rights claim in the context of sex and sexual orientation. The three Reports have as their major focus countries in which same-sex sexual acts are prohibited by law. However, as Robert Wintemute notes (in Chapter 6), the types of practical rights claim which are likely to be made by sexual minorities (and, by analogy, women) will vary depending on the level of social tolerance which already exists in whatever society is in issue. In many societies, sexual minorities are struggling at the basic level of asking for same-sex sexual acts to be decriminalized. It therefore comes as no surprise that social repression based on gender norms is particularly prevalent in such societies. The fact that so many people are struggling for very basic human rights relating to their gender or sexuality should not stop us, however, from thinking of—as human rights issues—those aspects of gender- or sexuality-based discrimination which present themselves *even in* societies where same-sex sexual acts are lawful. This point is reflected in contemporary human rights case law: in *Smith* v. *United Kingdom*, for example, lesbian and gay military personnel who were dismissed from the British armed services (after an extensive and highly intrusive military police investigation) due to their sexual orientation mounted a successful challenge to the discharge policy relying on the human right to sexual privacy protected by Article 8 of the European Convention.[53] An analogous point may be made about arguments for granting partnership rights to same-sex couples, in that these could be said to involve—in a fashion clearly analogous to more basic demands for the decriminalization of consenting sexual activity between persons of the same sex—the human right to be free from discrimination.[54]

We should now consider how the various questions and arguments discussed above are reflected in the chapters contained in this volume. The first chapter—by Judith Butler—is of significance at both theoretical and practical levels. Butler seeks to tackle what she describes as an apparent contradiction. On the one hand, calls for legal rights on behalf of

LGBT people tend to be seen as pertaining to individuals or to definable groups of individuals. After all, calls for bodily autonomy presuppose distinctness and individuality. Yet, on the other hand, it is through the body that gender and sexuality become exposed to others and implicated in social processes. By definition, therefore, gender and sexuality concern our relations *with others*. Desire, as an expression of sexuality, is (like grief or rage) about our relationship with another, and we fail to comprehend an important and basic aspect of our lives if we do not see that we are undone by one another. Butler is happy for us to talk of bodily autonomy and to use the language of 'my sexuality' or 'my gender', and to do so neither reluctantly nor for merely strategic reasons: for rights claims are part of the normative aspiration of any movement that seeks to maximize the protection and the freedom of sexual and gender minorities and of women. Nonetheless, she urges, we have to understand sexuality and gender as modes of being dispossessed, as ways of being for or by virtue of another, and to ask whether there are other normative aspirations that we might seek to articulate.

With this in mind, Butler suggests that the public assertion of lesbian and gay sexualities should seek to change the gender norms by which the world is defined. It is not so much a struggle for rights (as currently conceived) to be attached to our persons (as currently conceived): rather, the point is to be conceived as persons and to create a social transformation of the meaning of personhood. The assertion of sexual rights becomes a way of intervening in the social and political process by which the human is articulated: the point of asserting such rights is therefore not to prescribe new gender norms, but to encourage freedom. This ties in with Butler's deeper theory of gender as performative (an issue discussed by

Malcolm Bowie in his introduction): for the point of saying that gender is performative is to allegorize the ways in which reality is reproduced and contested. A more specific manifestation of the idea of cultural transformation is found in Butler's discussion of homophobic violence. As Butler points out, homophobic hate crimes often entail the most extreme and vicious acts of violence: something which suggests that a person's actual or apparent nonconformity with socially prescribed gender norms must arouse astonishing levels of anxiety on the part of those who engage in such violence. The desire physically to snuff out a person for nonconformity with gender norms implies that those norms underpin the attacker's sense of the world and sense of self in a very real way. This means, Butler suggests, that it will be necessary to reconceive and rearticulate what it means to be human, in the sense of being prepared to live with not knowing in advance what form humanness ought to take (as opposed, for example, to insisting on a binary gender-based view of the world) if we are to make genuine progress. A non-violent approach to life is one according to which we are prepared to live with not knowing in advance what holds us together as humans.

Butler makes five important points about how we conceive of human rights and the role of law. The first is that if we talk about sexual rights, we are bringing together two connected ways of being outside ourselves: namely, the dependence on others which Butler claims is inherent in the notion of sexuality, and the dependence on the protection of public and private spaces and of legal sanctions which goes with being part of a sexual minority that is frequently the target of aggression and violence. In consequence, when we speak of sexual rights, we are talking not merely of rights that relate to our individual desires, but of rights on which our very individuality depends. The discourse of rights underlines our dependency. Butler's second point is that it is quite right to campaign for the making available of marriage and domestic partnership rights to same-sex couples who want them, but that the 'traditional' notion of marriage should not be installed as a model for sexual legitimacy. Ties of kinship and community run more broadly than this and should not be shut down by the desire simply to buy into an existing ideal, which has faults as well as benefits. Butler's third key point is that affinities may be found between rights struggles centred on gender and sexuality, and those centred on physical disability and race. All of these struggles, she suggests, are attempts to counter social norms concerning what it is to count as human, and what form the human is required, culturally, to take. (One issue which Butler does not consider at this point, however, is the existence of prejudices of various types within already disempowered groups: the racist woman or gay man, for example, or the homophobic member of an ethnic minority group.)

Butler's fourth and fifth key points—concerning, respectively, the role of value judgements and cultural relativism—are interlinked. In relation to value judgements, Butler suggests that the fact that we cannot predict or control what permutations of the human might arise does not mean that we have to value *all possible* permutations. We can still struggle for the realization of normative values. However, a genuine struggle for normative values, she argues, must entail the acknowledgement that one's own position is not sufficient to elaborate the spectrum of the human. We need to keep our notion of the 'human' open to future articulation, and this is essential to the project of international human rights. However, Butler is quite clear that this should not lead us into a position of reductive cultural relativism, in which we are afraid to speak of international human rights since there can be only localized and provisional understandings of the concept. Morally, Butler insists, we are compelled to assess how well human rights work, and to use the language of rights to assert an entitlement to conditions of life that affirm the constitutive role of gender and sexuality. But to do so coherently, we must subject our categories—the 'human', 'gender' and 'sexuality'—to critical scrutiny, to accept that their boundaries are not fixed and that they can be open to reconception. For cultural transformation can involve the yielding up of our most fundamental categories. What is 'right' and what is 'good', Butler concludes, may well consist in staying open to the tensions that beset our most fundamental categories and in recognizing that unknowingness may lie at the core of what we know.

At a practical level, as Malcolm Bowie makes clear in his introduction, Butler's arguments provide a call to arms for those campaigning for the human rights of sexual minorities and of women. In fact, however, Butler's arguments could be said to be far more ambitious than those which are being put forward by many campaigning groups. For, as her treatment of partnership rights demonstrates, she is concerned to promote a new and more flexible understanding of human rights claims *per se*, at least when those claims are made in response to oppression instilled by prevailing social norms. Butler appears to be justifying human rights claims (and rejecting the attacks launched on international human rights norms by cultural relativists) as part of a broader project to promote cultural openness. Inevitably, this broader project gives rise to many questions. One is what role, more specifically, human rights claims play in that project. Butler tells us that she does not see them as rights to be advanced for purely strategic reasons, so does this mean that they have a normative weight of their own? If so, why and to what extent? Another question —perhaps more crucial still in the light of Butler's goals—is how human rights norms may be used, given the law's purported role as a device of social ordering, *without* shutting off some (or too many) potentially valuable options for reconceptualizing what it means to be human.[55] However such questions are answered, it is perhaps appropriate to conclude this section of the discussion by noting that for Butler, issues of gender and sexuality are intimately bound up together. Her discussion of homophobic violence clearly suggests that the common root of rights abuses relating to gender and sexuality is the victim's actual or perceived departure from powerful social norms concerning gender: in other words, just the same argument as that developed in the Amnesty Reports. It is only by reconceiving of gender—as Butler puts it, as part of the question of what it means to be human—and moving away from the need for rigid, preconceived answers, that we can make practical progress in combating such abuses.

Susan Moller Okin's wide-ranging analysis of women's rights at the end of the twentieth century also raises the issue of cultural relativism, alongside several other important points. Reflecting the view articulated in *It's In Our Hands* concerning the response of certain cultural, religious and ethnic movements to women's human rights claims,[56] Okin argues that in recent years we have witnessed one positive step forward, but two steps back. The positive step forward has been the recognition as human rights of rights that are of central practical importance to women's lives: something which has entailed a reconceptualization of the nature of human rights.

As discussed above, classic definitions of human rights have treated the state as the major or most likely oppressor of the individual, and the exercise of rights has been associated with the public sphere. In practice, however, the rights of women are more likely to be violated by people to whom they are close—such as fathers or husbands—and to be violated within the home rather than in the public sphere. The gradual reconceptualization of the nature of human rights to reflect this reality was, Okin argues, partly reflected in the *Platform for Action* adopted by the Fourth World Women's Conference in Beijing in 1995.

However, there have also been two steps back, the first of which relates to cultural relativism. Okin points out that, in the same time period that increasing emphasis has been placed on women's human rights, stress has also been placed on the rights of groups to their cultures, traditions and religions. Frequently, in international decision-making, deference has been paid to claims made on behalf of religious or cultural practices, even though such practices may involve the unequal treatment of women. Okin stresses that she would give priority to women's rights to be treated as equals over groups' rights to preserve their cultures (where those two rights conflict), and that where group rights are claimed on the basis of cultural or ethnic identity, women of the group concerned should be involved in the making of that claim. Okin suggests, partly by exploring the divorce laws of Israel and India, that considerable harm can ensue to women (and children) where group rights triumph. Okin acknowledges that certain other feminists have objected to the notion that anyone outside the group concerned can raise the issue of whether women's rights are truncated within that group's tradition, and stresses that she does not think that cultural and religious freedoms are unimportant. Indeed, they are often crucial to the members of the groups concerned, and understanding the relevant cultural and religious context is often essential in evaluating women's rights. However, where there is a conflict with women's rights, Okin is firmly of the view that there is no sound justification for group rights to take priority. Merely describing a practice as 'cultural' or 'religious' adds nothing to its innate goodness or badness. Furthermore, both religion and culture can be flexible, and can be encouraged to accommodate gender equality.

At this stage, two points should perhaps be made about Okin's argument: not least because her discussion of women's human rights fits neatly with her discussion of the competing claims of gender equality and group rights. The first point is that Okin's account of the competing claims raises in stark form the issue of the weight which should be given to local cultural and religious traditions. Perhaps because conceptions concerning 'appropriate' gender roles are so deeply embedded in so many cultures (and, indeed, subcultures), rights claims made on behalf of women and sexual minority groups are frequently opposed by representatives of some cultural tradition or another, in a way which—as Okin suggests—just would not happen in relation to other types of human rights claim. How to respond to this is a strongly contested issue, as the variety of stances advocated in different chapters in this volume suggests. The second point, raised by David Miller in his introduction to Okin's chapter, is about how we are to define women's human rights. Miller argues that there are conceptual differences between claims to human rights—which, he suggests, respond to basic harms—and claims to redress for inequalities. On this view, some inequalities are not serious enough to merit being described as basic harms which must be redressed by human rights. Miller's point in developing this argument is to suggest that supporters of Okin's position may need to think further about how far it is appropriate to use the language of human rights. Clearly, different theorists will disagree about this issue. However, the issue is significant for two reasons. First, it forces us to ask how far there is a fixed, conceptual definition of human rights, and how far we should label something as a human rights claim just because a particular group of actors (however large, sincere or deserving of respect) describes it as such. Second, our answer to the first question will determine whether we agree with Okin that the very definition of human rights (as opposed, say, to the ambit of the term) has been altered by the women's movement.

Returning to Okin's substantive argument, the second step back which she identifies relates to the treatment of less developed countries by global financial institutions such as the World Bank and the International Monetary Fund: for, she suggests, the theories of neoclassical economics which underlie the policies of these institutions contain mistaken assumptions about the quality of life and the role of women. On the quality of life, orthodox economic theory measures the success of a development project in terms of its impact on the gross domestic product (GDP) of the recipient country. However, this tells us nothing about the *distribution* of wealth or income. It tends to be assumed that a growth in GDP will make everyone better off, but this is no more than an assumption—and, Okin suggests, many large-scale development projects may in consequence have diminished the quality of life of those affected by them. On the role of women, Okin argues that orthodox economic theory either negates, or seriously misunderstands, the value of work traditionally done by women. Unpaid domestic labour—mainly carried out by women—tends not to be counted in economic assessments, even though there would be dramatic economic consequences if such labour suddenly became unavailable. In addition, given that the social division of labour between women and men can vary from one society to another, development agencies have sometimes made serious mistakes when they have based their calculations on the assumption that women's labour is not only costless, but also readily available whenever the male household 'head' requires it. Okin also draws attention to the savage implications, in terms of domestic budgets for health, education and other social services, of the domestic 'structural adjustment' programmes which global financial institutions require as a precondition for the renegotiation of loans made to debtor nations. These policies, she argues, have increased women's work, facilitated the spread of AIDS, and reduced the chances of population control.

Okin makes some pragmatic suggestions concerning how the second step back might be alleviated. First, debtor nations should be forgiven their debts, and structural adjustment requirements—which are slowly being amended due to doubts about their efficacy—should be ended. Second, emphasis should be switched from aid for large projects, directed via governments (whose members frequently waste or siphon off the money for personal use), to small-scale grants or loans paid directly to ordinary people for projects which they feel will improve their lives directly. As an example, Okin points to the work of the Global Fund for Women, a non-governmental organization (NGO) based in San Francisco, which makes small-scale grants on condition that the money will be used to empower women. NGOs, Okin suggests, are often far better placed than global financial institutions to understand the needs of individuals, and by bypassing often corrupt

national governments they can channel resources more effectively into projects which directly improve the quality of
people's lives.

In a broad survey of women's human rights in the Third
World (Chapter 3), Rajeswari Sunder Rajan takes up the
issues of cultural relativism and the definition of human rights.
On the first issue, Sunder Rajan advocates a rather different
position from that adopted by Okin. Sunder Rajan favours a
'difference approach', which emphasizes the values and interests *served by* rights claims, rather than the formal dictates of
the rights themselves. This approach, she suggests, allows us to
side-step conflicts between women's rights and group rights:
thus, in the context of divorce law, it may be preferable to
prioritize the implementation of Shari'a's relatively generous
provisions for divorced women rather than seeking formally
equal rights to divorce. Nonetheless, Sunder Rajan is in no
sense calling for priority to be given to group rights. She
believes that universality, humanity and rights are politically
valuable concepts which should not be abandoned, and that
cultural relativism can impede women's rights just as much as
can an overly rigid insistence on international standards. Her
argument is essentially a practical one. While the language of
human rights can often give wider appeal to claims made by
particular groups of women, the unthinking application of
international human rights norms can ignore cultural and
political issues which are important at local level. It does not
help disadvantaged women, Sunder Rajan suggests, to pit
them competitively against economically disadvantaged men.
Defining women so as to reflect the intersecting components
of their identity (relating, for example, to economic status,
caste status, place of residence) may offer a better guarantee of

understanding their situation than will be gained by emphasizing only their gender identity. The 'difference approach' is thus a pragmatic mechanism designed to facilitate improvements in the position of women by negotiation.

Although Sunder Rajan's conceptual approach differs from Okin's, the two would appear to agree about important issues. For example, both emphasize the particular burdens that women are forced to bear *as women* in circumstances of economic disadvantage, such as the burden of domestic work on top of exhausting work performed for pay; routine oppression, violence and discrimination in everyday life; and second-class status within patriarchal family and social structures. Both stress the role of cultural and religious practices, as well as the demands of the market, as sources of women's oppression. In addition, both are overwhelmingly concerned with the need to empower women who are currently facing extreme disadvantage. In this respect, Sunder Rajan is, on balance, a supporter (albeit, it would seem, a more hesitant one) of the types of micro-credit arrangement favoured by Okin. What is less clear—partly because neither author deals with the topic at length—is how far the two would agree about the definition of human rights in general, and what count as women's human rights in particular. Miller's critique of Okin's definition has already been discussed, and it may be the case that Sunder Rajan's position is closer to Miller's than to Okin's. For, having characterized the recording of indices of women's well-being in Human Development Reports as an encouraging development, Sunder Rajan notes that the fulfilment of basic needs of this kind is arguably a matter of women's fundamental rights *as citizens* rather than of human rights as such, although she also suggests that the position of women is perhaps strengthened if these rights are viewed as overlapping claims.

An important aspect of Sunder Rajan's chapter is her analysis of the role of the state in southern countries both as a potential defender against human rights abuses and as an inflictor of such abuses. Apart from the generic problem of police brutality against women, some states—for example, India—have at times promoted draconian birth control policies. Sunder Rajan also discusses the legal regulation of sexual behaviour. She examines changes in India, from a climate of pre-colonial tolerance towards lesbian and gay sexuality through to the sustained homophobia which is reflected in contemporary law and practice. Post-colonial states, she suggests, have sought to reify through law the role of women as wives and mothers, and to outlaw 'deviant' sexualities or expressions of sexuality. Laws protecting women—for example, against rape—thus tend to be motivated by a desire to entrench restrictive views of women's sexuality: for instance, by protecting women's chastity rather than their bodily autonomy. Sunder Rajan concludes that, as a result of these and other analogous practices, the state is something to be viewed—from the standpoint of women and sexual minorities—with some ambivalence.

In a challenging discussion, Alan Sinfield (Chapter 4) draws several analogies between points raised in *Crimes of Hate* and Shakespeare's play *Measure for Measure*, in order both to analyse gender-related oppression and to criticize the use of insufficiently reflective human rights-based campaigning in response to it. The premise of Sinfield's argument is that those who breach their society's prevalent gender norms have *always* been violently repressed. Thus Isabella's refusal to engage in 'conventional' sexual relations—for she wishes to enter a convent—incites Angelo's violent desire in *Measure for*

Measure, in much the same way as Katya Ivanova, the contemporary Russian woman whose plight is discussed in *Crimes of Hate,* was apparently singled out for repeated rape by policemen because of her nonconformity—as a lesbian—with the socially imposed heterosexual norm. Sinfield also points out that while the victims in the cases of violence, torture, rape and persecution disclosed in *Crimes of Hate* are people who defy their society's prevalent gender norms, only certain of these are people who would be neatly categorized as lesbian or gay in Northern societies (where—by contrast with some Southern societies—such social categorizations have a distinct meaning).

Although Sinfield does not discuss the issue, he appears to be adopting a constructionist approach to gender when categorizing the examples he discusses as instances of gender-based oppression. A constructionist approach typically maintains that 'male' and 'female' are not fixed and unchanging *social* categories, even if there have only ever been two *biological* sexes.[57] On this view, notions of gender are contingent: we use particular ideas about gender in order to understand a person's biological sex, but acknowledge that a person's biological sex may have been understood differently, or have assumed a different social significance, in other societies and/or at other times. If concepts of gender are themselves localized and socially constructed, it follows that the content of gender-based social norms—that is, rules governing 'appropriate' and 'inappropriate' behaviour for persons of a given gender—may themselves be seen as social constructs. By adopting this view—which has in recent years taken a powerful part in theoretical debates in literature and sociology—we can associate the rape of Katya Ivanova, or the persecution of a Latin American transgendered person, with those individuals' deviations from prescribed gender norms just as we can associate the attempted (and more 'conventional') seduction and molestation of Isabella in *Measure for Measure* with her perceived deviation from such norms. Any differences between the three examples become ones of type and degree ('how did the person concerned deviate from the imposed social norms, and to what extent?') rather than of category.

Sinfield also draws attention to connections between the persecutors and the persecuted in the examples he discusses. Echoing our earlier discussion, he suggests—drawing on *Crimes of Hate*—that at a deep level, those who engage in acts of violence against lesbians and gay men may well be acting out a sexual role when inflicting such violence, and are often as violent as they are because of what the victim's social identity can tell them about themselves. Perhaps more controversially, Sinfield asserts that this can be a two-way relationship, given that some gay men eroticize uniforms, assault and punishment. This relationship must, Sinfield suggests, lead us to reassess the prospects for human rights-based interventions to counter sexuality-related violence: for if torture is intimately associated with desire (by either side in the process), it will take more than fair-minded human rights protests to control it. A second question which Sinfield poses for human rights-based interventions is that if even Shakespeare cannot underwrite universal truth and justice in *Measure for Measure* (despite his apparent search for generally 'happy endings'), how can we as individuals hope to maintain a universal concept of human rights? In fact, Sinfield argues, co-opting the language of rights when calling for law reform measures can often resemble the invocation of seemingly random passages from Shakespeare: for the language of rights is now so popular that everyone—including *opponents* of the measures concerned—

tends to use it. This brings Sinfield to his third and deepest question: How can we affirm and support persecuted LGBT people everywhere without giving the impression that we are imposing, in an imperialist sense, Western conceptions of rights on countries whose social mores are resolutely different from our own? Fellow-feeling demands that we support those who are persecuted, but Sinfield suggests that we should adopt an approach based upon what he describes as civil, rather than human, rights. The rights for which LGBT people struggle (including, in Northern societies, partnership rights) may, Sinfield argues, be seen as 'civil' in the sense that they are the same rights as those possessed by everyone else in the society concerned. In some societies the scope of such rights may not be very wide, but at least they will be locally acknowledged and cannot be seen as imposed from above. Christopher Robinson thus concludes, in his introduction to Sinfield's chapter, that Sinfield's arguments should cause us to stop and think about how our critical responses should impinge upon the practical claims made by movements such as Amnesty International.

If Sinfield's contribution raises important questions about the value of human rights claims in the face of gender-based persecution, Rose George (Chapter 5) focuses in detail on a specific example of such persecution: namely, gang rape. George presents shocking evidence of the nature and prevalence of gang rape in the French *banlieue*—literally 'suburbs', but in fact areas of urban deprivation with impoverished and socially isolated immigrant populations. George's account is based partly on personal interviews—many of which are of an extremely disturbing nature—with victims, schoolteachers and social workers. George points out that until recently, the problem of gang rape was largely ignored—or treated as an unimportant issue—by the French news media and feminist community (a point reinforced by Michèle Le Doeuff in her introduction). This position has been altered only due to the courage of some women in speaking out, and because of a particularly horrific murder which (although it did not involve a rape) could not, because of its nature, be ignored.[58] George also presents important comparative evidence highlighting the incidence of gang rape in the United Kingdom: something which, she suggests, is ignored in analogous fashion by the British news media, probably due to its sheer unpleasantness.

The horror of gang rape is demonstrated with enormous power in the interviews recounted by George. In and of themselves, these interviews demand a response by the relevant national authorities. On a broader basis, however, George's account also illustrates two central themes of this volume. First, George argues that there is a close connection between gang rape and social perceptions of appropriate gender roles, a point which is also made by Le Doeuff in her introduction. In the *banlieue*, George suggests, young women are categorized either (and only) as 'good girls' or as 'sluts' and 'whores'. Cultural prejudices demand that until they marry they must be virgins, stay at home to look after male family members, and never go out alone. By contrast, the wearing of lipstick or any form of tight clothing—and certainly any form of independent social behaviour or association with males— counts as sufficient 'evidence' to 'justify' the conclusion that a young woman is a 'slut'. Gang rape tends to follow in the wake of such a categorization. Social perceptions of gender are, in other words, at the heart of a vicious and degrading social practice. A second issue taken up by George is the role of Islamic culture. Unlike some commentators, George is sceptical about the notion that Islam *per se* is to blame for the degradation of young women in the *banlieue*: for she suggests that prevailing social attitudes in some Islamic countries may in fact be more liberal than those which prevail in the *banlieue*. For George, the situation in the *banlieue* appears instead to rest on more localized cultural and/or religious factors: for example, the ready availability of pornography (seemingly to males of all ages), the enforced absence of ordinary social contact between young men and young women—both of these factors producing high levels of sexual frustration among young men—and the absence of any meaningful form of sex education. As a consequence of these factors, she suggests, some young men from the *banlieue* have trouble even understanding why rape is an extremely serious crime.

Given the endemic nature of the problem, George is reluctant to recommend specific solutions. However, Le Doeuff does so at a broad level. Having contrasted the realities of gang rape (and other varieties of sexual oppression) with what she categorizes as the glib assumptions of French politicians and theorists concerning gender issues, Le Doeuff calls for a renewed commitment on the part of feminists, coupled with the development of proper attitudes on the part of doctors, lawyers, administrators and police officers. She suggests that a new sense of commitment is needed to combat, through education, horrific practices such as gang rape. In some ways, it may be felt that this conclusion ties in with the localized advocacy of civil rights advocated by Sinfield.

A rather different stance is adopted by Robert Wintemute (Chapter 6). Wintemute's main focus is on constitutional claims to partnership rights made by same-sex couples. Before discussing the existing law and its potential for development, however, he constructs a full typology of the variety of legal claims which LGBT people have made in the face of adverse treatment due to their sexual orientation. As mentioned above, Wintemute points out that the types of ill-treatment which are highlighted in vivid detail in the Amnesty Reports relate only to the most *basic* human rights claims made by members of sexual minority groups: for example, claims to freedom from torture, from extra-judicial killing and from imprisonment without trial, as well as to freedom of expression, assembly and association. Once these rights are in place, Wintemute suggests, it is possible to campaign for 'sex rights': that is, rights which protect the individual's freedom from discrimination due to their sexual orientation or participation in consensual same-sex sexual activity, or because they have undergone or are undergoing gender reassignment. Such discrimination can include the criminalization of consensual sexual acts between persons of the same sex, the application of higher ages of consent to those acts than apply in the case of heterosexual activity, and the dismissal of individuals from their jobs because of their actual or perceived minority sexual orientation. As Wintemute observes, considerable progress has been made on these issues in Western European countries, and in many jurisdictions the more advanced issue of 'love rights'—that is, legal recognition and equal treatment of the relationships between LGBT individuals and their partners—is now firmly on the agenda.

Of course, the picture may in practice be somewhat more blurred than this: for, as Wintemute has himself observed, the British police engaged in campaigns against lesbian and gay bookshops, associations and individuals (that is, challenges to 'basic rights') long after sexual activity between consenting males was partly decriminalized in England and Wales in 1967.[59] Nonetheless, Wintemute's basic model is analytically useful. For he is clearly right to say, first, that the European Court of Human Rights is now basically committed to the principle that any discrimination against an individual because of their sexual orientation requires a strong justification, and second, that the key legal issue in Western Europe and North America is now the availability of partnership rights to same-sex couples. Furthermore, in discussing partnership rights, Wintemute offers us some powerful arguments of constitutional principle, together with some important observations concerning the extent to which partnership rights claims may be seen as universally applicable.

At the constitutional level, Wintemute suggests that the claims of same-sex couples to partnership rights are primarily claims to formal equality or freedom from direct discrimination. They are not claims (despite the rhetoric of some opponents) to special or distinct rights of any sort. Making benefits, including the availability of the institution of marriage, open to opposite-sex couples while closing them to same-sex couples is presumptively to discriminate on the basis of sexual orientation or sex. In consequence, once the general principle is established that there is a (constitutional) human right to be free from discrimination on the basis of sexual orientation or gender identity (and Wintemute analyses the case law from several jurisdictions when discussing the extent to which such a principle might be said to exist in national and international law), differences of treatment should not survive judicial scrutiny unless they can be supported by a strong and constitutionally recognized justification. Wintemute does not seek to analyse the specific justifications available under the rights instruments he examines, but chooses instead to discuss five essentially colloquial arguments which tend to be deployed by opponents of partnership rights for same-sex couples. Wintemute dismisses the first argument—based on tradition ('it's always been this way')—because plenty of other apparently discriminatory practices with long traditions have been abandoned without difficult social upheaval. The second set of arguments, based on religious objections to the recognition of same-sex partnerships, is dismissed because no religious institution should have the right to impose its doctrinal views on others through the vehicle of the law. The third argument, that marriage is designed for procreation and so should be unavailable to same-sex couples since they cannot procreate, is dismissed as over- and under-inclusive in significant ways. The fourth argument, based on the claim that the recognition of same-sex partnerships will inevitably lead to claims for the recognition of incestuous and polygamous marriages, is dismissed as a rhetorical trick: these latter issues, Wintemute suggests, can be considered on their own merits at the appropriate moment. Campaigners for same-sex partnership rights do not seek recognition for these other types of relationship, and it is wrong to confuse the two issues. The final argument—that same-sex marriage will devalue the institution for heterosexuals—is condemned as being no better than the argument that a whites- or men-only country club will be devalued if blacks or women are allowed to join.

Perhaps predictably, staunch opponents of same-sex partnership rights are unlikely to be convinced by Wintemute's rejoinders. Of greater practical importance is whether the rejoinders are likely to convince either a judge (given Wintemute's focus on constitutional litigation) or the reasonable but undecided voter or legislator. On reflection, it seems clear that the colloquial arguments—and Wintemute's rejoinders to them—will be relevant to legislators and voters rather than to judges. Most legislatures can legitimately consider a wide range of arguments—including the colloquial arguments Wintemute dismisses—when determining whether or not to grant partnership rights to same-sex couples. Wintemute's rebuttal is therefore important in the legislative context. However, litigation—especially constitutional litigation—should not depend upon colloquial argument. One of the key differences between legislatures and courts, as institutions, lies in the range of arguments which each can acceptably invoke when reaching a decision. If a court is to perform its proper constitutional function, its decisions need to relate to precedent and existing constitutional principle. Neither colloquial arguments nor rejoinders to them have a place, or at least not a significant place, in litigation concerning points of law (after all, one of the strongest criticisms which a lawyer can make of a judicial decision is that it was driven by policy or intuition rather than by solid legal reasons). In consequence, both supporters and opponents of same-sex partnership rights tend in practice to put forward legal/constitutional arguments where arguing the matter before a court. Colloquial arguments (and rejoinders) are saved for debates in the legislature. This can be supported by two specific examples. The first concerns Wintemute's dismissal of religious objections to same-sex partnership rights (his second set of colloquial arguments). Since the separation of church and state is embedded as a constitutional principle in many jurisdictions, including the USA, a justification for denying partnership rights to same-sex couples which could be shown—in a jurisdiction of this type—to be impermissibly closely related to religious doctrine ought not to pass muster before a court.[60] In such jurisdictions there is already a specific *constitutional* reason for rejecting the relevant colloquial argument: a rejoinder of the type offered by

Wintemute is therefore unnecessary in the context of litigation. Second, one of the reasons invoked most frequently by courts in order to justify a failure to extend legal protections to same-sex couples is that the court does not wish to usurp the role of the legislature: perhaps because the availability of partnership benefits is a sensitive social issue in itself, or because it has delicate fiscal implications, or for some other related reason.[61] Whatever the inner motivations of judges who rely upon deference-based arguments, such arguments are—at least officially—of a constitutional rather than a colloquial nature, and if they are to be overcome, constitutional counter-arguments must be used. It would be interesting to see how Wintemute would wish to deal with deference-related concerns of this type.

Nonetheless, it is fair to say that Wintemute provides a powerful rebuttal of the colloquial arguments considered on their own terms. He also offers some important observations concerning the potentially universal status of partnership rights claims. He states in stark terms that he does not subscribe to the view that local cultures can prevail over the human right to be free from discrimination: one should not leave discriminated-against individuals to their fates merely because of local cultural mores. However, Wintemute recognizes that, in practice, it will be very difficult to establish 'sex rights' or 'love rights' in the many countries where, as Amnesty International has documented, 'basic rights' are not guaranteed: for without the latter, campaigns for the former are highly unlikely even to operate, let alone succeed. Furthermore, he points out, religion has a strong influence over secular law in many non-Western countries. Wintemute regrets this fact, and concludes his chapter with a ringing endorsement of the need to separate religions and religious doctrine from state decision-making: something which, as Christopher McCrudden acknowledges in his introduction, raises many interesting questions concerning where and how that boundary should be drawn. Nonetheless, Wintemute accepts that any separation will take time, so that in many countries the journey from 'basic rights' to 'love rights' is likely to be a slow one. While this practical conclusion would probably be shared by Sinfield—who is similarly anxious not to leave people to their fate—it is clear that there is a strong difference of strategy between the two authors in terms of the types of claim that each would recommend campaigning groups to make in pursuit of legal protection for LGBT individuals and couples.

Claims and remedies are also central to Marina Warner's argument (Chapter 7), which focuses on the nature and role of apology. As Warner points out, recent years have witnessed an immense enthusiasm for the delivery of public apologies by institutions (e.g. governments, religious bodies) for acts of wrongdoing, seemingly as a result of the growth of identity politics. An apology has come to seem like a necessary bed-rock for the growth of social and human rights for groups that identify themselves as wronged. Furthermore, a refusal to make an official apology can be seen as a grave insult by those who feel that an apology is due to them. Warner thus notes, but does not develop at length, the point that Pope John Paul II has apologized on numerous occasions for wrongs done by the Catholic Church to Jews, women and minorities in general, while failing to make—when apologizing—any allusion either to the Vatican's apparent collusion with fascism during and before the Second World War, or to the Church's severely negative approach towards lesbians and gay men. Given the popularity of the public apology, it is clearly important to consider how it works and what it is intended to achieve, and also what use it may have in the context of human rights abuses. As Warner observes, these issues have a heavily gendered dimension: for not only are women frequently the subject of apparently gender-related wrongs (the widespread occurrence of rape of women in wars being a classic example), but saying 'sorry' is also frequently seen as a feminine way of resolving a dispute in that the apologist, by empathizing with the victim, must publicly shed his or her social authority to exculpate acts which were undertaken with that authority. The gender connotations of saying 'sorry' may thus be doubly significant in the context of human rights violations which implicate gender-based social norms.

Using a series of examples, Warner argues that to be effective an apology must involve a dialogue between the wrongdoer and the wronged party. The wronged party must acknowledge that an injustice has been done to them; the apologist must accept responsibility and express regret (and, implicitly, promise to reform); and the wronged party must accept the apology. There must also, presumably, be some sense of shared conviction that the apology will be enough to heal existing divisions or at least to allow the parties to live together peacefully in the future. When sought by an aggrieved community, an apology can therefore restore dignity and spread forgiveness: it is a formula which effects change.

As Warner observes, however, saying 'sorry' may in some circumstances simply not be sufficient as a remedy. The relationship of apology to legal redress is also problematical: for surely, Warner suggests, legal redress for human rights violations should be available whether or not the perpetrator apologizes. Thinking more cynically, apologizing may also imply an excuse not to do anything more about the injustice in question. Furthermore, the value of the apology can be devalued if it is used too often and too indiscriminately, or if—at the opposite end of the spectrum—it is accorded too limited an ambit. This, Warner argues, was one of the ironies of the process of truth-telling (which was not necessarily connected to the delivery of formal apologies) encouraged by the Truth and Reconciliation Commission in South Africa: an apparently feminine mode of discourse was not ultimately available to women themselves since the Commission was concerned only with 'political' crimes, with rapes inflicted on women (as a form of political oppression) being deemed to fall outside its ambit.

As Roy Foster observes in his introduction, Warner offers no easy answers to these complex problems. What should be clear, however, is that these problems must be considered if we are to find just and effective solutions to gender-based human rights violations. In this sense, the problems posed by the prevalence of the apology are analogous to those generated by the debate about how universal our commitment to human rights norms should be, since both bring into play questions concerning the absoluteness of our dispute-resolution mechanisms. The question whether the position of sexual minorities will be better advanced by a pragmatic appeal to local values (Sinfield's sense of civil rights) rather than by the bold assertion of secular universal rights (Wintemute's preferred position of principle) is thus similar in form to the question whether harmony will be better restored by apology and reconciliation rather than by an enforceable demand for redress. In the light of Warner's identification of the gendered nature of the apology as a dispute-resolution mechanism, we might also pause to consider how far each of these different approaches may be seen as gendered: an important point given the gendered nature of the wrongs at issue.

No collection of essays—still less one which is based on a series of lectures delivered by different people—can hope to provide a comprehensive account of a given subject-matter or area. This collection is no exception. What a collection such as this can realistically aim to do, however, is to highlight underlying unities, key themes and examples, as well as important questions and uncertainties in the area under scrutiny: or, indeed, some combination of all of these things. This volume's underlying unity may be said to lie in the claim that it *is* a human rights violation, and indeed a serious human rights violation, unjustly to penalize people because of their sex or sexual orientation. This issue demands our attention both because of the examples set out in the three Amnesty Reports—some being of a very graphic and violent nature—of prejudicial treatment of people who fail to live or act in a way which is considered 'appropriate' for a person of their biological sex, and because of the continuing disparities of treatment even in some liberal democracies. As the chapters in this collection illustrate, however, this underlying concern gives rise to many difficult questions, to which divergent answers are possible. Three such questions—whether we are dealing with examples of a common phenomenon when discussing rights violations based on sex and sexual orientation; whether the inclusion of these areas within the remit of human rights entails a reformulation of that concept; and what weight we should attach to competing claims made in the name of localized religious and cultural traditions—crop up again and again. Other important questions include how we can identify the best arguments for showing why gender- and sexuality-based prejudices are wrong; what role law has to play in combating social prejudice, as opposed to, say, education or economics; and how far we have come, and how far we have to go, in the quest for a world in which gender- and sexuality-related prejudice is eradicated.

As with the topics considered in previous series of Oxford Amnesty Lectures, a highly divergent range of answers can be produced, and only some of them will be canvassed in the pages which follow. However, since we are dealing with a serious human rights issue—one which, given the socially embedded nature of norms concerning gender roles, concerns people's ways of thinking about the world at a deep level—the questions raised in the previous paragraph must be debated with rigour. Given the depth and the scale of the prejudices in play in this area—prejudices which are reflected in the shocking examples of ill-treatment described in the three Amnesty Reports—glib and easy answers will not be sufficient. It is to be hoped that these chapters make some contribution to that debate.

Introduction to Judith Butler

Malcolm Bowie

Judith Butler's lecture, delivered in the Sheldonian on 6 March 2002, was a deeply moving occasion. In that tiered and ornamented space, through which so many local speech-makers had already passed and in which so many grandiloquent lectures on matters of public concern had previously been delivered, Butler spoke with unerring direct-ness about a matter that had seldom been addressed there, even obliquely. She spoke about the oppression of sexual minorities, and about the hope for humanity at large that an end to such oppression might bring. Inhumanity was her theme; and yet, as her successive propositions found their target, a new, enlarged and inclusive vision of what it is to be human began to emerge. The whole performance was compelling in its moral authority, and it is encouraging to know that the lecture will now reach a much wider audience by way of the printed page. Butler describes both the brutality and the subtle discriminatory practices to which gays, lesbians and transgendered people are exposed in Western and non-Western societies, and the exemplary courage and lucidity with which she proceeds will be a source of inspiration to campaign groups and concerned individuals around the world.

In some ways Judith Butler was not obviously suited to a public role of this kind, in spite of her prominence as a political activist in California and elsewhere. She was, and remains, an academic, a professor of rhetoric and comparative literature, and a cultural theorist not famous for the accessibility of her prose. In such collections as *Gender Trouble* (1990), *Bodies that Matter* (1993) and *Excitable Speech* (1997), she had created a strenuous literary idiom that even her admirers sometimes found exhausting. She had done this not by assembling a new technical lexicon for the field of sexual politics, but by hybridizing a number of existing theoretical languages, many of them French in origin, and overriding the seemingly ingrained differences of intellectual temper that certain of her admired predecessors displayed. In the new Preface to *Gender Trouble* which was published in 1999, Butler herself drew attention to the 'promiscuity' of her language. Only an American, she suggested, could have brought Lévi-Strauss, Foucault, Lacan, Kristeva and Wittig together at the syncretic meeting-place that her own volume proudly inhabited.

What she did not say, however, was that her own composite language serves to articulate a profoundly original view of human sexuality, and one that none of her mentors had prefigured. For Butler, 'gender' is a social construct rather than a biological datum; it is performed rather than prescribed; it is labile, multifarious, and now troubling, now exhilarating in its transformative capacity. The morphology and chromosomal pre-programming of the human body cannot be written out of the individual's sexual history, any more than the invisible pressures of the social group can be conjured away, but the individual's self-fashioning in speech is the very locus of human freedom. Performing one's gender is a fundamental right, and a right supremely worth protecting. However, defending that right—against homophobic bigotry, or against the array of repressive stereotypes that even supposedly liberal

societies bring to bear upon members of minority groups—
is a complicated matter. In the face of the crude simplicities
of judgement and expression to which gays and lesbians
were routinely subjected, the proponent of a new vision of
'performativity' in the sexual life needed to be complex,
paradoxical and guileful. Perhaps only a baroque rhetorician
could rise up against plain language that had become
tyrannical. For many of Butler's admirers, her difficulty, like
her eclecticism, was a necessary weapon in an unavoidable
war.

The chapter that follows is based on a lecture delivered
before a university audience, and at moments offers technical
terminology and polysyllabic display of the kind that professional academics from across the disciplines do indeed
sometimes favour. But what is remarkable about the lecture in
its institutional context, and as an event in Butler's own career
as a writer, is that it asks and answers such fundamental,
stripped-down questions as 'What does it mean to live a life?'
and 'What kind of life do I allow others to have in acting and
speaking as I do?' Butler's answers are complex and clear. She
speaks about the porosity of the human subject, which comes
into being in an intricate criss-cross of social relations, and
about the violent refusals of complexity to which the self-
appointed normalizers of sexual desire so readily resort.
She calls not only for a minimal set of legal safeguards, but also
for a plural and capacious social order in which the inter-
dependence of human beings is acknowledged even at their
moments of crisis and extremity. Previously stigmatized
sexual minorities must be allowed access to their humanity,
but not only in the tranquil daily transactions of civil society.
We need, Butler urges, 'to do justice to passion and grief and
rage, all of which tear us from ourselves, bind us to others,

transport us, undo us, implicate us in lives that are not our own, sometimes fatally, irreversibly'.

Judith Butler ends her lecture with a plea for the practice of 'cultural translation', which she defines as a continual process of exchange based on an openness to languages, societies and traditions other than those into which we ourselves happen to have been born. In addition, she associates herself with certain values—'democratic and non-violent, international and non-racist'—that will foster such translation both inside the minds of individuals and between human groups. This practice is of course already available to us in one highly visible form: in the work of great artists, many of whom have been, or still are, members of the sexual minorities under discussion here. In a way it is strange that Butler does not make more of the sexual, social and psychological pluralism that certain supreme art-works embody, and of the defiant self-emancipation from oppression that many gay artists have already achieved. Yet perhaps this choice of hers is not so very surprising. Western and non-Western societies alike have a long way to go if they are to guarantee the right to a 'liveable life' for all their members, and the existence of expert cultural translators among our artists does not of itself mean that general social progress is being made. Judith Butler's lecture is a call to action rather than to general reflection on cultural issues. It deserves the widest possible hearing among legislators, human rights professionals, and all those who seek to situate themselves freely in the performance space of human society.

On Being Beside Oneself: On the Limits of Sexual Autonomy

Judith Butler

What makes for a liveable world is no idle question. It is not merely a question for philosophers. It is posed in various idioms all the time by people in various walks of life. If that makes them all philosophers, then that is a conclusion I am happy to embrace. It becomes a question for ethics, I think, not only when we ask the personal question, what makes my own life bearable, but when we ask, from a position of power, and from the point of view of distributive justice, what makes, or ought to make, the lives of others bearable? Somewhere in the answer we find ourselves not only committed to a certain view of what life is, and what it should be, but also of what constitutes the human, the distinctively human life, and what does not. There is always a risk of anthropocentrism here, if one assumes that the distinctively human life is valuable, or most valuable, or the only way to think of the problem of value. But perhaps to counter that tendency it is necessary to ask both the question of life, and the question of the human, and not to let them fully collapse into one another.

I would like to start, and to end, with the question of the human, of who counts as the human, and the related question of whose lives count as lives, and with a question that has preoccupied many of us for years: *What makes for a grievable life?* I believe that whatever differences exist within the inter-

national gay and lesbian community—and there are many—
we all have some notion of what it is to have lost somebody.
And if we have lost, then it seems to follow that we have had,
that we have desired and loved, and struggled to find the
conditions for our desire. We have all lost in recent decades
from AIDS, but there are other losses that inflict us, other
diseases, and there is the fact as well that we are, as a community, subjected to violence, even if some of us have not
been. And this means that we are constituted politically in part
by virtue of the social vulnerability of our bodies; as a field
of desire and physical vulnerability, of a publicity at once
publicly assertive and vulnerable.

I am not sure I know when mourning is successful, or
when one has fully mourned another human being. I am
certain, though, that it does not mean that one has forgotten
them, or that something else comes along to take their place. I
do not believe it works that way. I think instead that one
mourns when one accepts the fact that the loss one undergoes
will be one which changes you, changes you possibly forever,
and that mourning has to do with agreeing to undergo a
transformation, the full result of which you cannot know in
advance. So there is losing, and there is the transformative
effect of loss, and this latter cannot be charted or planned. I do
not believe, for instance, that you can invoke a protestant ethic
when it comes to loss. You cannot say, 'Oh, I'll go through loss
this way, and that will be the result, and I'll apply myself to the
task, and I'll endeavour to achieve the resolution of grief that
is before me.' I think one is hit by waves, and that one starts
out the day with an aim, a project, a plan, and one finds oneself
foiled. One finds oneself fallen. One is exhausted, but does not
know why. Something is larger than one's own deliberate
plan or project, larger than one's own knowing. Something

takes hold, but is this something coming from the self, from the outside, or from some region where the difference between the two is indeterminable? What is it that claims us at such moments, such that we are not the masters of ourselves? To what are we tied? And by what are we seized?

It may seem that one is undergoing something temporary, but it could be that, in this very experience of undergoing, something about who we are is revealed, something which delineates the ties we have to others, which shows us that those ties constitute a sense of self, composed who we are, and that when we lose them we lose our composure in some fundamental sense: we do not know who we are or what to do. Many people think that grief is privatizing, that it returns us to a solitary situation, but I believe it exposes the constitutive sociality of the self, a basis for thinking a political community of a complex order.

It is not only that I might be said to 'have' these relations, or that I might sit back and view them at a distance, enumerating them, explaining what this friendship means, what that lover meant or means to me. On the contrary, grief displays the way in which we are in the thrall of our relations with others that we cannot always recount or explain, that often interrupt the self-conscious account of ourselves we might try to provide, in ways that challenge the very notion of ourselves as autonomous and in control. I might try to tell a story about what I am feeling, but it would have to be a story in which the very 'I' who seeks to tell the story is stopped in the midst of the telling. The very 'I' is called into question by its relation to the one to whom I address myself. This relation to the Other does not precisely ruin my story or reduce me to speechlessness, but it does, invariably, clutter my speech with signs of its undoing.

Let us face it. We are undone by each other. If we are not, we are missing something. If this seems so clearly the case with grief, it is only because it was already the case with desire. One does not always stay intact. It may be that one wants to, or does, but it may also be that despite one's best efforts, one is undone, in the face of the other, by the touch, by the scent, by the feel, by the prospect of the touch, by the memory of the feel. Thus when we speak about *my* sexuality or *my* gender, as we do (and as we must), we mean something complicated by it. Neither of these are precisely possessions, but both are to be understood as *modes of being dispossessed*, ways of being for another or, indeed, by virtue of another. It does not suffice to say that I am promoting a relational view of the self over an autonomous one, or trying to redescribe autonomy in terms of relationality. The term 'relationality' sutures the rupture in the relation we seek to describe, a rupture that is constitutive of identity itself. This means that we will have to approach the problem of conceptualizing dispossession with circumspection. One way of doing this is through the notion of ecstasy.

We tend to narrate the history of the broader movement for sexual freedom in such a way that ecstasy figures in the 1960s and 1970s, and persists mid-way through the 1980s. But perhaps ecstasy is more historically persistent than that; perhaps it has been with us all along. To be ec-static means, literally, to be outside oneself, and this can have several meanings: to be transported beyond oneself by a passion, but also to be *beside oneself* with rage or grief. I think that if I can still speak to a 'we', or include myself within its terms, I am speaking to those of us who are living in certain ways *beside ourselves*, whether it is in sexual passion, or emotional grief, or political rage. In a sense, the predicament is to understand what kind of community is composed of those who are beside themselves.

We have an interesting political predicament, since most of the time, when we hear about 'rights', we understand them as pertaining to individuals, or when we argue for protection against discrimination, we argue as a group or a class. In that language and in that context we have to present ourselves as bounded beings, distinct, recognizable, delineated, a subject before the law, a community defined by sameness. Indeed, we had better be able to use that language to secure legal protection and entitlements. But perhaps we make a mistake if we take the definitions of who we are, legally, to be adequate descriptions of what we are about. Although this language may well establish our legitimacy within a legal framework ensconced in liberal versions of human ontology, it fails to do justice to passion and grief and rage, all of which tear us from ourselves, bind us to others, transport us, undo us, implicate us in lives that are not our own, sometimes fatally, irreversibly.

It is not easy to understand how a political community is wrought from such ties. One speaks, and one speaks for another, to another, and yet there is no way to collapse the distinction between the other and myself. When we say 'we', we do nothing more than designate this very problematic. We do not solve it. And perhaps it is, and ought to be, insoluble. We ask that the state, for instance, keep its laws off our bodies, and we call for principles of bodily self-defence and bodily integrity to be accepted as political goods. Yet it is through the body that gender and sexuality become exposed to others, implicated in social processes, inscribed by cultural norms, apprehended in their social meanings. In a sense, to be a body is to be given over to others even as a body is, emphatically, 'one's own', that over which we must claim rights of autonomy: this is as true for the claims made by lesbians, gays and bisexuals in favour of sexual freedom as it is for transsexual and transgender claims to self-determination, as it is to intersex claims to be free of coerced medical, surgical and psychiatric interventions, as it is for all claims to be free from racist attacks, physical and verbal, as it is for feminism's claim to reproductive freedom. It is difficult, if not impossible, to make these claims without recourse to autonomy and, specifically, a sense of bodily autonomy. Bodily autonomy, however, is a lively paradox. I am not suggesting, however, that we cease to make these claims. We have to, we must. And I am not saying that we have to make these claims reluctantly or strategically. They are part of the normative aspiration of any movement that seeks to maximize the protection and the freedoms of sexual and gender minorities, of women, defined with the broadest possible compass, of racial and ethnic minorities, especially as they cut across all the other categories. But is there another normative aspiration that we must also seek to articulate and to defend? Is there a way in which the place of the body in all of these struggles opens up a different conception of politics?

The body implies mortality, vulnerability, agency: the skin and the flesh expose us to the gaze of others, but also to touch, and to violence. The body can be the agency and instrument of all of these as well, or the site where 'doing' and 'being done to' become equivocal. Although we struggle for rights over our own bodies, the very bodies for which we struggle are not quite ever only our own. The body has its invariably public dimension: constituted as a social phenomenon in the public sphere, my body is and is not mine. Given over from the start to the world of others, bearing their imprint, formed within the crucible of social life, the body is only later, and with some uncertainty, that to which I lay claim as my own. Indeed, if I seek to deny the fact that my body relates me, and against my will, and from the start, to others I do not choose to have in proximity to myself (the metro or tube is an excellent example of this dimension of sociality), if I build a notion of 'autonomy' on the basis of the denial of this sphere or a primary and unwilled physical proximity with others, then do I precisely deny the social and political conditions of my embodiment in the name of autonomy? If I am struggling *for* autonomy, do I not need to be struggling for something else as well, a conception of myself as invariably in community, impressed upon by others, impressing them as well, and in ways that are not always clearly delineable, in forms that are not fully predictable?

Is there a way that we might struggle for autonomy in many spheres, but also consider the demands that are imposed upon us by living in a world of beings who are, by definition, physically dependent on one another, physically vulnerable to one another? Is this not another way of imagining community in such a way that it becomes incumbent upon us to consider very carefully when and where we engage violence, for violence is, always, an exploitation of that primary tie, that primary way in which we are, as bodies, outside ourselves, for one another?

If I may then return to the problem of grief, to the moments in which one undergoes something outside of one's control, finds that one is beside oneself, not at one with oneself, perhaps we can say grief contains within it the possibility of apprehending the fundamental sociality of embodied life, the ways in which we are, from the start, and by virtue of being a bodily being, already given over, beyond ourselves, implicated in lives that are not our own. Can this situation, one which is so dramatic for sexual minorities, one which establishes a very specific political perspective for anyone who works in the field of sexual and gender politics, supply a perspective by which to begin to apprehend the contemporary global situation?

Mourning, fear, anxiety, rage. And in the USA after 11 September 2001, we have been everywhere surrounded with violence, of having perpetrated it, having suffered it, living in fear of it, planning more of it. Violence is surely a touch of the worst order, a way in which the human vulnerability to other humans is exposed at its most terrifying, a way in which we are given over, without control, to the will of another, the way in which life itself can be expunged by the wilful action of another. To the extent that we commit violence we are acting upon another, putting others at risk, causing damage to others, expunging, annihilating. In a way, we all live with this particular vulnerability, a vulnerability to the other which is part of bodily life, but this vulnerability becomes highly exacerbated under certain social and political conditions. Although the dominant mode in the USA has been to shore up sovereignty and security to minimize or, indeed, foreclose this vulnerability, it can serve another function and another ideal. The fact that our lives are dependent on others can become the basis of claims for non-militaristic political solutions, one which we cannot will away, one which we must attend to, even abide by, as we begin to think about what politics might be implied by staying with the thought of corporeal vulnerability itself.

Is there something to be gained from grieving, from tarrying with grief, remaining exposed to its apparent tolerability and not endeavouring to seek a resolution for grief through violence? Is there something to be gained in the political domain by maintaining grief as part of the framework by which we see our international ties? If we stay with the sense of loss, are we left feeling only passive and powerless, as some fear? Or are we, rather, returned to a sense of human vulnerability, to our collective responsibility for the physical lives of one another? The attempt to foreclose that vulnerability, to banish it, to make ourselves secure at the expense of every other human consideration, is surely also to eradicate one of the most important resources from which we must take our bearings and find our way.

To grieve, and to make grief itself into a resource for politics, is not to be resigned to a simple passivity or powerlessness. It is, rather, to allow oneself to extrapolate from this experience of vulnerability to the vulnerability that others suffer through military incursions, occupations, suddenly declared wars, police brutality. That our very survival can be determined by those who we do not know and over whom there is no final control means that life is precarious, and that politics must consider what forms of social and political organization seek best to sustain precarious lives across the globe.

There is a more general conception of the human at work here, one in which we are, from the start, given over to the other, one in which we are, from the start, even prior to individuation itself, and by virtue of our embodiment, given over to an other: this makes us vulnerable to violence, but also to another range of touch, a range which includes the eradication of our being at the one end, and the physical support for our lives at the other.

We cannot endeavour to 'rectify' this situation, and we cannot recover the source of this vulnerability, for it precedes the formation of 'I'. This condition of being laid bare from the start, dependent on those who we do not know is one with which we cannot precisely argue. We come into the world unknowing and dependent and, to a certain degree, we remain that way. We can try, from the point of view of autonomy, to argue with this situation, but we are perhaps foolish, if not dangerous, when we do. Of course, we can say that for some this primary scene is extraordinarily loving and receptive, a warm tissue of relations that support and nurture life in its infancy; for others this is, however, a scene of abandonment or violence or starvation; they are bodies given over to nothing, or to brutality, or to no sustenance. No matter what the valence of that scene is, however, the fact remains that infancy constitutes a necessary dependency, one that we never fully leave behind. But they must still be apprehended as given over, part of understanding the oppression of lives is precisely to understand that there is no way to argue away this condition of a primary vulnerability, of being given over to the touch of the other, even if, or precisely when, there is no other there, and no support for our lives. To counter oppression requires that one understand that lives are supported and maintained differentially, that there are radically different ways in which human physical vulnerability is distributed across the globe. Certain lives will be highly protected, and the abrogation of their claims to sanctity will be sufficient to mobilize the forces of war. And other lives will not find such fast and furious support and will not even qualify as 'grievable'.

What are the cultural contours of the notion of the human at work here? And how do the contours that we accept as the cultural frame for the human limit the extent to which we can avow loss as loss? This is surely a question that lesbian, gay and bi-studies has asked, in relation to violence against sexual minorities; that transgendered people have asked as they have been singled out for harassment and sometimes murder; that intersexed people have asked, whose formative years have so often been marked by an unwanted violence against their bodies in the name of a normative notion of human morphology. This is no doubt also the basis of a profound affinity between movements centred on gender and sexuality with efforts to counter the normative human morphologies and capacities that condemn or efface those who are physically challenged. It must, as well, also be part of the affinity with anti-racist struggles, given the racial differential that undergirds the culturally viable notions of the human, ones we see acted out in dramatic and terrifying ways in the global arena at the present time.

So what is the relation between violence and what is 'unreal', between violence and unreality that attends to those who become the victims of violence, and where does the notion of the ungrievable life come in? It would be one thing to argue that first, on the level of discourse, certain lives are not considered lives at all, they cannot be humanized; they fit no dominant frame for the human, and that their dehumanization occurs first at this level, and then this level gives rise to a physical violence that in some sense delivers the message of dehumanization that is already at work in the culture.

So it is not just that a discourse exists in which there is no frame and no story and no name for such a life, and that violence may be said to realize or apply this discourse. Violence against those who are already not quite lives, who are living in a state of suspension between life and death, leaves a mark that is no mark. If there is a discourse, it is a silent and melancholic writing in which there have been no lives, and no losses, there has been no common physical condition, no vulnerability that serves as the basis for an apprehension of our commonality, and there has been no sundering of that commonality. None of this takes place on the order of the event. None of this takes place. How many lives have been lost from AIDS in Africa in the last few years? Where are the media representations of this loss, the discursive elaborations of what these losses mean for communities there?

I began this chapter with a suggestion that perhaps the interrelated movements and modes of enquiry that collect here might need, on the one hand, to consider autonomy as one dimension of their normative aspiration, one value to realize when we ask ourselves: In what direction ought we to proceed, and what kinds of values ought we to be realizing? I suggested as well that the way in which the body figures in gender and sexuality studies, and in the struggles for a less oppressive social world for the otherwise gendered and for sexual minorities of all kinds, is precisely to underscore the value of being beside oneself, of being a porous boundary, given over to others, finding oneself in a trajectory of desire in which one is taken out of oneself, resituated irreversibly in a field of others in which one is not the presumptive centre. The particular sociality that belongs to bodily life, to sexual life, and to becoming gendered (which is always, to a certain extent, becoming gendered *for others*) establishes a field of ethical enmeshment with others and a sense of disorientation for the first person, the perspective of the ego. As bodies, we are always for something more than, and other than, ourselves. To articulate this as an entitlement is not always easy, but perhaps not impossible. It suggests, for instance, that 'association' is not a luxury, but one of the very conditions and prerogatives of freedom. Indeed, the kinds of association we maintain importantly take many forms. It will not do to extol the marriage norm as the new ideal for this movement, as the Campaign for Human Justice has erroneously done. No doubt, marriage and same-sex domestic partnerships should certainly be available as options, but to install either as a model for sexual legitimacy is precisely to constrain the sociality of the body in acceptable ways. In light of seriously damaging judicial decisions against second parent adoptions in recent years, it is crucial to expand our notions of kinship beyond the heterosexual frame. It would be a mistake, however, to reduce kinship to family, or to assume that all sustaining community and friendship ties are extrapolations of kin relations.

Kinship ties that bind humans to one another may well be no more or less than the intensification of community ties, may or may not be based on enduring or exclusive sexual relations, may well consist of ex-lovers, non-lovers, friends, community members. In this sense, then, the relations of kinship arrive at boundaries that call into question the distinguishability of kinship from community, or which, perhaps, call for a different conception of friendship. When these modes of association work to produce sustaining webs of relation, they constitute a 'breakdown' of traditional kinship that not only displaces the central position of biological and sexual relations from its definition. In addition, the incest taboo that governs kinship ties, producing a necessary exogamy, does not necessarily operate among friends and in networks of communities. As a result, sexuality is no longer exclusively regulated by the rules of kinship at the same time that the durable tie is situated outside of the conjugal frame. Sexuality becomes open to a number of social articulations that do not always imply binding relations or conjugal ties. That not all of our relations last or are meant to last, however, does not mean that we are immune to grief. On the contrary, sexuality outside the field of monogamy may well open us up to a different sense of community, intensifying the question of where one finds enduring ties, and so become the condition for an attunement to losses that exceed the private realm.

Nevertheless, those who live outside of the conjugal frame

or who maintain modes of social organization for sexuality that are neither monogamous nor quasi-marital are more and more considered unreal, and their loves and losses less than 'true' loves and 'true' losses. The derealization of this domain of human intimacy and sociality works by denying reality and truth to the relations at issue. *The question of who and what is considered real and true is apparently a question of knowledge, but it is also, as Foucault makes plain, a question of power. Having or bearing 'truth' and 'reality' is an enormously powerful prerogative within the social world, one way which power dissimulates as ontology.* According to Foucault, one of the first tasks of a radical critique is to discern the relation 'between mechanisms of coercion and elements of knowledge?'[1] Here we are confronted with the limits of what is knowable, limits that exercise a certain force but are not grounded in any necessity, limits that can only be tread or interrogated by risking a certain security through departing from an established ontology: '[N]othing can exist as an element of knowledge if, on the one hand, it . . . does not conform to a set of rules and constraints characteristic, for example, of a given type of scientific discourse in a given period, and if, on the other hand, it does not possess the effects of coercion or simply the incentives peculiar to what is scientifically validated or simply rational or simply generally accepted, etc.'[2] Knowledge and power are not finally separable, but work together to establish a set of subtle and explicit criteria for thinking the world: 'It is therefore not a matter of describing what knowledge is and what power is and how one would repress the other or how the other would abuse the one, but rather, a nexus of knowledge–power has to be described so that we can grasp what constitutes the acceptability of a system.'[3]

What this means is that one looks both for the *conditions*

by which the object field is constituted, and for the *limits* of those conditions. The limits are to be found where the reproducibility of the conditions is not secure, the site of their contingency and their transformability. In Foucault's terms, 'schematically speaking, we have perpetual mobility, essential fragility or rather the complex interplay between what replicates the same process and what transforms it'.[4] To intervene in the name of transformation means precisely to disrupt what has become settled knowledge and knowable reality, and to use, as it were, one's unreality to make an otherwise impossible or illegible claim. I think that when the unreal lay claim to reality, or enter into its domain, something other than a simple assimilation into prevailing norms can and does take place. The norms themselves can become rattled, display their instability, become open to resignification.

In recent years, the new gender politics has offered numerous challenges from transgendered and transsexual peoples to established feminist and lesbian/gay frameworks, and the intersex movement has rendered more complex the concerns and demands of sexual rights advocates. If some on the Left believed that these concerns were not properly or substantively political, they have been under pressure to rethink the political sphere in terms of its gendered and sexual presuppositions. The suggestion that butch, femme and transgendered lives are not essential referents for a refashioning of political life, and for a more just and equitable society, fails to acknowledge the violence that the otherwise gendered suffer in the public world, fails as well to recognize that embodiment denotes a contested set of norms governing who will count as a viable subject within the sphere of politics. Indeed, if we consider that human bodies are not experienced without recourse to some ideality, some frame for experience itself, and that this is as true for the experience of one's own body as it is for experiencing another, and if we accept that that ideality and frame are socially articulated, we can see how it is that embodiment is not thinkable without a relation to a norm or a set of norms. The struggle to rework the norms by which bodies are experienced is thus crucial not only to disability politics, but also to the intersex and transgendered movements as they contest forcibly imposed ideals of what bodies should be like. The embodied relation to the norm exercises a transformative potential; to posit possibilities beyond the norm or, indeed, a different future for the norm itself, is part of the work of fantasy, when we understand fantasy as taking the body as a point of departure for an articulation that is not always constrained by the body as it *is*. If we accept that altering these norms that decide normative human morphology and, as a result, give differential 'reality' to different kinds of humans, then we would be compelled to affirm that transgendered lives have a potential and actual impact on political life at its most fundamental level: who counts as a human, and what norms govern the appearance of 'real' humanness.

Moreover, fantasy is part of the articulation of the possible; it moves us beyond what is merely actual and present into a realm of possibility, the not yet actualized or the not actualizable. The struggle to survive is not really separable from the cultural life of fantasy, and the foreclosure of fantasy— through censorship, degradation or other means—is one strategy for providing for the social death of persons. Fantasy is not the opposite of reality: it is what reality forecloses and, as a result, it defines the limits of reality, constituting it as its constitutive outside. The critical promise of fantasy, when and where it exists, is precisely to challenge the contingent limits of what will and will not be called reality. Fantasy is what allows us to imagine ourselves and others otherwise; it establishes the possible in excess of the real; it points elsewhere, and when it is embodied, it brings the elsewhere home.

How do drag, butch, femme, transgender, transsexual enter into the political field? They not only make us question what is real, and what 'must' be, but they also show us how the norms that govern contemporary notions of reality can be questioned and how new modes of reality can become instituted. These practices of instituting new modes of reality take place in part through the scene of embodiment, where the body is not understood as a static and accomplished fact, but an ageing process, a mode of becoming that, in becoming otherwise, exceeds the norm, reworks the norm, makes us see how realities to which we thought we were confined are not written in stone. Although some people have asked me, what is finally the use of simply increasing possibilities for gender, I tend to answer: possibility is not a luxury; it is as crucial as bread. I think we should not underestimate what the thought of the possible does for those for whom the very issue of survival is most urgent. If the answer to the question, is life possible, is 'yes', that is surely something significant. It cannot, however, be taken for granted as the answer. That is a question whose answer is sometimes 'no', or one that has no ready answer, or one that bespeaks an ongoing agony. For many who can and do answer the question in the affirmative, that answer is hard won, if won at all, an accomplishment, one that is fundamentally conditioned by reality being structured or restructured in such a way that the affirmation becomes possible.

One of the central tasks of lesbian and gay international rights is to assert in clear and public terms the reality of homosexuality, not as an inner truth, not as a sexual practice, but as one of the defining features of the social world in its very intelligibility. In other words, it is one thing to assert the reality of lesbian and gay lives as a reality, and to insist that these are lives worthy of protection in their specificity and commonality; but it is quite another to insist that the very public assertion of gay-ness calls into question what counts as reality, what counts as a human life. Indeed, the task of international lesbian and gay politics is no less than a remaking of reality, a reconstituting of the human, and a brokering of the question, what is and is not liveable? So what is the injustice here? I would put it this way: to be called unreal, and to have that call, as it were, institutionalized as a form of differential treatment, is to become the other against whom (or against which) the human is made: it is the inhuman, the beyond the human, the less than human, the border that secures the human in its ostensible reality. To be called a copy, to be called unreal, is thus one way in which one can be oppressed, but consider that it is more fundamental than that. To be oppressed means that you already exist as a subject of some kind, you are there as the visible and oppressed other for the master subject, as a possible or potential subject, but to be unreal is something else again. To be oppressed you must first become intelligible. To find that you are fundamentally unintelligible (indeed, that the laws of culture and of language find you to be an impossibility) is to find that one has not yet achieved access to the human, to find oneself speaking only and always *as if one were* human, but with the sense that one is not, to find that one's language is hollow, that no recognition is forthcoming because the norms by which recognition takes place are not in one's favour.

We may think that the question of how one does one's

gender is merely a cultural question, or an indulgence on the part of those who insist on exercising bourgeois freedom in excessive dimensions. The point of saying, however, that gender is performative is not simply to insist on a right to produce a pleasurable and subversive spectacle, but to allegorize the spectacular and consequential ways in which reality is both reproduced and contested. This has consequences for how gender presentations are criminalized and pathologized, how subjects who cross gender risk internment and imprisonment, why violence against transgendered subjects is not recognized as violence, why this violence is sometimes inflicted by the very states which should be offering such subjects protection from violence.

What if new forms of gender are possible, how does this affect the ways we live, the concrete needs of the human community? And how are we to distinguish between forms of gender possibility that are valuable and those that are not? First, I would say that it is not a question merely of producing a new future for genders that do not yet exist. The genders I have in mind have been in existence for a long time, but they have not been admitted into the terms that govern reality. Thus it is a question of developing, within law, within psychiatry, within social and literary theory, a new legitimating lexicon for the gender complexity that we have been living for a long time. Because the norms governing reality have not admitted these forms to be real, we will, of necessity, call them 'new'.

What place does the thinking of the possible have within political theorizing? Is the problem that we have no norm to distinguish among kinds of possibility, or does that only appear to be a problem if we fail to comprehend 'possibility' itself as a norm? 'Possibility' is an aspiration, something we might hope will be equitably distributed, something that might be socially secured, that cannot be taken for granted, especially if it is apprehended phenomenologically. The point is not to prescribe new gender norms as if one were under an obligation to supply a measure, gauge or norm for the adjudication of competing gender presentations. The normative aspiration at work here has to do with the ability to live and breathe and move, and would no doubt belong somewhere in what is called a philosophy of freedom. The thought of a possible life is only an indulgence for those who already know themselves to be possible. For those who are still looking to become possible, possibility is a necessity.

It was Spinoza who claimed that every human being seeks to persist in his own being, and he made this principle of self-persistence, the *conatus*, into the basis of his ethics and, indeed, his politics. When Hegel made the claim that desire is always a desire for recognition, he was, in a way, extrapolating upon this Spinozistic point, telling us, effectively, that to persist in one's own being is possible only on the condition that we are engaged in receiving and offering recognition. If we are not recognizable, if there are no norms of recognition by which we are recognizable, then it is not possible to persist in one's own being, and we are not possible beings; we have been foreclosed from possibility. We think of norms of recognition perhaps as residing already in a cultural world into which we are born, but these norms change, and with the changes in these norms come changes in what does and does not count as recognizably human. To twist the Hegelian argument in a Foucaultian direction: norms of recognition function to produce and to de-produce the notion of the human. This is made true in a specific way when we consider how international norms work in the context of lesbian and gay human rights, especially as they insist that certain kinds of violence are impermissible, that certain lives are vulnerable and worthy of protection, that certain deaths are grievable and worthy of public recognition.

To say that the desire to persist in one's own being depends on norms of recognition is to say that the basis of one's autonomy, one's persistence as an 'I' through time, depends fundamentally on a social norm which exceeds that 'I', which positions that 'I' ec-statically, outside of itself in a world of complex and historically changing norms. In effect, our lives, our very persistence, depend upon such norms or, at least, on the possibility that we will be able to negotiate within them, derive our agency from the field of their operation. In our very ability to persist, then, we are dependent on what is outside of us, on a broader sociality, and this dependency is the basis of our endurance and survivability. When we assert our 'right', as we do and as we must, we are not carving out a place for our 'autonomy'—if by 'autonomy' we mean a state of individuation, taken as self-persisting prior to and apart from any relations of dependency on the world of others. We do not negotiate with norms or with Others subsequent to our coming into the world. We come into the world on con-dition that the social world is already there, laying the groundwork for us. This implies that I cannot persist without norms of recognition which support my persistence: the sense of possibility pertaining to me must first be imagined from somewhere else before I can begin to imagine myself. My reflexivity is not only socially mediated, but socially consti-tuted: I cannot be who I am without drawing upon the social-ity of norms that precede and exceed me. In this sense, I am outside of myself from the outset, and must be, in order to survive, and in order to enter into the realm of the possible.

To assert sexual rights, then, takes on a specific meaning against this background. It means, for instance, that when we struggle for rights, we are not simply struggling for rights that attach to my person, but we are struggling *to be conceived as persons*. There is a difference between the former and the latter. If we are struggling for rights that attach, or should attach, to my personhood, then we assume that personhood as already constituted. But if we are struggling not only to be conceived as persons, but to create a social transformation of the very meaning of personhood, then the assertion of rights becomes a way of intervening in the social and political process by which the human is articulated. International human rights is always in the process of subjecting the human to redefinition and renegotiation. It mobilizes the human in the service of rights, but also rewrites the human, and rearticulates the human when it comes up against the cultural limits of its working conception of the human, as it does and must.

Lesbian and gay human rights takes sexuality, in some sense, to be its issue. Sexuality is not simply an attribute one has, a disposition or patterned set of inclinations. It is a mode of being disposed towards others, including in the mode of fantasy, and sometimes only in the mode of fantasy. If we are outside of ourselves as sexual beings, given over from the start, crafted in part through primary relations of dependency and attachment, then it would seem that our being beside ourselves, outside ourselves, is there as a function of sexuality itself, where sexuality is not this or that dimension of our existence, not the key or bedrock of our existence, but, rather, as co-extensive with existence, as Merleau-Ponty once aptly suggested.

I have tried here to argue that our very sense of personhood is linked to the desire for recognition, and that desire places us outside of ourself in a realm of social norms which we do not fully choose, but which provide the horizon and the resource for any sense of choice that we have. *This means that the ec-static character of our existence is essential to the possibility of persisting as human.* In this sense we can see how 'sexual rights' brings together two related domains of ecstasy, two connected ways of being outside of ourselves. As sexual, we are dependent on a world of others, vulnerable to need, violence, betrayal, compulsion, fantasy; we project desire, and we have it projected on to us. To be part of a sexual minority means, most emphatically, that we are also dependent on the protection of public and private spaces, on legal sanctions that protect us from violence, on safeguards of various institutional kinds against unwanted aggression imposed upon us, and the violent actions they sometimes instigate. In this sense, our very lives, and the persistence of our desire, depend on there being norms of recognition which produce and sustain our viability as human. Thus, when we speak about 'sexual rights', we are not merely talking about rights that pertain to our individual desires, but to the norms on which our very individuality depends. This means that the discourse of rights avows our dependency, the mode of our being in the hands of others, a mode of being with and for others without which we cannot be.

I served for a few years on the board of the International Gay and Lesbian Human Rights Commission, a group that is located in San Francisco, but which is part of a broad international coalition of groups and individuals who engage in a struggle to establish both equality and justice for sexual minorities, which includes transgender and intersexed individuals, and also includes all persons who live with HIV or AIDS.[5] What astonished me time and again was how often the organization was asked to respond to immediate acts of

violence against sexual minorities, especially when that violence was not redressed in any way by local police or state
government in various places around the globe. I had to
reflect on what sort of anxiety is prompted by the public
appearance of someone who is openly gay, or presumed to be
gay, someone whose gender does not conform to norms,
someone whose sexuality defied the public prohibition upon
it, someone whose body does not conform with certain mor-
phological ideals. What motivates those who are driven to kill
someone for being gay, to threaten to kill someone for being
intersexed, who would be driven to kill simply through the
public appearance of someone who is transgendered? The
desire to kill someone, or killing someone, for not conforming
to the gender norm by which he or she is 'supposed' to live
suggests that life itself requires a set of sheltering norms, and
that to be outside it, to live outside it, is to court death. The
person who threatens violence proceeds from the anxious and
rigid belief that a sense of world and a sense of self will be
radically undermined if such a being, uncategorizable, is permitted to live within the social world. The negation, through
violence, of that body is a vain and violent effort to restore
order, to renew the social world on the basis of intelligible
gender, and to refuse the challenge to rethink that world as
something other than natural or necessary. This is not far
removed from the threat of death, or the murder itself, of
transsexuals in various countries, and of gay men who read
'feminine' or gay women who read 'masculine'. These crimes
are not always immediately recognized as criminal acts. Sometimes they are denounced by governments and international
agencies; sometimes they are not included as legible or 'real'
crimes against humanity by those very institutions.

If we oppose this violence, then we oppose it in the name

of what? What is the alternative to this violence, and for what transformation of the social world do I call? This violence emerges from a profound desire to keep the order of binary gender natural or necessary, to make of it a structure, either natural or cultural, or both, that no 'human' can oppose, and still remain human. If someone opposes these norms not just by having a point of view on them, but if this opposition is incorporated into the body, the corporeal style of this person, and that stylized opposition is legible, then it seems that violence emerges precisely as the demand to undo that legibility, to question its possibility, to render it unreal and impossible in the face of its appearance to the contrary. This is, then, no simple difference in point of views. To counter that embodied opposition with violence is to say, effectively, that this body, this challenge to an accepted version of the world, is and shall be unthinkable. The effort to enforce the boundaries of what will be regarded as real requires stalling what is contingent, frail, open to fundamental transformation in the gendered order of things.

An ethical query emerges in light of such an analysis: how might we encounter the difference that calls our grids of intelligibility into question without trying to foreclose the challenge that the difference delivers? What might it mean to learn to live in the anxiety of that challenge, to feel the surety of one's epistemological and ontological anchor go, but to be willing, in the name of the human, to allow the human to become something other than what it is traditionally assumed to be? This means that we must learn to live, and to embrace, the destruction and rearticulation of the human in the name of a more capacious and, finally, less violent world, not to know in advance what precise form our humanness does and will take, but to be open to its permutations in the name of non-violence. Emmanuel Levinas has taught us, wisely, that the question we pose to the Other is simple and unanswerable: 'Who are you?'[6] The violent response is the one which does not ask, and does not seek to know. It wants to shore up what it knows, to expunge what threatens it with not-knowing, what forces it to reconsider the presuppositions of its world, their contingency, their malleability. The non-violent response lives with its unknowingness about the Other, in the face of the Other, since sustaining the bond that the question opens is finally more valuable than knowing in advance what holds us in common, as if we already have all the resources we need to know what defines the human, what its future life may be.

That we cannot predict or control what permutations of the human might arise does not mean that we must value all possible permutations of the human; it does not mean that we cannot struggle for the realization of certain values, democratic and non-violent, international and anti-racist. The point is only that to struggle for those values is precisely to avow that one's own position is not sufficient to elaborate the spectrum of the human, that one must enter into a collective work in which one's own status as a subject must, for democratic reasons, become disoriented, exposed to what it does not know.

The point is not to apply social norms to lived social instances, to order and define them (as Foucault has criticized), nor is it to find justificatory mechanisms for the grounding of social norms that are extra-social (even as they operate under the name of the 'social'). There are times when both of these activities do and must take place: we level judgments against criminals for illegal acts, and so subject them to a normalizing procedure; we consider our grounds for action in collective contexts, and try to find modes of deliberation and reflection about which we can agree. But neither of these is all we do with norms. Through recourse to norms, the sphere of the humanly intelligible is circumscribed, and this circumscription is consequential for any ethics and any conception of social transformation. We may try to claim that we must *first* know the fundamentals of the human in order to preserve and promote human life as we know it. But what if the very categories of the human have excluded those who should be described and sheltered within its terms? What if those who ought to belong to the human do not operate within the modes of reasoning and justifying 'validity claims' that have been proffered by Western forms of rationalism? Have we ever yet known the 'human'? And what might it take to approach that knowing? Should we be wary of knowing it too soon or of any final or definitive knowing? If we take the field of the human for granted, then we fail to think critically—and ethically—about the consequential ways in which the human is being produced, reproduced and de-produced. This latter enquiry does not exhaust the field of ethics, but I cannot imagine a 'responsible' ethics or theory of social transformation operating without it.

The necessity of keeping our notion of the 'human' open to a future articulation is essential to the project of international human rights discourse and politics. We see this time and again when the very notion of the 'human' is presupposed; the human is defined in advance, in terms that are distinctively Western, very often American, and, therefore, partial and parochial. When we start with the 'human' as a foundation, then the 'human' at issue in human rights is already known, already defined. And yet, 'the human' is supposed to be the ground for a set of rights and obligations that

are global in reach. How we move from the local to the international (conceived globally in such a way that it does
not recirculate the presumption that all humans belong to
established nation states) is a major question for international
politics, but it takes a specific form for international lesbian,
gay, bi, trans- and intersex struggles as well as for feminism.
An anti-imperialist or, minimally, non-imperialist conception
of international human rights must call into question what is
meant by the human, and learn from the various ways and
means by which it is defined across cultural venues. This
means that local conceptions of what is 'human' or, indeed, of
what the basic conditions and needs of human life are, must
be subjected to reinterpretation, since there are historical
and cultural circumstances in which the 'human' is defined
differently, and its basic needs and, hence, basic entitlements
are made known through various media, through various
kinds of practices, spoken and performed.

A reductive relativism would say that we cannot speak of
the human or of international human rights, since there are
only and always local and provisional understandings of these
terms, and that the generalizations themselves do violence to
the specificity of the meanings in question. This is not my
view. I am not ready to rest there. Indeed, I think we are
compelled to speak of the human, and of the international,
and to find out in particular how 'human rights' do and do
not work, say, in favour of women, of what 'women' are, and
what they are not. But to speak in this way, and to call for
social transformations in the name of women, we must also be
part of a critical democratic project, one which understands
that the category of the 'human' has been used differentially
and with exclusionary aims, that not all humans have been
included within its terms, that the category of 'women' has

been used differentially and with exclusionary aims, and that
not all women have been included within its terms, and that
women have not been fully incorporated into the human, and
that both categories are still in process, underway, unfulfilled,
that we do not yet know, and cannot ever definitively know, in
what the human finally consists. This means that we must
follow a double-path in politics: we must use this language to
assert an entitlement to conditions of life in ways that affirm
the constitutive role of sexuality and gender in political life,
and we must also subject our very categories to critical scrutiny, find out the limits of their inclusivity and translatability,
the presuppositions they include, the ways in which they must
be expanded, destroyed or reworked both to encompass and
open up what it is to be human and gendered. When the UN
conference at Beijing met a few years ago, and we heard there
a discourse on 'women's human rights', or when we hear
from the International Gay and Lesbian Human Rights
Commission, it strikes many people as a paradox. Women's
human rights? Lesbian and gay human rights? But think about
what this coupling actually does. It performs the 'human' as
contingent, that it has in the past, and continues in the present,
to define a variable and restricted population, which may or
may not include lesbians and gays, may or may not include
women. It says that such groups have their own set of human
rights, that what 'human' comes to mean when we think
about the humanness of women is perhaps different from
what 'human' has meant when it has functioned as presumptively male. It also says that these terms are defined, variably, in
relation to one another. And we could certainly make a similar
argument about race. Which populations have qualified as
the 'human' and which have not: what is the history of this
category? Where are we in its history at this time?

I would suggest that in this last process we can only rearticulate or resignify the basic categories of ontology, of being human, of being gendered, of being recognizably sexual, to the extent that we submit ourselves to a process of cultural translation. The point is not to assimilate foreign or unfamiliar notions of gender or humanness into our own, as if it is simply a matter of incorporating alienness into an established lexicon. Cultural translation is also a process of yielding our most fundamental categories—that is, seeing how and why they break up, require resignification when they encounter the limits of an available episteme: what is unknown or not yet known. It is crucial to recognize that the notion of the human will only be built over time in and by the process of cultural translation, where it is not a translation between two languages which stay enclosed, distinct, unified. But rather, *translation will compel each language to change in order to apprehend the other*, and this apprehension, at the limit of what is familiar, parochial and already known, will be the occasion for both an ethical and social transformation. It will constitute a loss, a disorientation, but one in which the 'human' stands a chance of coming into being anew.

When we ask what makes a life liveable, we are asking about certain normative conditions that must be fulfilled for life to become life. And so there are at least two senses of life: one which refers to the minimum biological form of living, and another which intervenes at the start, which establishes minimum conditions for a liveable life with regard to human life.[7] This does not imply that we can disregard the merely living in favour of the 'liveable life' but that we must ask, as we asked about gender violence, what humans require in order to maintain and reproduce the conditions of their own liveability. And what are our politics such that we are, in whatever way is possible, both conceptualizing the possibility of the liveable life, and arranging for its institutional support?

There will always be disagreement about what this means, and those who claim that a single political direction is necessitated by virtue of this commitment will be mistaken. But this is only because to live is to live a life politically, in relation to power, in relation to others, in the act of assuming responsibility for a collective future. To assume responsibility for a future, however, is not to know its direction fully in advance, since the future, especially the future with and for others, requires a certain openness and unknowingness; it implies becoming part of a process in which no one subject can predict the outcome. It also implies that a certain agonism and contestation over the course of direction will and must be in play. Contestation must be in play for politics to become democratic. Democracy does not speak in unison; its tunes are dissonant, and necessarily so. It is not a predictable process; it must be undergone, like a passion must be undergone. It may also be that life itself becomes foreclosed when the right way is decided in advance, when we impose what is right for everyone and without finding a way to enter into community, and to discover there the 'right' in the midst of cultural translation. It may be that what is 'right' and what is 'good' consists in staying open to the tensions that beset the most fundamental categories we require, to know unknowingness at the core of what we know, and what we need, and to recognize the sign of life in what we undergo without certainty about what will come.

2

Introduction to Susan Moller Okin

David Miller

It is both an honour and a pleasure to introduce Professor Susan Okin's Amnesty lecture on women's human rights in the late twentieth century. Before her tragic and untimely death, she was, in my view, unsurpassed as a political philosopher writing on feminist issues. The most notable features of her work, reaching back nearly a quarter of a century to the publication of *Women in Western Political Thought* in 1979, are the lucidity with which she wrote, and her overriding concern to use theoretical analysis to address issues of practical political relevance. This is in contrast to much contemporary work in political philosophy, including feminist political philosophy, which often seems to involve producing concepts and theories of ever-increasing obscurity with no practical aim in sight. From this point of view, *Women in Western Political Thought*, which examined how women were represented in the political theories of Plato, Aristotle, Rousseau and John Stuart Mill, was her most 'academic' book. In her next book, *Justice, Gender and the Family*, published a decade later, she turned the spotlight on to contemporary theories of social justice, and especially their treatment of gender issues. She highlighted the way in which the nuclear family in its current form works to women's disadvantage, and ought therefore to be (though it rarely is in practice) a central concern of such theories.

More recently, Susan Okin turned her attention to the

implications for women of multiculturalism, the political perspective whose main aim is to argue for policies that provide special protection for minority cultures. In her provocatively titled essay 'Is Multiculturalism Bad for Women?', which provoked a heated debate, Okin argued that cultural protection often means the protection of cultural practices which control and subordinate women, and so feminists ought at the very least to subject to close critical scrutiny proposals to give special rights to groups whose internal cultures are patriarchal. Her focus in this essay was on minority groups within Western liberal societies, but in her Amnesty lecture that follows she broadened her scope to include developing nations whose whole culture may be opposed to liberal ideas of gender equality.

Okin's argument is that the growing success of the movement for women's human rights—success in the sense that the validity of these rights has been proclaimed in documents such as the *Platform for Action* adopted by the UN World Women's Conference in Beijing in 1995—has been contradicted on the ground by two counter-forces. One is the ability of cultural groups throughout the world to have women's rights set aside in the name of cultural traditions—to protect practices such as unequal marriage and divorce laws, discrimination at work and so forth. The other is the imposition by external bodies such as the IMF of economic policies that are insensitive to the realities of women's position in developing countries, especially the work they do that is unpaid and that therefore does not register in conventional measures of economic growth. The combined effect of these two forces has been to undermine the human rights of many of the world's most vulnerable women, the official documents notwithstanding.

The case that Okin makes in this lecture is a powerful and persuasive one, and I have no wish to question her critique of ill-thought-out economic policies that have damaged women's economic prospects in many places, or her suggestions for new policies to take their place. I would, however, like to reflect briefly on the question of human rights as it bears on the position of women in non-Western societies. The idea of human rights has deservedly become a popular weapon for attacking policies and practices that are harmful to women, and in many cases—for instance, the issue of female circumcision—it provides an appropriate standard against which to judge them. There is a danger, however, that human rights are expanded to include claims and demands that are prominent in Western liberal thought, but may not be applicable to societies with different cultural backgrounds. When this happens it is all too easy for human rights to be written off as nothing more than an expression of Western liberalism. To avoid the danger, we need to be clear about which claims and demands genuinely belong on the list of human rights, and which are better seen as principles or ideals to which those of us who live in Western societies may be deeply committed, but are not essential to human lives in all circumstances.

Okin does not say explicitly how she understands human rights, relying to a considerable extent on the *Platform for Action* that emerged from the 1995 World Women's Conference. However, the issues which the *Platform* addresses range from those that clearly involve breaches of human rights—for instance, violence against women, female malnutrition and inadequate access to health care—to those that involve gender inequality, but not so obviously violations of human rights—for instance, 'stereotyping of women and neglect of women's perspectives in the media'. However regrettable this may be, the harm involved is not the kind of basic harm that corresponds to a human right.

More generally, I detect in Okin's essay a tendency to run together the question of women's human rights with the question of gender inequality. We need to ask when inequalities become so damaging to women's interests that their human rights are put in question. It is well known that in Western societies women are typically paid less than men for doing the same job. This is clearly a social injustice, but it does not amount to a violation of human rights except in cases where the pay difference means that the women involved are not getting a wage that is adequate to cover their basic needs. In non-Western societies, gender inequality often takes the form of excluding women from certain occupations (for instance, from holding religious or political offices). This offends our idea of equality of opportunity. But from a human rights perspective, the question we should ask is whether the effect of the exclusions is to put in jeopardy basic rights such as the right to a living wage or to freedom of expression.

None of this is meant to challenge the particular example that Okin focuses on in this part of her study, namely, the inequalities that disfigure Muslim and Jewish laws governing marriage and divorce. Her claim is that these laws leave women in such communities vulnerable to oppression and economic exploitation. Thus on human rights grounds we have good reason to confront these cultures in their present form, and I agree with Okin that 'cultural rights' should not be interpreted so as to protect them from such a confrontation. My claim is only that women's human rights and women's equality are different, albeit sometimes overlapping, issues, and that we need to consider them separately if we want to avoid making human rights a synonym for all the political values that we Western liberals treasure.

Women's Human Rights in the Late Twentieth Century: One Step Forward, Two Steps Back

Susan Moller Okin

It is well known that, virtually worldwide, awareness of women's rights and of the ubiquitous and frequent violation of these rights has grown exponentially in the past two decades. A broad-based international women's movement, originating in the mid-1970s, became focused during the 1980s on gaining recognition as human rights for rights that are of central importance in women's lives. This movement to expand global awareness of women's rights, and to integrate them fully into the human rights recognized in international law, has had untold positive effects. It has brought together groups of women throughout the world, in all its social and cultural variety, to discuss problems and injuries that they have experienced in common, as well as those that are more particular to women from their different local, national or regional contexts. It has helped many non-feminists as well as feminists throughout the world to realize that human rights must be reconceptualized in crucial ways if they are to address the multiple and serious ways in which the rights of women are violated *because they are women*. This movement and its effects are the very significant 'one step forward' of my title. First, I will give a brief summary of its history. Then, I shall go on to discuss the 'two steps back'—movements or courses of action that, I shall argue, have set back the cause of women's rights during the same two decades. The idea at the basis of the first of these steps is the claim that women's human rights are justifiably limited by the rights of peoples to the protection of their cultures or to their freedom of religious practices. The ideas behind the second step are the supposedly gender-neutral but actually male-biased assumptions of neoclassical economics, in particular, development economics.

One Step Forward

The global movement for women's human rights was, to some extent, co-ordinated and funded from above, by non-governmental organizations (NGOs)—by feminist groups such as the Center for Women's Global Leadership and Women Living Under Muslim Laws, and by human rights advocates such as Human Rights Watch and Amnesty International, as well as by the United Nations. To a very significant extent though, as I shall explain, it was a grass-roots movement.[1] Prior to the United Nations Conference on Human Rights, held in Vienna in 1993, 900 non-governmental organizations (NGOs), which had been established for a variety of causes concerned with the well-being or empowerment of women, participated in a vast petition drive aimed at the explicit recognition, at the Vienna meeting, of women's human rights. Promulgated in twenty-four languages, the petition was signed (with signatures ranging from names to thumb prints) by nearly half a million women, including women from 124 of the world's countries. The petition called upon the 1993 conference 'to comprehensively address *women's* rights at every level of its proceedings' and demanded 'that gender violence, a universal phenomenon which takes many forms across culture, race, and class, be recognized as a violation of human rights requiring immediate action'.[2] Testimonials from women around the world whose basic rights had been violated by various kinds of violence against them made up a dramatic event in Vienna. Widely reported on by the media, this instance of what might be called auto-biographical documentary made a striking impression on the NGO representatives and (in a shortened form) on the members of the official (government) delegations, many of whom had little or no previous experience of the concept 'women's rights as human rights'.

Once such attention had been beamed on women's rights at a major international human rights conference, and the Fourth World Women's Conference was being planned for Beijing in 1995, the role and actions of grass-roots women's organizations around the world became even more important. Women from all over the world—brought together as members of community action groups, such as the Self Employed Women's Association (SEWA) in India, or members of micro-credit organizations, such as the Grameen Bank, which was started in Bangladesh—contributed to an agenda that was forged at local, national and regional levels in prepar-ation for the international conference. From the ground up, then, though with some catalysing and funding from above, were developed the conceptions of women's needs, situations, problems and rights that were later to be articulated at Beijing. While many viewpoints emerged about what does or does not constitute discrimination against women or violation of women's rights more broadly conceived, certain common themes soon emerged. Unlike previous conceptions of human rights, the emerging way of thinking did not view the state as the major or most likely violator of women's human rights.

Instead, these rights were seen as far more likely to be violated by persons, usually but not only men, to whom the women were closely related—including both fathers and husbands or other male partners. Second, these rights violations were often masked or hidden by the public/private dichotomy, which depicts family or domestic life as private in the sense that it is beyond the range of rights talk and concerns. As a vivid example, take the Universal Declaration's Article 12, which protects a right-holder from 'arbitrary interference with . . . his privacy, family, home . . . [and] attacks upon his honour'. This clause, which on the surface may seem merely a benign protection of the privacy of all 'persons', has sometimes been interpreted in a way that endangers women and children: as a constraint on the authority of states to *protect* women and children in their homes from violations of their rights by more powerful family members.[3]

The reports and recommendations of the many local, national and regional meetings around the world held in preparation for Beijing provide excellent evidence of what women in many different socioeconomic and cultural circumstance consider most basic to their well-being and indispensable in their lives. Again, as in the lead-up to the Vienna Conference, violence against women of many kinds—ranging from domestic abuse to rape (including marital rape) and from the forced or otherwise coerced marriage of girls to female genital mutilation—was considered by most of those reporting at the meetings to be a major issue. For strategic purposes, including the need to present a united front and to make a strong impact on powerful, influential people and governments who were apathetic or uninformed about gender inequity, the movement coalesced around the issue of violence against women. It was this issue above all which led to the realization that human rights needed to be reconceived in order adequately to address women's rights. For, as those at the grass roots made clear, women were more likely to suffer from violence in the private sphere, from men with whom they lived intimately—men in their own families—as they were to suffer violence in the public sphere, from the state, which had been the preeminent concern of previous human rights advocates. Having drawn attention to women's rights through the dramatic example of violence, and having reconceived human rights so as to fully include rights that were of particular relevance in women's lives, the women's rights as human rights movement then compiled—again, working from the grass roots—a substantial and varied list of rights of sufficient significance to be considered human rights of all women, everywhere.

The final *Platform for Action*, adopted in Beijing in September 1995—in the case of some clauses after considerable political struggle—emphasizes above all the following 'critical areas of concern' for the world's women: the burden of increasing poverty—including overwork (paid and unpaid), underpay and malnutrition; unequal and inadequate education; unequal and inadequate health care; many forms of violence against women and other effects of violent conflict on women; unequal access to power, decision-making, resources and management of the environment; stereotyping of women and neglect of women's perspectives in the media; and persistent discrimination against and violation of the rights of the girl child.[4] There is no doubt from this document, as well as from the struggles of the movement to get it adopted, that the voices of the poor and disadvantaged were able to penetrate the walls of the official government forum as well as the NGO forum. These voices confirm the views, heard but often then lost in the clamour at many of the previous UN human rights and even women's conferences, that their highest priorities are the fulfilment of women's basic needs, the acquisition of the resources and skills that constitute their capacity to make a living for themselves and their children, and the attainment of more control over central aspects of their lives.[5]

In a move which presages one of the two steps back that I shall be addressing below, the *Platform* also states clearly that the conventional ways of thinking of neoclassical economics, translated into the policies of the world's most powerful financial institutions, have contributed to the problems of many women, especially poor women, in LDCs, and must be changed. 'Insufficient attention to gender analysis,' it states, has meant that 'women's contributions remain too often ignored in economic structures. . . . As a result, many policies and programs may continue to contribute to inequalities between women and men. Where progress has been made in integrating gender perspectives, program and policy effectiveness has also been enhanced.'[6] Explicit focus is aimed at problems arising from the structural adjustment policies that have been pursued by the World Bank and the International Monetary Fund from the late 1970s, especially their measures for reducing public expenditure on social services such as health care. In the *Platform*'s initial discussion of the recent 'expansion of unspeakable poverty' in many parts of the world, structural adjustment programmes and the harm done by them to vulnerable and disadvantaged groups are targeted for criticism numerous times. The document points out that such policies have 'led to a reduction in social expenditures, thereby adversely affecting women', have 'shifted . . . responsibilities for basic social services . . . from Governments to women', 'have had a disproportionately negative impact on women's employment' and 'have not always been designed to take account of their impact on women and girl children, especially those living in poverty'—whose numbers have grown.[7]

In a move which refers to the other of the two steps back that I will turn to below, the *Platform*'s stances on the relationship between both religion and culture on the one hand, and women on the other hand, is more nuanced and less straightforwardly positive than those of previous human rights documents. On the one hand, it endorses the importance of religious freedom, acknowledging that religion 'plays a central role in the lives of millions of women and men', and that it 'may, and can, contribute to fulfilling women's and men's moral, ethical, and spiritual needs'. However, it by no means highlights religion or spirituality as somehow essential to a complete human life. It also specifically points out that 'any form of [religious] extremism may have a negative effect on women and can lead to violence and discrimination'.[8]

Moreover, the *Platform* adopts the strongest position yet taken at a United Nations human rights meeting on the priority of women's human rights over the claims coming from 'various historical, cultural, and religious backgrounds', in cases where the two come into conflict. The conference discussions made a breakthrough in that they addressed head-on the conflict between the rights of peoples or cultural groups and the rights of women. As voiced by Hilary Charlesworth a year earlier, the problem is that collective rights, which are sometimes called 'third generation rights', such as the right to 'self-determination' or to 'cultural development', have not infrequently been 'invoked, and supported, recently in a number of contexts to allow the oppression of women'.[9] As we shall see, while the Beijing *Platform* strongly endorses anti-relativist positions, it also stresses the importance of understanding and evaluating women's rights and their violations with particular attention to cultural context. This brings us to discussion of the first step back: culturally relativist claims against women's equality.

A First Step Back: Cultural Rights Claims Against Women's Equality

One of the greatest problems—both theoretical and practical —of recent developments in international human rights results from the coincidence of the increasing emphasis on women's human rights with the rising claims of the rights of various kinds of groups, or peoples, to the integrity of their various cultures, traditions and religions. On the one hand, we have the phenomenon I have been discussing up to now: the increasing recognition that the earlier, post-World War II conceptions of human rights were built on the unspoken assumption that the right-holder was a male household head, rather than each individual person. Thus much needed to be rethought and much remained to be done if even women's most basic human rights were to be realized. On the other hand, especially in the context of recent colonialism, it is widely believed that attending to the human rights of individuals does not suffice: the right of self-determination has been held to belong to groups or to peoples. While there is undoubtedly legitimacy to this claim, those who make it have paid little attention to 'the fact that the most prominent identity [of such groups] is usually a construct of the most powerful players in this group'—who are usually older, male members of the group.[10] The tension between the two claims—that women must be fully included in human rights

90

talk and protections, and that 'peoples' have claims to some important human rights—was clearly evident at the 1995 UN Fourth World Conference on Women in Beijing. After much debate and dispute, the final *Platform* stated: 'While the significance of national and religious particularities and various historical, cultural and religious systems must be kept in mind, it is the duty of states, regardless of their political, economic and cultural systems, to promote and protect all human rights and fundamental freedoms.'[11] In its coverage the following day, the *New York Times* expressed the view that this 'affirmation that women's rights should supercede national traditions [was] arguably the most far-reaching stance on human rights ever taken at a United Nations gathering'.[12] We feminists are quite divided about issues where the two types of rights conflict. Some, including myself, tend to favour women's rights to be treated as equals over groups' or people's rights to preserve and promote their cultures in cases where the two conflict, and argue that it is, at the very least, incumbent on anyone claiming group or people's rights on the basis of cultural or ethnic identity to ensure that the women of the cultural or religious group are involved in the making of such claims and the associated discussions.[13] On the other hand, some feminists consider it highly objectionable—a crime akin to colonialism—for anyone outside of a particular religious or cultural community even to raise the issue of whether women's rights are truncated within that community's tradition.[14]

The tension between a number of women's rights and the claims of various religious or cultural groups is considerable. I shall argue that where religious or cultural claims trump women's claims to equality, considerable harm often accrues to women, and consequently to their children as well. In a number of countries in the less economically developed world, including some of the most populous ones, the laws of marriage and divorce are religiously based and are biased towards giving men additional power within marriage and in the event of divorce. I will discuss how and why such marital laws (or 'personal laws', as they are often called) are explicitly justified, against claims in favour of the equal treatment of women, by appeals to culture or religion. I believe that such attempts at justification fail (except in certain very specifically defined circumstances that are most unlikely to exist in practice). In short, then, claims based on culture or religion often *do*, but, I argue, *should not*, trump women's equality with men. However, this is not in any way to deny that understanding the relevant cultural or religious context is essential for evaluating women's rights and violations of such rights.

In the context of current discussions in political theory about multiculturalism (in which the focus is often on the rights of minority groups *within* the various nation states), it needs to be emphasized that the claim that cultural particularities should have special recognition is made by sovereign states as well as by groups within states. On the one hand, the Universal Declaration of Human Rights of 1948 claimed, quite remarkably, that women and men have equal rights; the document purportedly applies to both men and women equally. Thirty years later, since it was obvious that many countries of the world, if not all, retained laws and policies that clearly discriminated, treating women and men very differently, in the great majority of cases favouring the former, the Convention on the Elimination of All Forms of Discrimination Against Women was formulated and promulgated. Whatever one thinks about the practical effectiveness of such documents or the movements that give rise to them, one can learn quite a lot by countries' reactions to them. Of all the international human rights documents, this Convention has had by far the most 'reservations' expressed by signatory countries. A number of these have to do with all or parts of the Convention's clause stating that women and men are to be equal in marriage and divorce, and most of them base their objections on religious or cultural grounds. Of those (almost all) countries that have signed and/or ratified the Convention—the United States has signed but not ratified it—India, Bangladesh, Iraq, Jordan, Morocco and Israel are among those that have expressed reservations against Article 16, which specifies that men and women are to have 'the same rights and responsibilities during marriage and at its dissolution'. Most of these countries state, more or less explicitly, that because their marriage and divorce laws are in accord with the Islamic Shari'a, which holds that husbands and wives have different, complementary roles and rights, they cannot agree to the 'same rights and responsibilities' clause. Some, notably India and Israel, express reservations to the same article on the grounds that the terms of marriage and divorce are in the hands of the *various* religious communities officially recognized in these countries.

In this context it is worth noting that reservations based on culture or religion are by no means the order of the day in international law. A recent study by Joel Paul shows that such justifications for the unequal treatment of women stand a considerably higher chance of being accepted than culturally based claims made about other issues.[15] No such reservations, or recourse to such claims, for example, were expressed by countries signing the 1965 Convention on the Elimination of all forms of Racial Discrimination. Moreover, when the Afrikaaner-dominated regime made parallel claims about its culture, and about the notion that apartheid was necessary for its preservation, it simply reinforced its status as international pariah. In addition, culturally based claims for exceptions to treaties or conventions on subjects such as whaling and cutting down the rain forests have considerably less chance of gaining international legal recognition than do culturally based exemptions from clauses of the anti-discrimination Convention on Women. That is to say, in short, that culture or religions do *not* usually trump in cases involving such matters as eliminating racial discrimination or protecting the rain forest; far more often, culture or religion *have been allowed to* trump where the issue of women's equality is concerned.

As many have noted, women's equality and cultures or religions have been on a collision course for a long time. During the colonial period, the treatment of women within a number of colonized cultures was one of the issues that was often taken up by colonial powers as proof of the inherently less civilized or progressive aspects of the indigenous culture. These chauvinistic and often hypocritical claims for the more equal treatment of women set the stage for later antagonism. Perhaps with some awareness of this potential, the 1948 Declaration boldly pronounced, in the face of myriad practices and laws that violated each, both the equal rights of women and the right of all to culture and to freedom of religious belief and practice. The tension was further highlighted when 'third generation' rights—the rights of peoples, or culturally distinct groups, to preserve their cultures and traditions—were promulgated as part of the Convention on Social, Economic and Cultural Rights, in 1966. Those who, like myself, are concerned about this tension do not think that cultural and religious freedoms are unimportant. Far from it, especially in the wake of centuries of colonialism. In many cases they are of crucial importance to the members of religious or cultural groups who suffer under oppressive conditions or would be likely to live in states of continual conflict, without the explicit protection of their rights to their separate and distinct religious or cultural practices. That some peoples—whether they make up a single nation state or a minority group within a nation state—need certain rights and protection in order to preserve and protect their languages, beliefs and customs is by now well established. At the same time there is a very real conflict, in many cases, which affects hundreds of millions of the world's women, between such protections and women's equality. Martha Nussbaum has written eloquently about what she terms 'the liberal dilemma' of respect for religious freedom when it comes into conflict with the commitment to other human rights, including women's right to equal treatment and respect.[16] Let us look now at how this conflict occurs in practice, even within liberal democratic states which in many respects place a value on the legal equality of each and every one of their citizens. Let us take the cases of group rights in India, the world's second most populous state and its largest liberal democracy, and in Israel, as our examples.

In both India and Israel, marriage and divorce are controlled by the various religious groups, or communities, as they are termed in India, within them. For various reasons, some having to do with the colonial past (during which little of indigenous cultures was often left standing except customs having to do with women, marriage and families), some having to do with connections between religions and male control, and some having to do with the fact that frequently it is women within families who are the primary transmitters of cultures, many cultural and religious groups have come to have a particular stake in regulating the relations between spouses and within families. This means, among other things, that the many millions of Indian *Muslim* women can be divorced unilaterally by their husbands at any time, but have no similar right to leave a miserable marriage. Rather, they depend for this ability on the ruling of a religious court judge, which is given only for specific, limited reasons, such as a husband's desertion or failure to provide economic support. Moreover, according to the Shari'a law as practised in India, a Muslim woman is not entitled to any continued support from her husband in the event of divorce, no matter how the marriage was dissolved and regardless of the extent to which the division of labour within the marriage leaves the wife economically vulnerable. A particularly infamous case during the late twentieth century in India involved a woman who had raised five children and was unilaterally divorced, and who was left homeless and destitute after a forty-year marriage to a successful lawyer.[17] She was supposed, according to Muslim law, to rely on her family of origin, or charity, to support her for the rest of her life. When the Indian Supreme Court ordered the husband to pay her a small maintenance, major disputes broke out between the Muslim minority, which claimed its communal right of religious freedom was being violated, and the Hindu majority, which claimed to be upholding the rights of Muslim women. Not surprisingly, as is so often the case, women within the minority group who were concerned with Muslim women's inequality were in an impossible situation, as was the divorced woman—Shah Bano—herself. Either they were for women's rights and regarded as traitors to their community; or they were for Muslim rights and considered traitors to the advancement of women. The end of the affair was not good for Muslim women; in response to the uproar, the Indian Parliament passed the oddly named 'Muslim Women (Protection of Rights on Divorce) Bill'—which restored the status quo ante, and thereby did anything *but* protect the rights of Muslim women on divorce.

In the case of Israel, I shall take Jewish family law as my example of how the group-based religious personal laws affect the rights and the lives of women. Orthodox Jewish law regulates marriage and divorce between all Jews within Israel. The only way for a Jewish Israeli to avoid the inequalities of Orthodox marriage and divorce law is to get married outside of Israel; thus many marrying couples head off to Cyprus to marry legally, returning to Israel for the celebrations. In the absence of such resources there is no choice but to marry the Orthodox way. Orthodox Jewish marriage and divorce law is ultimately based on one Torah passage, from the Book of Deuteronomy, Chapter XXIV, 1–4, which reads:

A man takes a wife and possesses her. She fails to please him because he finds some indecency about her, and he writes her a bill of divorcement, hands it to her, and sends her away from his house; she leaves his house and becomes the wife of another man; then the second man rejects her, writes her a bill of divorcement, hands it to her, and sends her away from his house. . . .

Throughout the early period of Judaism, the 'taking', 'possessing' and 'sending away' of wives included polygamy, as marriage still does in Islam, as well as the extreme inequality of male-controlled unilateral divorce. About a thousand years ago, the progressive Talmudic scholar Rabbi Gershom saw to it that Halakhic marriage was reformed. It was no longer permitted for a Jewish man to marry multiple wives; neither, from then on, could he divorce his wife unilaterally, without her consent. However, the original inequality persists regarding the husband's control over giving his wife the 'bill of divorcement', or *get*.

This remaining substantial inequality in Halakhic law has a significant effect on the lives of many women in Israel. The 'better' outcome for a divorcing Jewish woman who has been married in Israel is to have her husband throw the *get* in her face, as he is permitted and even expected to do during the rabbinical court's divorce proceedings. The worse outcome is for him to refuse to give her the *get*. For unless a husband gives his wife a *get*, she is not released from the marriage, though it is, for all practical purposes, over. She cannot remarry; nor can she bear children who are regarded as legitimate, Jewish children; any she bears will be termed 'bastards' and not permitted to marry Jews who are not also bastards like themselves. But a divorcing wife has no such power over her husband, even though without the giving of the *get* he too is formally still married to her. Obvious inequality results, since he can not only manacle his wife, but can also proceed with his own life virtually unimpeded. He can father legitimate Jewish children, and can in some circumstances even marry a second wife with the permission of a rabbinical court. His 'first wife' of the incomplete divorce, however, is stuck in life as if she were still in reality his wife—stuck in a marriage that has long since died, and frequently subjected to extortion by a man who is able to move on.

It seems clear on the face of it that women are seriously disadvantaged by such personal laws. However, a defender of religious group rights in the Indian or Israeli case might say: 'Yes, women are disadvantaged, in that they do not have equal rights within their religious groups' laws of marriage and divorce. But controlling personal or family law is of especial importance to these groups, even more so when they are in a minority, because of the part such law plays in the preservation of their religion and culture. It is, with all its unequal treatment of women, an important aspect of their religious freedom. Moreover, overall, the women, too, benefit from having their group's way of life protected. In India, for example, surely women as well as men have suffered greatly from communalist violence; and surely Muslim women would suffer, as well as Muslim men, were the Hindu majority to gain control over the Muslim minority. So surely the protection of her religious community is as important to a woman as it is to a man?'

These claims have considerable weight. They help to explain why, so often, women who are members of a minority or otherwise oppressed cultural or religious group defend laws and practices that seem to disadvantage and subordinate them within their own group. Yet I believe each of the claims can be answered. To be sure, control of family or personal law is of special, central importance to religious or cultural minority groups, although at least part of the reason for this is a matter of historical contingency, in that these were often parts of the law that it was of less interest, and more potential trouble, for colonizers to control. However this may be, one must surely take into consideration that issues having to do with personal and family law are *also* of special, central importance to *women*. If the availability and the terms of divorce are not equal, this inequality affects the whole of marriage and family life. For women especially, inequality within marriage and family life, in turn, reverberates throughout their entire lives.

Albert O. Hirschman's work on the relationship of exit to voice provides a theoretical basis for the importance of the unequal terms of divorce within marriage.[18] His theory, though developed in the context of quite different social institutions and relationships, clearly seems to apply also to marriage. If the terms of divorce are considerably less favourable to one party in a marriage, or if they even enable one party to exit the marriage far more easily than the other, surely this must affect the marriage, giving more power to the party for whom exit is an easier or more feasible option. Even when the terms of divorce are equal, as Martha Fineman and I and others have argued, the traditional division of labour between the sexes tends to make divorce less advantageous for women than for men—who usually possess far more of the couple's human capital, and are less likely to live, post-divorce, with dependent children.[19] However, the effect of the inequality of divorce on an ongoing marriage is, surely, likely to be far greater if the *terms* of divorce are very different for wives than for husbands, as is so often the case when religious law governs marriage. In such situations, it seems extremely unlikely that a woman would be able to exert influence equal to that of her husband over major or even minor decisions made within her marital family—even decisions governing her own day-to-day life and conduct. Empirical work done on these issues by economists such as Amartya Sen and Partha Dasgupta confirms this hypothesis.[20] Such inequalities cannot but be disadvantageous for children, too; for women's control over family resources and income is well known to be far more closely correlated with their children's nutrition, health care, education and other basic well-being than is men's.

On top of all this, as feminists as long ago as Mary Wollstonecraft and John Stuart Mill pointed out, if women are not equal within marriage, they cannot be equal in any other sphere of life: wage work, politics, the marketplace and so on.[21] All other equal rights for women can be virtually nullified by this single inequality in their lives. Thus in a way, for countries to sign and ratify the CEDAW, but to express reservations about equality within marriage, is not very different from their not signing or ratifying it at all.

In responding to the second point, that overall women too benefit from the type of religious or cultural group rights that exist in India and Israel, I argue that it presents a false dichotomy: *either* cultural or religious group rights *or* equality for women. Of course, historically and contingently, this is the question. But is there any justice in it? Are men ever required to sacrifice their rights to equal treatment in order to protect or preserve their cultural or religious identity? I cannot readily think of an example. And so one may well ask: why aren't women's human rights always given first priority? Since, at least from a liberal perspective, any group right must be justified by the benefits it brings to individual human beings, why isn't the equality of persons—including the women and the men—within the group always made a prerequisite for the granting of any group right? During the late twentieth century, this standard came to be applied where *racial* (in)equality was concerned, without provoking an outcry about limiting religious freedom; why not to sex (in)equality? Shouldn't any religious or cultural group that enjoys official recognition or privilege within a liberal political society have to first reform its rules and practices so as to bring them in line with the equality of men and women?[22] (This should apply to groups with tax-exempt status such as the Catholic Church as much as it would to Orthodox Jews in Israel or Muslims in India.) The burden of justification surely lies with those arguing differently. But though this is where the fundamental equality of human beings that lies at the basis of both liberalism and human rights would lead us, it does *not* seem to be the direction in which contemporary international politics are moving. As feminist international lawyers Hilary Charlesworth and Christine Chinkin wrote recently: 'While the right to gender equality on the one hand, and religious and cultural rights on the other, can be reconciled by limiting the latter, in political practice cultural and religious freedom are accorded much higher priority nationally and internationally.'[23]

I have given some reasons why we should regard such prioritizing as unjustified. We should view the contemporary successes of cultural and religious claims against women's equality as a temporary political setback—fuelled in the global South by reasonable resentment about the damage done by colonialism and by continued economic imperialism, and both accepted and rationalized (as Joel Paul demonstrates) more than other culture-based claims because of the persistence of patriarchy in the global North. There is no soundly argued justification for such claims that warrants their permanent acceptance. Culture, religion, and the groups that base their claims on them should not take permanent priority over each individual human being's right to be treated with equal dignity and respect. Culture is not sacred—even though it is often made to appear so, by reference to ancient text, law and tradition. It is, after all, in the end just 'ways of doing things', and some of these can and do change without greatly affecting all of the other aspects of a culture. Religions, too, have undergone considerable reform over time. Most if not all religions, in some of their forms and in some periods of their histories, have included repugnant doctrines and despicable practices. That such doctrines and practices have the imprimatur of being 'religious' does not make them any more justified or less horrible. Surely religions should be able to encompass sex equality, just as most of them have come to encompass racial equality and an anti-caste principle. Finally, neither culture nor religion is either hegemonic or non-contested; both are often contested and open to question. Those versions of culture and religion that resist the accommodation of gender equality should lose recognition in a global order with any serious aspirations toward the fulfilment of the human rights of women.

A Second Step Back: Economics, Gender and Structural Adjustment Policies

Development Economics and Gender

The second step back, a step away from the fulfilment of many women's human rights, has been due to the misconceptions of most development theories and the consequent graphic failure of policies based on them—*especially* during the last quarter century of development. Both neglect of issues of gender and misunderstandings about gender have affected international development policies from the early post-World War II period, though I cannot cover the earlier period in any depth here. A large part of the problem has to do with some of the fundamental assumptions and ways of thinking of neoclassical economics, which have prevailed virtually unchallenged within official circles in the global North and, more importantly, in the two most important global financial institutions, the World Bank and the International Monetary Fund. Only in around 1990 were such assumptions seriously questioned within some parts of these institutions, and the challenge is being taken seriously only very belatedly.

Let us look at three particularly troubling assumptions and ways of thinking that are at the core of widely held theories of development economics. The neoclassical theories that still tend to prevail in powerful places typically measure the success or lack of success of development only in terms of economic growth, which is measured in terms of per capita gross domestic product (GDP). The assumption has been that as countries grew economically, their people would be better off. Growth was thought to lead to the more equal distribution of improved standards of living and to the reduction of poverty, as well as to better average standards of living.[24] Thus the development projects, programmes, loans and economic aid that were delivered to the less from the more developed world were aimed at economic growth, primarily through industrialization on the one hand, and making agriculture more high tech on the other. In the early decades of development, vast amounts of money were spent on large-scale development projects such as dams.

That the growth of GDP is a misleading measure of development—except when the latter is very narrowly construed—is easily illustrated: the GDP of the United States is ten times that of Costa Rica, yet life expectancy, which is a reasonable measure of health, an important aspect of human well-being, is only one year shorter in Costa Rica than it is in the USA. How can this be so? One reason is that per capita GDP tells us nothing at all about the *distribution* of wealth or of income. The belief that economic development as defined by the growth of GDP would lead to greater equality, both among the different countries of the world and within them, has turned out to be seriously wrong. Even where GDP has risen markedly, in many cases inequality has increased—the gap between the rich and the poor has grown. This has happened within many of the most and of the least industrialized of the world's countries over the past few decades. At the same time, economic inequality *among* countries has grown, with the rich becoming richer and many of the poor becoming poorer. Per capita GDP tells us nothing about whether (as is the case in many countries of the world) there is a small wealthy elite and the vast majority of people are very poor, or whether wealth and income are distributed far more evenly. Likewise, the growth of per capita GDP tells us nothing at all about how a society uses its resources and its productivity. One of the evident reasons why Costa Rica's life expectancy almost equals that of the USA is that the country has no military; thus a far greater proportion of its public expenditure is on education and health care. So long as one focuses on measuring the growth of GDP, one knows little about how the people of a country are actually thriving. Yet, apart from a brief period in the early 1970s, it was not until the 1990s that the World Bank—by far the largest development agency in the world—seriously began to take notice of this. Many development projects, especially large-scale ones such as dams, on which most development funds were spent until recently, may have contributed to the growth of GDP at the same time as they actually detracted from the quality of life of the people. As a West African woman participant said to me recently during a discussion of World Bank programme evaluations: 'Sometimes the programme is declared a success, even though the people have died.'

A second important, and importantly misleading, assumption of neoclassical economics is the way GDP is measured, which is by adding the value of all the new goods and the services that are produced and sold within a society in a given year. The only work or productivity that has economic value is that which is transacted in the marketplace. All the unpaid labour that is done, the vast majority of it by women, does not count and is, literally, not counted, by economists. This, too, is problematic and can be seriously misleading even in the countries of origin of those who claimed to be development experts. Their blindness about gender and ignorance of relations between the sexes often led such experts to make ridiculous assumptions, which often led, not surprisingly, by highly complex processes of reasoning to equally ridiculous conclusions.

Why would highly intelligent economists make the mistake of not counting unpaid labour, no matter how socially necessary such labour is? Since economics aspires to the status of a science, it aims to be as theoretically sparse and as quantitative as possible. This means that, if something is not readily quantifiable, economists tend to ignore it. Anything that is not exchanged in the market and so does not have a market price is hard for economists to measure. Therefore, they do not 'count' such labour or productivity as having economic value (as contributing to GDP, for example). Thus all the work that women typically do as wives and mothers, in bearing and raising children, cleaning houses and clothes, shopping and cooking, taking care of the sick and aged, volunteer work in schools and in the community at large, does not count economically.[25] A hypothetical example easily illustrates the magnitude of this omission. If every homemaker in the USA were one day to start paying the homemaker living immediately to the south of her (or him, in the rare case) to do her daily work, no more work would be done than had been done the day before, but the country's total GDP would suddenly escalate by hundreds of billions of dollars. Since far more of women's labour is unpaid in the less industrialized parts of the world than in the more industrialized—subsistence farming is done mostly by women in many parts of the world, as is the time-intensive carrying of water and fuel for daily needs—the failure of economists to count such labour is even more misleading in these contexts, and the policy decisions based on their consequent calculations are even more likely to lead to unintended results.

Another, in this case actual, historical example illustrates the absurdities that the assumption that unpaid labour is without economic value can lead to in cost–benefit analyses.[26] An economist-led study of the costs and benefits of breast-feeding as compared with formula feeding of infants in developing countries counted, on the credit side, the nutritional and health benefits in terms of height, weight and resistance to infectious diseases (all easily measurable), comparing those of the breast-fed children with those of the bottle-fed children. On the debit side, the study counted the costs of formula and bottles, compared with . . . zero, yes, *nothing at all*. Women's breasts and the milk and calories they provide are apparently 'free'. Anyone who has ever breast-fed a baby knows this to be ludicrous. Of course breast-feeding has costs: it takes considerably longer than bottle-feeding; it uses up a considerable amount of calories, which the mother has to replace if she is not to become undernourished herself; and it requires that the mother, rather than any other care provider, be present to feed the infant, which of course means considerable opportunity costs for the mother. However, since breast-feeding is *not* typically exchanged in the market, even though it might be, economists cannot easily put a price on it, and seem not to be bothered to try to estimate the real costs—in time, calories and lost opportunities for paid work—that it has for women. It is not even that these factors are impossible to measure; all of them can and no doubt would be measured if so much of women's work were not so easily dismissed by the dismal science of economics. Not surprisingly, perhaps, the assumption that unpaid labour has no economic value has led to some very serious mistakes on the part of development economists, and thereby to some disastrously mistaken policies by the global institutions ruled over by economists—the World Bank and the International Monetary Fund.

The third badly misleading assumption typically made by economists is that households or families can be treated as if they were individuals. This too, as I shall explain below, is even more of a problem in the context of the less developed than the more developed world. For a couple of decades now, feminists have challenged economists' assumptions about households; but only recently have mainstream economists begun to take any notice.[27] In general, of course, economics is about individual 'economic actors', who are assumed to be self-interested and rational. That is to say, each is assumed to have a distinct aim or end ('his utility function' in economic parlance) and to pursue the least costly means to that end. While economists know, of course, as the rest of us do, that households usually contain a number of distinct persons, they have a very strong incentive to assume that each household can be treated as if it were a single individual. For if the different members of each household were acknowledged to have distinct economic aims or utility functions, it would introduce into economic theories complications that economists are unwilling to cope with. Such complications would undoubtedly reduce the parsimony of their theories. Earlier economists simply *assumed*, without explanation, that households could be treated as if they were single individuals. More recently (perhaps as part of a general late twentieth-century trend in many disciplines to recognize, finally, that women are distinct persons) they have thought it necessary to explain this assumption.

The most popular way of doing this is best known from the work of an economist of the Chicago School, Nobel Prize winner Gary Becker. In Becker's *A Treatise on the Family*, he first argues that, just as with an individual, a family's economic motivation may be assumed to be maximizing its utility.[28] He then moves on to suggest that the heads of households can be assumed to be beneficent altruists. In *this* capacity they do not act self-interestedly but rather the opposite: each such 'head' takes account of the interests of all other members of his family equally with his own. Thus, for example, a husband is assumed, according to Becker, to regard additional labour on his wife's part as just as costly as additional labour done by himself. Similarly, his wife's or child's leisure or desire for goods is to count equally with his own. (Becker modifies this somewhat in the light of what he claims is the greater importance to the family of the primary earner's (or family head's) leisure, satisfaction of desires and so on.) While most of us may be happy to accept this as a model of how those with the most power or authority in families *should* behave, few people who have ever been in any position in a household other than that of the household head would seriously put it forward as a model of the way families actually *do* behave. In addition, it seems directly in tension with the problematic assumption discussed above—the complete devaluation of unpaid labour by economists.

As I have suggested, in the context of many less industrialized countries, economists' assumptions are even more misleading than they are in the industrialized world. Thus the policy mistakes these assumptions lead to can be even more serious. Let us look at the example of a policy initiative whose flaws are traceable to all three (but especially the second and third) of the flawed assumptions of economists I have discussed above. Between 1966 and 1980 in the Gambia, West Africa, a succession of rice-growing initiatives attempted by *three* rather different development agencies—the government of the People's Republic of China, the Taiwanese government and the World Bank—all failed to meet the planners' expectations.[29] They failed partly because they were aimed at aggregate growth rather than specifically at people's well-being, but largely because in each case the project planners directed their initiatives—credit, expertise, training and other inputs—to the African men. Each assumed, in addition, that the men would have available to them the free labour of their wives and children. This makes sense according to Gary Becker's conception of household economics; all contribute as much as they can to increasing the economic gains of the household to which they belong, because each has the reasonable expectation of benefiting equally from these gains.

So why did the projects fail? They failed because this theory of family economics bears little relation to reality anywhere, and because they took no account of the fact that gender roles were quite different in the Gambia than in the USA, and even more different in the Gambia than they are in the fantasy lives of Western economists. In the Gambia, 71 per cent of women are estimated to be in the labour force, and they constitute at least half of the agricultural workforce, doing 60 per cent of the 'visible', paid agricultural work. (This means, of course, that they do a great deal more of the actual agricultural work than this, since much of their work is unpaid subsistence farming.) They have primary responsibility for processing the grains, which takes approximately six hours per day; and they collect fuel and water, clean the house, cook and do the other domestic work. They also have an average of 6.4 children each (one of the highest fertility rates in the world). Not surprisingly, these women work from 5 or 6 a.m. until 9 or 10 p.m., but none of their unpaid work—which constitutes a great proportion of their work—was noticed or counted by the development economists planning the projects. Moreover, according to customary obligations and ideas about gender in the Gambia, it was in fact the women, not the men, who were the primary cultivators of rice. Not only was this so, but they cultivated their rice both on communal land and on land they had cleared themselves, the product of which belonged to them. Not surprisingly, confounding the experts—communist no less than capitalist—these women were not about to add to their already back-breaking workloads by contributing labour to cultivating or harvesting their husbands' rice, as the projects all assumed would happen. The projects failed to meet their goals largely because there was a critical shortage of labour available at times in the season that were crucial for rice growing. Rather than being available at no cost at such times, the women were busy harvesting their own rice, on land that was not even part of the development experts' various projects.

Meanwhile, during the implementation of the rice-growing projects, more than 50 per cent of children in the Gambia continued to die before the age of 5, due in no small part to the chronic overwork and malnutrition of their mothers, which did not show up on the economists' maps. Thus what the economist planners had counted on as 'free labour' was not only not free but not available, both because the women did their own farming and because they literally could not do any more work than they were already doing. The assumptions that women's time is both free and elastic (infinitely stretchable), and that members of a household will pool their resources because they expect to benefit equally from the product of these resources, turned out to be fatally wrong in this context. The failure of the three successive projects demonstrates some of the limitations not only of development economists' assumptions but also, it seems, of their powers of observation where matters concerning gender are concerned.

From Bad to Worse: Structural Adjustment and Globalization

Lenin was wrong, strictly speaking; the imperialism of the nineteenth and early twentieth century was not 'the final stage of capitalism'. However, in a larger sense, he seems to have been right. What happened in the last two decades of the twentieth century, commonly known by the rather neutral term 'globalization', is perhaps better understood as yet another stage in the history of imperialism. For much of globalization is not simply a process that happened, or was participated in equally by the richer and the poorer of the world's nation states. Rather, in large part, it has been, like colonialism before it, imposed by the economically more powerful on the economically less powerful. In their quest to modernize during the 1950s and 1960s, the less developed countries had incurred large foreign debts. Their indebtedness greatly increased during the 1970s, when both their demand for and supply of loans suddenly increased due to the oil price hikes that OPEC was able to effect. (International banks literally hawked large-scale loans, due to unusually large OPEC deposits.) When interest rates soared at the end of the 1970s on these variable-rate loans, many less developed countries were unable to keep up with their loan payments. Often, they were unable even to pay the increased interest, so that the principal amounts they owed grew year by year.[30]

This was, at least in retrospect, an opportunity almost too good to be true for the governments of the wealthier countries, by 1981 led by Thatcherite Britain and by the USA under Reagan—both bedazzled by the potential of free-market capitalism and opposed to most elements of the welfare state. The IMF and (to a lesser extent) the World Bank—far more influenced in policy directions by the wealthier than the poorer members—offered the severely strapped debtor nations a deal they literally could not afford to refuse: their loans would be restructured, with longer periods for repayment and in some cases other renegotiated terms, if and only if their governments adopted 'structural adjustment programmes' (SAPs). What did these amount to? In a word, thoroughgoing free marketization, called 'liberalization' by economists. The indebted countries were told to end subsidies to domestic industries, abolish import controls, float their currencies free of controls, and do their utmost to balance their budgets. Interestingly, they were *not* encouraged to cut arms purchases or other military spending. This the 'Washington consensus' considered too intrusive of their sovereignty.[31] It meant that the full weight of the cuts fell on their budgets for health, education and other social services. Forced to cut back in these areas, they were also encouraged to charge 'user fees' for basic health care and public education.

Even when these policies were first enacted in the early to mid-1980s, feminist scholars of development foretold that, and explained why, they would be disastrous for many women and children, and very hard on many others. These scholars, for example, Gita Sen and Karen Grown, the main authors of *Development Alternatives for a New Era: Development, Crises, and Alternative Visions*, argued strongly that the policies would both retard development and violate many women's and children's human rights to be able to fulfil their basic needs.[32] No attention was paid to these forewarnings, but they have turned out, not surprisingly, to be right. Countless studies now suggest that SAPs have had very deleterious effects on many of the world's very poorest people, and have been particularly hard on women and children. Since, as we have seen, a great deal of the work done by women, especially in less developed countries, is not counted in economics, and since, as we have also seen, women's and girls' getting less food, health care or leisure time does not get noticed in economics as it happens within the supposedly altruistic family, the international financial institutions have remained unaware of a large proportion of these costs. Ironically, perhaps the only way in which women's unpaid work has been 'counted' is that its supposed 'elasticity' has been one of the factors on which these institutions have relied in order to make government spending more 'efficient'. For example, cutting the times of (costly) hospital stays has relied on women's (supposedly cost-free) labour as carers for the sick, thereby in theory producing greater economic efficiency, but in practice resulting in overworked and fatigued women and girls in many poor communities.

In addition to such hidden costs, there is so far, twenty years later, little evidence that the SAPs have had the effects they were supposed to have on economic growth. Opening the world up to market forces was supposed to enable the GDPs of all countries to grow, with each benefiting from comparative advantage. Instead, the average GDP of less developed countries has actually stagnated—0.02 per cent growth per annum during the two decades since the policies were implemented. Two particular effects of SAPs seem especially unfortunate, along with the near zero per cent rates of growth:

cuts in health care and educational expenditure. In South Asia and in much of sub-Saharan Africa, the levying of user fees and cuts in public health expenditure have certainly not helped in curbing the catastrophic spread of AIDS/HIV, to which women, especially young women, are the most vulnerable part of the population. In addition, cuts in education and the charging of school fees have undoubtedly contributed to ongoing population growth. It has been a well-established fact in social science at least since the late 1970s that the single most important factor enabling women to control their own fertility, resulting in fewer births, is their levels of educational attainment.[33] However, with SAPs forcing reductions in public spending on education and health care, girls and young women are often the first to suffer—being those pulled out of school first, whether as education becomes costlier or as help is needed to care for a sick family member at home. It may be hard to believe, but for two crucial decades at the close of the twentieth century, the world's chief financial institutions were not just advocating but forcing on the less developed world policies that increased women's work, facilitated the spread of AIDS, and reduced the chances of population control. Not only for the less developed world but for the world as a whole, given the dangers of both international instability and global climate change, this could hardly be regarded as wise public policy.

Towards Women's Human Rights via a Better Development Policy?

Given not only the current economic disparities, but also this very unfortunate history of relations among them, what do the world's wealthier nations, and especially the more affluent individuals in them, owe to the poorer ones? How can we restart the promotion of women's human rights that was attempted but severely limited by the two steps backward that I have discussed here? In my view, the very least that the world's wealthy can do is to forgive the alleged 'debt' of the less developed nations, and to finish ending Structural Adjustment, which is already undergoing considerable adjustments due to growing doubts about its efficacy in promoting economic growth. Undoing some of the harm done is surely the least that can be expected. In addition, though, it is being increasingly realized that the best economic aid does not come in the form of giant projects or plans for modernization and/or industrialization. It is also being suggested that the most effective aid may not be given through governments—where it has all too often been wasted by nepotism and bribery, squandered in civil war and repression, or siphoned off into the Swiss bank accounts of corrupt elites.[34] Many people, though unfortunately not yet enough at places such as the World Bank, are realizing that the best way to offer aid may be in relatively small amounts, and to ordinary people. In addition, rather than the donors deciding what should be done with the aid, they should listen more to the people at the bottom who need it. More and more, non-governmental aid-giving agencies are asking ordinary people: 'What is not working well here? What do you need? What changes could make your lives healthier, safer, better?'

This mode of operation is what has made foundations and other NGOs such as the Global Fund for Women, based in San Francisco, so successful. The Global Fund solicits applications from grass-roots groups, or individuals seeking to start such groups, throughout the world. The only requirement is that the applicant show how the requested funds (up to $15,000) will be used 'to empower women'. It is not enough that they be used to help women, if this means treating them as passive recipients of aid; women must be helped by the funding in a way that empowers them and promotes their rights.

Sometimes, there isn't even any need to ask people what they need, since they are already stating it clearly. This was the case at the meeting I attended in spring 2000 at the World Bank, where women delegates from many of the countries of sub-Saharan Africa kept saying: 'Women in our countries need micro-credit. Please give us funds for making small-scale loans, especially to women.' (Micro-credit refers to small, unsecured loans, generally given to persons as members of a group; group membership and peer pressure substitute for collateral, since if one member's loan is not repaid, subsequent members of the group are not issued loans.) Yet when I asked the World Bank's chief economist for Africa, during the coffee break, whether the Bank was likely to respond positively to this request, he said he was doubtful, because it would involve bypassing governments. Apparently, it is fine to pressure governments of less wealthy countries to cut back on spending on education, health care and social services, but unacceptable to bypass them by making available small-scale loans to people to improve their lives. Given the extent of corruption, and in particular of siphoning off of financial aid by corrupt governments, bypassing governments—especially in sub-Saharan Africa—seems an excellent way forward. Unfortunately, the world's most powerful economic institutions have long been too state-centric to be able to take this route. So far it has been NGOs, often small grass-roots organizations working in close connection with those they are helping, that have achieved some of the most important advances affecting the world's least advantaged women.

It is to be hoped that the more powerful international economic institutions and the governments of the more affluent countries will be able to learn, both from the less powerful and less state-oriented organizations and from their own past mistakes, how to improve on decades of basically failed development policies. Only when development is decoupled from economic growth as conventionally measured, rather than being seen as strongly linked to it, and only when development is viewed consistently as having to do primarily with the quality of men's, women's and children's lives, will there be any hope of substantial positive changes. Only then, it is to be hoped, will the enormously misleading assumptions of economists begin to cede to measurements of contributions, productivity and rewards that bear some real relation to people's daily work and experience, their daily responsibilities and needs. Only when development experts are able to think consistently in terms of real people, women and children as well as men, will we be able to make significant further progress in turning women's rights as human rights from platforms and pronouncements into policies.

3

Women's Human Rights in the Third World

Rajeswari Sunder Rajan[1]

There can be no question that, in order to be meaningful, human rights in their full range must be available to everyone everywhere—which means to the most underprivileged women living in the Third World. This necessarily universal reach of human rights has tended, however, to turn the cause of women in the Third World into a battlefield for contending parties: between those who insist that they *shall* have such rights and those who would deprive them by pronouncing on their behalf that 'they don't want rights'.[2] If we are to avert such a situation we shall need to achieve clarity about the issues that surround women's human rights in the South.

I

We may begin by asking if and how universal human rights apply, conceptually and practically, to (poor, rural, tribal, dalit) women in the South. The 'universal' and the 'human' are categories conceptualized precisely as a way of covering everyone everywhere, both singly and in tautologous combination with one another. What we find in reality is of course a striking absence of consensus—frequently, indeed, active contestation—about their applicability to everyone everywhere. The 'regional' contradicts the 'universal', and 'women' is in conflict with the 'human'.

The first is because—and this has become a postmodern cliché by now, as well as the tired retort of intellectuals in the non-West—'universal' values are too often the disguise worn by dominant liberal values of the West emanating from the Enlightenment. Their imposition upon other cultures evokes fear and suspicion, especially since they gain their further legitimacy by inferiorizing or demonizing the latter for their putative 'difference'. The status of women has been systematically and often spectacularly deployed as a civilizational index in this way, and made to serve as a pretext for intervention.

The conflict between 'women' and the 'human', on the other hand, is the result of the widespread tendency to view gender as particularistic and the female sex as separate and specific in contrast to the 'larger' category of the human. It is odd to have to *assert*, consequently, that women's rights are human rights—as if women were thought not to be human or that their rights were distinct from the rest of the human race's. 'Women's rights' also tend to be viewed as a programme having its historical origins in the West: hence 'Westernized'. It is in light of both of these tendencies— women's contradictory exclusion from and subsumption within the 'human', as well as the taint of 'Westernization' that 'women's rights' carries—that we must understand the necessity to clarify that women's rights are human rights— and vice versa, that human rights are also women's (rights).

As a result of these limits and contestations of the categories of the universal and the human, women in the Third World are at two removes from an international human rights regime. This distance would appear to be a matter of a *constitutive* contradiction in the concept of universal human rights, operating at a foundational level. But universality, humanity and rights—and their combination—are concepts too politically valuable for us not to make the attempt to 'save' them even if historically they may have operated against their spirit in exclusionary ways. Therefore I offer the failure of human rights politics in the form of empirical observations—as *failures*, hence susceptible to correction. My brief, like that of other such critiques, will be that it is not by means of uniformity and by fiat, but only through the negotiation of context-specific differences that their reach can be ensured. This chapter attempts, in conclusion, to identify instances of such negotiation in process in the countries of the South, as a way forward.

II

Women in the South are vulnerable to human rights violations of two kinds. Violence of an *exceptional* kind occurs during situations of crises such as war, riots or communal conflicts, where the punishment of women (and through them of the men of their community) takes the form of sexual violation (rape, abduction, sexual humiliation, torture). Violence of this kind also appears in the form of typical culturally enforced practices. The other form that violence takes is of an *everyday* kind expressed in women's routine oppression, deprivation and discrimination. This form of everyday, indeed commonplace, violence, even where it is the product of general overall poverty, is particularly marked against women who bear its major burdens in the form of overwork, food deprivation, medical neglect, illiteracy and excessive childbearing. Sexual violation too is not of course only exceptional: it is also routine, especially when used as a form of regulating and chastising women. The connection between spectacular and structural violence is therefore a deep-seated one. Both kinds of violence are employed against women *as women*, and serve patriarchies of various kinds.

Human rights have to be invoked not only to condemn and punish women's sexual violation during periods of crises, but to produce an understanding of wrongdoing in the first place, so historically routine have such violations become in times of war. As You-me Park has argued (in the context of the apology demanded of the Japanese government for the forcible enslavement of Korean 'comfort women'), they have also gained such widespread sanction that in this instance the demand for apology was the cause of puzzlement.[3] In the recent violence in the state of Gujarat in India, unspeakable horrors—rape and torture—were inflicted upon Muslim women by Hindu men on the rampage, collectively and with impunity—and explained away by the community's leaders, by state officials, and even by members of investigative commissions as a somehow inevitable or, worse, a natural lapse that is bound to occur when (male/communal) 'passions' are 'inflamed'. Human rights discourse has the task of creating new forms of sensitization and conscientization that will function as a taboo against such violations—as of course against the violence itself—different from the attacked community's sense of outrage against *its* honour which only provokes 'revenge', often of precisely the same kind.

Exceptional, or culturally specific, forms of violence are also the product of traditional practices, whose manifestations as they apply to the non-Christian world are too glibly named in terms of the exotic—as female genital mutilation, the enforced wearing of the veil, honour killings, *sati*—battling modernity in the name of custom or religion. Typically they are preserved (indeed reinvented) as signifiers of communitarian identity, borne upon the bodies of women. These practices tend to be taken as representative of Third World women's situation as such—even of the Third World itself—as Chandra Mohanty has observed, warning against the dangers of an ethnocentric feminism repeating the cognitive moves of Orientalism.[4]

'Culture' in the non-Western world quickly comes to be equated with 'religion'. This metonymic passage of meaning results in viewing religious practices—which, increasingly, are being formulated as rights, the cultural rights of minorities— as the main obstacle to women's liberation, since they demand their conformity to oppressive traditional practices. It is not of course the case that it is only minority religious communities that discriminate against women. Judging from the regressive personal laws of all religions (in India there are four bodies of such religious laws), as well as the claims made upon women in the name of 'tradition', historically but also into the present, by different fundamentalisms which includes the Christian right, in matters such as dress, birth control, observance of religious ritual and so on, women have no reason to expect equality, autonomy or freedom (of exit, among other things) from the vested interests of religious patriarchies.

A uniform secular law achieved through the elimination of personal laws is then offered as the quick-fix solution to achieving a human rights regime. But both legal uniformity and its opposite, cultural relativism, can impede women's rights. Indeed, cultural relativism—the 'belief that no universal legal or moral standard exists against which human practices can be judged'—has been described by the UN Special Rapporteur on Violence against Women in a recent report as 'the greatest challenge to women's rights and the elimination of discriminatory laws and harmful practices'.

The Rapporteur does not trivialize the reasons for local opposition to international norms of women's rights that invokes cultural relativism: she recognizes the force and validity of its causes, listing the histories of colonialism experienced by many parts of the non-Western world, the feeling of siege in societies targeted by Western imperialism (especially following the events of 11 September 2001), and the vulnerability of minority communities seeking to safeguard their practices. It is nevertheless the case, she points out wryly, that 'it is only with regard to women's rights, those rights that affect the practices in the family and the community, that the argument of cultural relativism is used'.[5]

International human rights activism has tended to focus its energies on battling the forms of violence against women which are attributable to indigenous cultural practices—arguably at the cost of ignoring systemic forms of deprivation that endanger Third World women's health and well-being on a less spectacular everyday basis. This is in part at least because the latter (caused in many instances by First World structural adjustment policies) are so invisible that the broader global culpability for such gender deprivation tends instead to be displaced on to, and marked as the disability of, 'culture'. An encouraging sign of change is that the indices of women's well-being have recently begun to be recorded and ranked by the Human Development Reports as a way of tracking the progress that governments make towards implementing ameliorative measures.[6] The fulfilment of basic needs of this kind are arguably a matter of women's fundamental rights as citizens rather than human rights issues as such; but as overlapping claims they help to strengthen women's entitlements from the state.

By foregrounding sexual violence, international human rights discourse has also created a sense of violence as the generic condition of being for women in the Third World—so much so that we then run the risk of ignoring other sexuality-related issues. Female sexuality in the South has therefore tended to be viewed in human rights and also feminist discourse primarily as a site of violence, rather than in terms of sexual pleasure, autonomy and freedom. What recent scholarship on gay and lesbian sexuality in India, for instance, marks as a 'generally tolerant tradition' in pre-colonial times has yielded to sustained homophobia (often taking the form of denial of the existence of 'deviant' sexualities in the Indian 'tradition'), or at best silence.[7] Even the women's movement has been slow to press for acceptance of alternative sexualities, or for women's 'liberation' as such, viewing them trivially as 'sexual preference' or 'lifestyle' (and attributed to Western fashions).[8] Such repression, whether pursued actively by law—homosexuality in India continues to be condemned under a colonial anti-sodomy statute, Section 377 of the Indian Penal Code—or silently effected by cultural and political practices, is equally a mode of violence.[9]

III

So far I have tried to describe the broad international framing of issues of Third World women, chiefly in terms of sexual violence, whose agents are interchangeably identified as (indigenous) societies/cultures/religions. I now turn to the context of the nation state, both as a matter of what happens to women *within* national boundaries and as an examination of the postcolonial *state*'s role and functions.

The state, through constitutional provisions of equality and fundamental rights to women as citizens, as well as the establishment of national human rights commissions and

participation in international conventions, is the most powerful guarantor of human rights. At the same time, the despot-
ism of the state—i.e. its legitimized access to the machinery of
law and order and defence, and hence the use of armed
force—is also responsible for the most overt examples of
human rights abuses against women. The most familiar and
scandalous type of such abuse in India, for example, has been
the rape of women in custody by the police—hence 'cus-
todial' rape—around which significant feminist and human
rights struggles have repeatedly taken place.[10] The same scale
of operations that makes the state the inescapable resource for
ensuring the fundamental rights as well as the welfare of its
citizens also means that its disregard and flouting of such
expectations will have the most damaging and punishing consequences, amounting to violation of human rights.

More fundamentally, the postcolonial state seeks to regulate 'morality' by means of legislation that promotes normative forms of family and outlaws 'deviance' (prostitution,
lesbianism), thereby reifying women's roles as wives and
mothers. Jacqui Alexander has argued that the state 'actively
sexualizes relationships between men and women and has an
active stake in promoting and defending conjugal masculinity'. Her example is the Sexual Offences Bill in Trinidad and
Tobago, 1986, which sought to regulate a number of sexual
practices under the umbrella of a single law. Among other
issues, it re-criminalized male homosexuality (using the high
incidence of AIDS in the Caribbean as the reason) as well as
lesbian sex; it also restricted its earlier proposal to criminalize
rape in marriage to certain very narrow conditions. It thereby
revealed its capacity 'to create new political constituencies
(in this instance a category called lesbians)' and 'to exercise
power within "the family" '.[11] Laws 'protecting' women are

invariably conservative in intention and practice, while also providing the means for the state's control over them. In India, politicians stand ever-ready to pass more stringent laws to prevent rape, impelled by self-righteous notions of protecting women's 'chastity'. Such a putative protection has also motivated the Indian state's framing of laws such as the Indecent Representation of Women Act (an anti-obscenity law), and recent laws against sexual harassment. Women's groups, alert to the implications of measures such as these, have been opposed to laws that primarily empower the state in its control of women by further entrenching traditional notions of female sexuality. The National Commission of Women (NCW), for instance, has taken a firm stand against the proposed death penalty for rape, on the grounds that the already miniscule rate of conviction in rape cases is likely to go down even further if such an irrevocable penalty applied. The NCW has also proposed that all sexual violation of women be included under the broad category of 'sexual assault' so that penetration is not fetishized as the single or even the most serious offence of the many sexual crimes against women. Women's groups have also demanded that the existing Victorian terminology— 'indecency', 'carnal knowledge', 'outraging the modesty' and so on—which codes women's chastity as value be replaced by a feminist rationale that will acknowledge women's sexual autonomy and rights to bodily integrity.[12]

In developing nations, another imperative, that of 'development', similarly makes the state both the source of support and an obstacle to women's well-being. Population control has become in the majority of developing nations (prominently India) a major developmental preoccupation, and towards this end, draconian family control measures targeting women's bodies have been pursued. At a succession of recent international forums these measures have been resisted, and in its place a more humane, gradualist and indeed radically different understanding of reproductive rights for women has been proposed and disseminated.[12] Commenting on the Indian government's National Population Policy proposal of 2000, the noted human rights and constitutional scholar Upendra Baxi praised the document for the non-coercive and participatory approach it recommends, its sensitivity to 'women's empowerment', and its attention to issues of reproductive health, in line with the Cairo and Beijing conferences' directives—at the same time that he delivered a resounding rebuke for its 'silences': the absence, first, of any mention of (let alone apology for) the family planning excesses of the Indian state in the past (notoriously during the Emergency regime); and second, the silence on reproductive rights or reproductive self-determination. 'The articulation of a *human rights-free* national population policy is a cause for alarm', he warned.[14] It is also true that the overriding arguments for augmenting women's well-being have largely been instrumentalist in nature (the dramatic decline in fertility rates with the increase of women's literacy, for example, has been a significant fact in persuading policy-makers of the efficacy of education for girls)—not the recognition of their intrinsic rights of bodily autonomy and control.

We cannot afford to lose sight of the fact that developmental excesses have impacted upon women's rights in multiple and uneven ways. Women's efficient use of micro-credit loans, for instance, has made them exemplary beneficiaries of the state's developmental aid programmes—but this means of course that consequently they are forced to bear the double burden of supporting the family while continuing to perform their traditional domestic functions within the household.

Gayatri Spivak is critical of the encouragement of women's micro-enterprise (widely praised as a success story in development circles) for another reason: that, in the absence of a proper developmental infrastructure, it is no more than a form of 'credit-baiting'.[15] It is true, nonetheless, that women-focused development programmes have had positive outcomes, among them the increased participation of women in local-level government and administration. On the whole the double benefit from promoting women's well-being—overall development alongside the 'empowerment' of women themselves—is probably to be welcomed rather than deplored.

Through the foregoing examples I have tried to show that the postcolonial state's role in human rights administration, and, equally, its neglect, distortion or actual violation of such rights, must be taken seriously in any discussion of women's human rights in these regions of the world. But current wisdom has it that the state is being increasingly relegated to a minor role as a globalized regime takes over and national economies in the South come under the regulation of markets and of international funding agencies promoting 'structural adjustment' policies. This is undoubtedly the case—but in the Third World the state nevertheless is and will continue to be called upon to play the mediating role between markets and people. The 'liberalization' of the economy in developing countries such as India has had a major adverse impact on welfare programmes run by the state, on other poverty alleviation schemes, and on wage and tax structures. Understandably, women have suffered the most from these shifts in economic policy, from loss of employment, difficulty of access to privatized medical care, and the removal of subsidies in the informal sector and in agriculture.[16]

Yet at the same time a new kind of agency is made available

to women in globalization in recognition of their earning and spending capacities. This is true particularly of countries in East and South-east Asia, whose economies depend to a significant extent on women's labour in industry and the informal sector at home, in Free Trade Zones, and abroad (the foreign remittances sent by women through employment outside their countries is a major boost to these national economies). All this produces a somewhat ambivalent recognition of their role in development as workers and producers.[17] While the new market regimes give women visibility in national economic profiles, it also makes them vulnerable to a number of work-related problems: at the work site, sexual harassment as well as health hazards; discrimination in pay; confinement to arduous low-end jobs; vulnerability to lay-offs; poor arrangements for childcare; rapid and unsettling transformations of familial and other social relations; and of course the double burden of work and family. The spread, success and reach of women's labour organizations with transnational linkages is an indication that these problems are now being tackled at a global level, with attention given to their human rights implications.[18]

In the foregoing sections I have identified the main sources of women's oppression as located, broadly speaking, in: society (cultural norms and practices, religion); the state and its agencies; and the market/economy; and argued that these are also the very forces that can and must be called upon to ensure women's freedom. In the following section I consider the benefits but also the limits of human rights politics and policies in the South, and the cautions to be observed in finding their application in this context.

IV

There can be no doubt that when violations of women's rights—as they relate to bodily autonomy, labour and well-being—are (re-)coded as human rights issues they may expect better hope of redress, or at least attention, in forums such as the local and international media, as well as from governments. As I indicated at the start, women's rights have a tendency to be trivialized or to be dismissed as irrelevant to 'traditional' societies. The articulation of rights, in particular those based in claims for gender equality, do not find an immediate or adequate response in such contexts. Human rights language, by contrast, is more likely to find an echo within, and to appeal to, a larger constituency. A greater degree of magnitude and seriousness is also attributed to violations named in the language of human rights. The likelihood that human rights issues will have greater visibility gives a spurt, in turn, to local activism. It is significant, for instance, that political opposition to traditional forms of oppression is now being reformulated in a new and different (i.e. human rights) idiom—as in the demand by dalits (former 'untouchables') to have caste discrimination in India included as a human rights issue on the agenda of the World Conference against Racism (Durban, 2001). In addition, there is an inestimable value that derives from the publicity and consciousness-raising which such processes engender that must be counted as gain, even if the cause should fail.[19] The greater resonance of human rights is therefore something that activists and NGOs seek to exploit in their activist concerns.

However, in doing so, and in applying human rights norms to women of the South, certain cautions about the mechanism of their functioning would need to be borne in mind.

How, for instance, do human rights travel from international norm-setting forums to their local 'delivery' points, and vice versa? While the circuitry between local contexts and global forums is of undeniable significance, it is also true that much may be lost in transmission both ways. The setting up of lines of communication is therefore of crucial importance. The role of intermediaries—primarily non-governmental organizations (NGOs), but also the state—is central in creating linkages; and their functioning needs to be monitored and adjusted periodically.

In these transmissions, human rights bodies would need to be particularly alert to the danger that uniform norms do not lead to a disregard of the complexities of the situation on the ground, whether cultural or political: this is a strategic matter of the politics of internationalizing issues that may in fact require resolution 'on the ground', as it were.[20] International pressure to conform to human rights agendas has been known to cause a backlash when it produces (feelings of) threat to national sovereignty, a particularly sensitive issue in countries in the South.[21] There is also the danger of media exploitation of stories of human rights violations.[22] I do not dwell here on the cynical deployment, masking self-interested economic motives, of benevolent human rights concerns on behalf of people of the South by distant adjudicating bodies.[23] When women's issues become sites of conflict, as in the examples cited above, the gains made through any rights that may have been achieved are threatened. Therefore strategic considerations about conducting political struggles around human rights agendas via more conciliatory and participative processes such as negotiation, coalitions and alliances, mobilization of public opinion, international resources, and networking, are imperative.

At a more conceptual level, it may be worth suggesting that human rights for women are not profitably articulated in terms primarily of equality demands, even though it might be argued that rights ought to oppose discrimination as much as they do oppression. Pitting disadvantaged women competitively against men in a similar position within their society does not greatly benefit them, and indeed distorts the picture.[24] Defining women so as to reflect the many intersecting determinants of their identity (e.g. as poor, rural, tribal or dalit), offers a better guarantee of understanding their situation than insisting solely on their gender identity—particularly in terms of their imbrication with the community and the locality they inhabit.[25] Since rights often conflict with other rights or with practices and imperatives of a different kind, they can end up driving a wedge between women and men of a community in ways that must be guarded against, as a matter of tact and strategy but also of common sense. Thus, for example, equal rights in divorce for Muslim women with men (a favoured cause among Western feminists on behalf of women under Islam) should arguably be less of a priority than implementing Sharia's (quite generous) provisions for divorced women.

While many of the above observations relate to the practical aspects of making human rights prevail, they also point to the need to rethink the concept itself in more expansive ways, beyond mere legalism and a fixed idea of right(s). No one seriously advocates refusing the ideal of universal access to human rights. What creates resistance and unease among the opponents and critics of a universal human rights regime is its hegemonic implications, but also its conceptual limitations, as the above discussion has tried to show. By way of conclusion, in the following section I identify some proposals for negotiating human rights for women that might side-step such conflict and, more tentatively, for revisioning human rights in a genuinely universal (i.e. *trans-cultural*) framework.

V

The recognition of the problem of conflicting rights as the major obstacle to ensuring women's human rights in the South has led to a great deal of productive discussion among political theorists seeking a way forward. The conflict between sexual equality and cultural autonomy produces the political problem of assuring minorities of their cultural autonomy while *also* ensuring justice for the 'minorities within minorities' (who are usually the women of the community). While in some cases the envisaged solution has taken the form of a more strident assertion of the priority of liberal individual rights under all circumstances,[26] in others it has led to an emphasis on *process*, which will allow communities to arrive at solutions to conflicts through internal deliberations. Such process-based solutions may of course end by simply abandoning women to their communities' patriarchies, since it is the latter who dominate deliberative proceedings. If such processes are required to follow democratic standards, which would allow everyone equal participation in the deliberations (as recommended by Partha Chatterjee in the Indian context of a 'crisis of secularism'),[27] they are in effect being asked to guarantee equality to women—which may be precisely the issue at stake.

It is this predicament that leads Avigail Eisenberg to propose the 'difference approach' that I endorse here as a potential theoretical and political model of resolution.[28] Eisenberg draws our attention to the shift of emphasis he proposes: from 'rights themselves' to 'the *values and interests* that rights are often meant to protect'.[29] Thus, in my example, above, if the intention was to secure assured maintenance provision for divorced Muslim women, then this outcome would weigh more in the approach to the issue—even if it meant privileging Shari'a—than replicating the liberal divorce laws available to women in the West. The difference approach sidesteps the formulation of the problem as a conflict of rights, which invariably only produces an impasse. Above all, it insists on respecting the 'cultural, religious and historical contexts' in which the interests and values take shape.[30]

More radically, we may want to broaden the concept of *human rights* beyond its European liberal provenance and its present cultural and imaginative limits, to embrace, for example, other traditions of humane-ness, or to challenge the hegemonic definitions of personhood. For instance, some (non-Western) cultures' traditional relations to the environment, their practices of non-violence (*ahimsa*), the respect shown towards age, or their different forms of egalitarianism, may be regarded as potential resources for a richer and more inclusive notion of human rights. Nor is it necessarily only tradition and 'other' cultures which provide such alternatives. New categories of person emerge from contemporary struggles for human rights themselves, such as, for example, the 'girl child'. Speaking on the occasion of the final anniversary of the SAARC (South Asian Association for Regional Cooperation) Girl Child Decade (1990–2000), Razia Ismael of the Woman's Coalition drew attention to this naming of the girl child:

the recognition of the girl child was not a small feat. . . . If we are investing in measures for the advancement of our female citizens . . . we must recognize that nearly half of them are children. . . . Should these [resources] not be very specific to the different needs of the many clusters within the 0–18 age range? That's where the girl child lives, in the range between surviving foeticide and exercising her franchise as a voter. . . . Gender disaggregation of data is something we are constantly reminded to ensure. Age disaggregation of gender information is something we are not reminded to ensure, but should ensure. But if we do not measure either our ideas or our actions by these two vital markers, the girl child's prospects remain bleak.[31]

Following the SAARC initiative, the UN Conference on Women in Beijing (1995) for the first time included the concerns of the girl child in every section of its *Platform for Action*, and added the girl child's neglect as a new, crucial issue.[32]

We are witnessing, too, the beginnings of a radical questioning of species boundaries—where does the 'human' end and the 'non-human' begin?—in the work of several writers and philosophers. The expansion of the concept of the 'human' beyond ethnocentrism, sexism and logocentrism feeds into— but has been equally impelled by—the human rights movement. What is also indicated, as a practical consideration, is the need to find a context-sensitive and flexible application of human rights norms—as activists in the Third World have long been urging and as political theorists such as Eisenberg have recently begun to recommend. Women in the Third World stand to gain significantly from such critique and rethinking.

4

Introduction to Alan Sinfield

Christopher Robinson

Although the primary role of language in fashioning and limiting our apprehension of fundamental issues about the self and its relationship with others has long been accepted, it is only recently that people have begun to recognize the specific part played in that process by the most complex manifestation of language, namely, literary language. Literature, especially if by that term we mean what is recognized by the intellectual establishment as 'great' literature, for the most part includes and excludes, confirms and denies, according to the officially promoted value system of the society of which it is the product. This had long been, and continues to be, a source of confusion and despair for all those belonging to minoritized or disempowered groups who find themselves, for reasons of gender, sexual orientation, class or race, outside the value system which such literature reflects or has been made to reflect in the discourse of traditional criticism. As a teenage boy I remember coming to the conclusion that I must be some sort of historical 'sport', since the only place I could find a reflection of the emotions and desires akin to those I was beginning to feel was in the literature of Greece and Rome. When I did, by accident, find a modern novel (Mary Renault's *The Charioteer*) which suggested that I was not alone in the world, I kept it out of the local library for six months and reread it avidly (even though it is shot through with a symbolism which equates homosexuality with physical disability) just because it seemed to confirm my right to exist. It was only many years later that I realized a second important truth about literature: namely, that traditional ways of interpreting it have often disguised the degree to which it diverges from official values, disrupts or betrays their limits. This is not a British problem, I hasten to add: even overtly homosexual writers such as Cavafy, Lorca and Proust have had their sexuality virtually edited out of serious critical interpretation until very recently, and the mere suggestion that the sex or gender of canonical writers such as Henry James and George Eliot might have any bearing on the way they write still elicits howls of rage from conservative critics. With works such as *Faultlines: Cultural Materialism and the Politics of Dissident Reading* (1992) and *Cultural Politics—Queer Reading* (1994), Alan Sinfield has been a ground-breaker in British critical discourse designed to reveal the subversive dimension of literature, just as, in his time as Professor of English in the School of Culture and Community Studies at Sussex University, he has helped to establish the academic 'respectability' of courses of study which acknowledge the importance of sexuality and explore its catalytic role in the unravelling of cultural politics.

In the chapter which follows, Sinfield gives a reading of *Measure for Measure* which reflects pointedly on the situation of people who are persecuted on account of their gender and sexuality, acknowledging the moral complication raised by the fact that violence is often a central facet of desire rather than a perversion of it. More provocatively, he argues that the play reveals a tendency to avoid, even to gloss over, the consequences of corruption and exploitation in the ruling class in a way which suggests that universals may be harder to come by in the realm of truth and justice than traditional liberal thinkers would have us believe. The significance of the chapter is dual. First, it demonstrates the way in which classic literature and everyday modern experience can be brought into contact in a significant way—as Sinfield indicates, he juxtaposes Shakespeare and human rights with a view to unsettling established attitudes towards both. Second, it frankly acknowledges that proponents of queer theory and more broadly of sexual rights are dangerously prone to a form of cultural imperialism in their assumptions about the sexual norms of non-Western cultures, and invites further thought in an area where activists are frequently loath to venture. The ways in which we can legitimately pronounce upon the sex and gender systems of other societies without appearing to reduce the human to a category of Western thought are now being explored in many intellectual *fora* (notably, for example, in cross-disciplinary international workshops held at University College London). As well as showing us how reading literature can give us insights into conceptual problems raised by our relationship with the world around us, Sinfield also invites us to pause and consider how our critical responses to such issues can and should impinge on the essential practical activities of a great international movement such as Amnesty.

Rape and Rights: *Measure for Measure* and the Limits of Cultural Imperialism

Alan Sinfield

Pleasures of Domination

In Shakespeare's *Measure for Measure* the state is asserting itself. Two familiar distractions are being applied by the ruling elite. One is military enterprise abroad: 'If the Duke, with the other dukes, come not to composition with the King of Hungary, why then all the dukes fall upon the King' (I.ii.1–3).[1] Another is a witch-hunt for alleged dissidents at home. Declaring that he is construed by the people as having been lax, the Duke thinks it better to absent himself and allow his deputies to put the laws into effect. In a further tyrannical-paranoid move, he disguises himself as a friar so that he can spy on his deputies, and recruits a shady network of holy brothers.

Some bawds and their clients are harassed, but the system starts to bite when upper-class people are involved. The attempt to rescue Claudio leads to Angelo's attempt to exploit Isabella. Claudio begs for her help:

> Implore her, in my voice, that she make friends
> To the strict deputy: bid herself assay him.
> I have great hope in that. For in her youth
> There is a prone and speechless dialect
> Such as move men.
>
> (I.ii.167–74)

This last thought proves all too true. Angelo is moved sexually by Isabella. 'She speaks, and 'tis such sense / That my sense breeds with it' (II.ii.142–3). He offers to save Claudio if Isabella sleeps with him. When she refuses he becomes brutal:

> I have begun,
> And now I give my sensual race the rein:
> Fit thy consent to my sharp appetite;
> Lay by all nicety and prolixious blushes
> That banish what they sue for. Redeem thy brother
> By yielding up thy body to my will;
> Or else he must not only die the death,
> But thy unkindness shall his death draw out
> To ling'ring sufferance. Answer me tomorrow,
> Or, by the affection that now guides me most,
> I'll prove a tyrant to him.
>
> (II.iv.158–68)

We may discern here the misogyny of the rapist, who desires to spoil the pure, to violate, to hurt and degrade.

In 2001 Amnesty International published a powerful booklet about prisoners who are being detained and ill-treated because of their gender and sexuality: *Crimes of Hate, Conspiracy of Silence* (hereafter '*C.H.*').[2] This is one of the cases:

In 1997, Katya Ivanova, a lesbian living in Moscow in the Russian Federation, went to the local police station to lodge a complaint against neighbours who had assaulted and threatened her. She showed the officer dealing with her complaint the notes her neighbours had pushed under her door containing threats and homophobic abuse. As soon as he saw these, the officer began to sexually harass her. . . . 'He threatened that my neighbours might kill me, but that he would be able to help me. Then he told me that the only way he would help me is if I slept with him. When I attempted to resist him, he grabbed me and threw me on the table. He beat me in the face and raped me, right there in his office.' In the next few months she was summoned on a number of occasions by the same officer. (*C.H.*, p. 23)

Measure for Measure, I mean to show, helps us to see some things about this kind of assault; others it obscures.

In both instances the woman has indicated that she rejects marriage and prefers to live in community with women. Of course, nuns are not the same as lesbians. However, we are told that Isabella's intimate relationship hitherto has been with Juliet—her 'cousin'—'Adoptedly, as schoolmaids change their names/By vain though apt affection' (I.iv.46–8). In her introduction to *Breaking Silence: Lesbian Nuns on Convent Sexuality*, Rosemary Curb observes some apt analogies between the two situations:

groups of nuns or Lesbians are often mistaken for one another today, since we often travel in female packs oblivious to male attentions or needs . . . both nuns and Lesbians are emotionally inaccessible to male coercion . . . a male-defined culture which moralizes about 'sins of the flesh' and the pollution and evil of women's carnal desires sees both nuns and Lesbians as 'unnatural' but at opposite poles on a scale of virtue.[3]

It is that oblivion to 'male attentions or needs' which informs Isabella's inability to comprehend what Angelo is proposing, whereas Claudio, the Provost and Lucio understand very well.

Like Katya, Isabella finds that refusal of conventional relations with men incites the desire of the officer. Angelo uses her admission of female frailty to challenge her bid for autonomy:

> I do arrest your words. Be that you are,
> That is, a woman; if you be more, you're none.
> If you be one—as you are well express'd

By all external warrants—show it now,
By putting on the destin'd livery.
(II.iv.133–7)

The badge of the female is sexual subjection to men. The other characters also assume this. The woman who attempts to exclude herself is to be forcibly repatriated. This urge to put the dissident woman back in her place is found repeatedly in the Amnesty International reports. Norah was arrested in Uganda: 'Nasty remarks were made that I should just be punished for denying men what is rightfully theirs, and that who do I think I am to do what the president feels to be wrong. They even suggested that they should show me what I am missing by taking turns on me' (*C.H.*, p. 2). In Russia, again, investigators raped Irina—'to teach her a lesson', they said, and to 'reorient' her sexual identity (*C.H.*, p. 42).

Crimes of Hate observes a special virulence in the treatment of lesbians and gay men:

As a 1997 report by the Southern Poverty Law Center in the USA commented: 'When gays and lesbians are attacked it's particularly vicious. . . . They aren't just punched. They're punched and kicked. They're beat and spit on. They're tied up and dragged behind cars. It's almost as if the attacker is trying to rub out the gay person's entire identity'. (*C.H.*, p. 47)

We may think of the brutal murder of Matthew Shepard in Laramie, Wyoming.[4] It might be supposed that this fervour occurs because the sexual dissident is ineluctably alien. I think, however, that lesbians and gay men are specially victimized because they cannot be filtered out from the social organization and, in particular, the penal system. In Abu Ghraib, the Iraqi prison, sexual mistreatment was experienced as especially repugnant.

Typically, the subject of torture is perceived by his or her persecutors as other. Often he or she belongs to a different race, region or religion; or political commitment positions him or her as beyond the orbit of civil society, and hence as not entitled to the usual protection. But lesbians and gay men cannot be cordoned off. We rarely have gay parents; we are produced from within the family, the community, the state. Consider the consequences of the Holocaust: there are few Jews in Central Europe, but there are many homosexuals. This is because it needs Jews to produce Jews, whereas homosexuals are born into straight communities. This pattern, whereby the deviant is a swerving away from the dominant, rather than being its antithesis, has been described as a 'perverse dynamic' by Jonathan Dollimore: 'The perverse dynamic signifies that fearful interconnectedness whereby the antithetical inheres within, and is partly produced by, what it opposes.'[5]

This implication of sexual dissidents and their host community is particularly intense in reports of interrogations and prison brutality. Time and again, the assaults of police and guards on lesbians and gay men documented in *Crimes of Hate* display a blatant sexual aspect. 'If that's what you want, I'll give it to you', guards told Luciano Rodriguez Linares in prison in Mexico, as they held him down and inserted a finger into his anus; police in Chicago rammed a baton into the rectum of Frederick Mason; police in Venezuala forced transgender people to perform sexual acts in return for release (*C.H.*, pp. 30, 21, 27). It is plain to us that the torturer, in such cases, is himself involved in sexual acts. He may tell himself initially that he is imposing just and even corrective punishments; he may believe that he is upholding public decency. However, at some level of awareness he is likely to know that he, himself, is implicated in the deviant sexuality that he abhors. It is because of this complicity that the sexual dissident must be not only punished, but destroyed; because of what he tells the torturer, not about subversives, but about himself. Despite his bargain to reprieve Claudio in return for Isabella's compliance, Angelo orders his immediate execution.

Conversely, a prominent scenario in gay male pornography and chat lines dwells upon police and military uniforms, punishment, bondage and assault. Some of us entertain fantasy investments in the scenes of our own humiliation; indeed, it is the humiliation that we desire. Of course, heterosexuals do this as well. But the concern of many gay men with the machismo that despises and threatens them is germane, Leo Bersani has argued, to 'the logic of homosexual desire', which 'includes the potential for a loving identification with the gay man's enemies'. The dominant definitions of masculinity, which the gay man must resist because they are the ground of his oppression, are, Bersani adds, 'in part constitutive of male homosexual desire'.[6]

If violence is not an aberration in desire, but integral with it, and the good guys are involved psychically with the bad guys, where does this leave Amnesty? Traditionally, it apprehends its project through a broadly Enlightenment framework, in which the state acts from a rational estimate of its own interests, licensing or tolerating torture and inhumane treatment because they seem likely to secure its continuing domination. Of course, we know also that sadistic individuals will get themselves into positions where they can exercise their desires, but that is generally seen as incidental. However, where the sexuality and gender of the victimized person is the matter at issue, the sexual component in the oppressors makes manifest the implication of the oppressor with the victim. This involvement should affect our estimate of the scope of

Amnesty interventions. If torture is imbricated with desire, it will take more than fair-minded protests to control it.

Pleasures of the Text

Thus far, it may appear that I am following the standard procedure of literary criticism, especially where Shakespeare is concerned. I take a theme of importance to me today, and discover, with only a little pressured reading, that it has been anticipated by the Bard. Thereby resistance to the oppression of lesbians and gay men may seem to be a universal imperative, and Shakespeare's authority is enhanced as well. However, if *Measure for Measure* helps us to see more clearly some aspects of the situation of people who are persecuted on account of gender and sexuality, it also has troubling aspects.

Shakespeare did not invent the story of Isabella and Angelo; it was circulating, in various versions, in sixteenth-century Europe. Basically, a woman appeals to a magistrate for the life of her condemned husband; the magistrate exploits her sexually and, despite his promise, takes the life of the husband. The woman appeals to the ruler of the land, who decrees that the magistrate must marry the widow to restore her honour, and must then be executed. The leading motifs evidently concern the importance of integrity in office, the frailty of fidelity in women, and the ultimate trustworthiness of the ruling elite.[7]

The function of such tales is to facilitate debates about key topics in that society. By placing this or that particular inflection upon a story, authors offer diverse implicit propositions about how the world goes, and how it should go. Giraldi Cinthio in his *Hecatommithi* (1565) changed the ending by making the woman plead successfully for the life of the magistrate. Thereby, J.W. Lever comments in his Arden edition,

'Through the heroine's love and the emperor's virtue, mercy was combined with justice, and marriage instead of blood-retaliation made amends.'[8] Shakespeare in *Measure for Measure* adopts this more civilized version.

But is it enough? The play is still premised on the unquestioned assumption that sexual offenders will be whipped and executed; much of it is set on death row. Pompey, a bawd, is given the alternatives of serving as assistant to the hangman or 'your full time of imprisonment, and your deliverance with an unpitied whipping' (IV.ii.10–12). These were the common punishments in early modern Europe. Compare the end of *Henry IV Part II*, where we see Mistress Quickly and Doll Tearsheet being taken to be whipped to inaugurate the new reign. Or consider the end of *Othello*, where Lodovoci orders 'the censure of this hellish villain', Iago—'The time, the place, the torture: O, enforce it!'[9] There is no place here for a debate about whether torture can be justi-fied; in context, it seems only right. Similarly when Henry V orders the summary execution of Cambridge, Scroop and Grey. These are the practices that Amnesty condemns when they are perpetrated by the Taliban and the USA.

Measure for Measure repeatedly evades the implementation of these cruel, but not unusual, punishments by a cunning process of doubling. At each major point of conflict, a substi-tute character appears who can fulfil the demands of the story without distressing thematic consequences. The play begins with the Duke's doubling of himself: Angelo is to be the severe deputy while he himself is exonerated from state vio-lence. Another woman, Mariana, is found to fulfil Angelo's sexual demands instead of Isabella. Then the execution of Claudio is avoided by sending to Angelo the head of another prisoner, Ragozine, who has died of natural causes. Thus

Isabella retains her purity, and Angelo, his fatal purposes having been thwarted, need not be executed. Angelo can marry Mariana, and Isabella is available for the Duke's proposition that she abandon the sisterhood and marry him. Compare the deployment of the twins in *Twelfth Night*: the threat that Orsino may love a boy and Olivia may love a girl—both of them Viola—is evaded by the arrival of Viola's twin, Sebastian. Now there is a conventionally appropriate partner for everyone.

Thus Shakespeare's version of these stories appears more humane: no one has to be whipped or killed. Yet, thanks to the substitutions, this has been accomplished without any challenge to the system. Because Isabella is split into two—the woman who refuses Angelo's demand and the woman who accedes—the rape is smoothed over, rather than confronted. At each point the incoherence and oppressiveness of state ideology is magicked away. The Duke's devices rescue not only individual characters, but also the reputation and stability of the state and the penal system in particular.

Act V is a sustained demonstration of how difficult it is to confront a dictatorial regime; as Angelo forecast, his word is believed rather than that of citizens. However, like the ruler in other versions of the story, the Duke is there finally to expose Angelo as a double and to restore faith in the system. Yet (and this is surely disconcerting) to gain his ends the Duke himself uses the full battery of dictatorial processes—arbitrary manipulation of the constitution, co-option of other institutions (the Church), undercover surveillance, entrapment by an *agent provocateur* (in the Duke's exchanges with Lucio), impersonation (of a friar), abuse of confidence and suborning of witnesses; all under the shadow of corporal and capital punishment. The answer to the problems produced by tyrannical rule, it appears, is a strong ruler and an elaborate state espionage apparatus.

To my mind, the Duke's rule is made more sinister by the delight he takes in his contrivances. He tells Isabella:

I do make myself believe that you may most uprighteously do a poor wronged lady a merited benefit; redeem your brother from the angry law; do no stain to your own gracious person; and much please the absent Duke, if peradventure he shall ever return to have hearing of this business. (III.i.198–204)

The gleeful tone here is unsettling; the Duke is gaining too much enjoyment from his manipulations.[10] There are other ways, besides rape, of exerting power over women and subordinates; consider the Duke browbeating Claudio with the worthlessness of his life (III.i.5–41), and his withholding of the truth from Isabella 'To make her heavenly comforts of despair' (IV.iii.109). Nor does the text suggest that he undergoes any corrective process of self-knowledge.

It might be pleasant to suppose that Shakespeare has observed all this, with the intuitive political and ethical insight of poetic and dramatic genius, and is displaying it to incite in an audience suspicion of the ruling elite and of the system that sustains it. Kiernan Ryan posits something similar in the brief moment of Barnardine's resistance. Barnardine refuses to double for Claudio because he has been drinking all night and is in no condition to meet his maker. The answer: another split. Barnardine need not be executed because Ragozine has died of natural causes. Ryan finds something further in Barnardine, namely:

the outward sign of the play's inward drive to clear a space within which a superior conception of justice can secretly flourish. I say 'secretly', because the play's visionary displacement of the Viennese regime is mainly achieved by subliminal means, by the structural manipulation of perspective and supposition rather than by overt assertion.[11]

Now, I am not against subliminal readings. In effect, this is the critical practice theorized by Pierre Macherey, and still necessary, in my view, for a sophisticated approach to reading and textuality. Closure is always inadequate; no text can contain within its project all the potential significance that it must release in pursuance of that project. Reading for the gaps and silences discloses the unconscious of the text.[12] Even so, I do not find in Barnardine a sufficient prompt for Ryan's 'superior conception of justice'.

As I read *Measure for Measure*, it is the other way around. The doublings appear to offer a humane path to a just system, but the 'subliminal means' which effect the pleasure of the text require the reader to go along with the Duke's manipulations, underlying values, and eventual achievement. To enjoy the play, other than in a self-consciously perverse manner, you have to be pleased that Isabella is not raped and that Claudio is not executed. Therefore you have to allow, with whatever reservations, the Duke's devices.[13] The contrivances of the Duke are coterminous with the organization and closure of the play. This is what reading is: picking up the coded signals of the text as they develop, and entering into the complicated sequence of anticipation, frustration and resolution.

That the doublings are evasions is evident if we think again about the Amnesty booklet. In real life there are no substitutes, there is just the one independent woman, and she is raped; just the one victimized brother, and he is executed; just the one magistrate, and no effective appeal. If *Measure for Measure* offers a humane gloss upon some of the stories that preceded it, it still fails to meet the standards of justice and rule that we demand today. The other choice, of course, is to read the play against the grain—as I am doing—pointing up the embarrassments in the theme and evasions in the plot.

Human Rights and Civil Rights

I have derived notable insights from reading *Measure for Measure*. However, if this play can help us to highlight certain kinds of wisdom and understanding, by the same token it may promote reactionary ideas. But can the Bard be on the wrong side when it comes to torture, rape and murder? This is the pivot of my essay: if even Shakespeare cannot underpin universal truth and justice, how can we hope to ground a universal concept of human rights, upon which Amnesty may depend?

The rhetoric of rights currently affords a lever for lesbians and gay men. The European Convention on Human Rights was incorporated into UK law by the Human Rights Act 1998, and a decision of the Court of Human Rights suggests that the anti-discrimination Article 14 may be applied to sexual orientation.[14]

Nonetheless, we know very well that the 'rights' we would now claim have not been recognized universally throughout history, and are not recognized throughout the world today. As Jeffrey Weeks succinctly puts it:

Rights do not exist in nature. They are products of social relations and of changing historical circumstances and balance of forces, so the claim for rights is always in terms of some rights rather than others. . . . By arguing for a more extended definition of rights, we are actually changing the definition of what can be regarded as a right.[15]

Claiming that your preference is a right is like quoting Shakespeare: it is a strategic way of adding emphasis to a position. Anti-choice campaigners speak of a 'right to life'; their opponents of a 'right to choose'; the anti-gay legislation, Section 28, was promoted by a Parents Rights Group. When ACT UP demonstrated at the Roman Catholic service of Cardinal O'Connor in New York, it was complained that they had 'denied Catholic parishioners their freedom of religion'.[16]

When President Sam Nujoma of Namibia describes gay men as 'unnatural' and contrary to the will of God,[17] or President Robert Mugabe of Zimbabwe brands gays 'less than human' (*C.H.*, p. 4), we reply that our practices are natural and human to us. However, we are merely swapping truth claims. Mugabe declares:

If we accept homosexuality as a right, as is being argued by the association of sodomists and sexual peverts, what moral fibre shall our society ever have to deny organised drug addicts, or even those given to bestiality, the rights they might claim and allege they possess under the rubrics of individual freedom and human rights?[18]

It is not easy to fault Mugabe's logic.

As with other features I have discussed, the drawing of gender and sexuality into the orbit of human rights may provoke some rethinking of Amnesty's principles. While torture may be regarded as unacceptable on any terms, intervening in the sex/gender systems of other cultures necessarily involves disputing, not only the laws or the abuses, but the mores of those cultures. This is acknowledged in *Crimes of Hate*:

Whereas most governments either deny practising human rights violations or portray them as rare aberrations, the repression that LGBT people face is often openly and passionately defended in the name of culture, religion, morality or public health, and facilitated by specific legal provisions. (*C.H.*, p. 4)

An endemic problem for the rights activist intervening over-seas is that anything he or she does is open to the construction that it is an imperialist intrusion.

It is indeed arrogant to take it for granted that metropolitan ways of doing things are superior, let alone more natural or more human. We should not expect to find the gradual emer-gence, step by step, of something like our present-day array of lesbian, bisexual, gay, transvestite, transsexual and transgen-dered relations, as if other peoples should be developing in our direction (on the analogue of supposedly 'developing nations'). In fact, concepts of gender and sexuality are contested within metropolitan societies. After all, repressive laws on sexuality in the Caribbean derive from British colonial rule; male homo-sexuality was legalized in England and Wales only thirty-seven years ago, and not in all contexts; sodomy remains illegal in some states of the USA; until 1991 Amnesty resisted the adoption of sexuality as a human right.

Despite all diversity, fellow-feeling demands that metro-politan lesbians and gay men affirm and support persecuted sexual dissidents everywhere. It should demand also, by the same token, that we respect their difference—their difference from us. This respect should generate a close attention to local self-understandings; wherever possible, our protests should build on local campaigns. 'If there is no universal pattern of sex and gender identities then how is a universally applicable guarantee of rights possible?', Paul EeNam Park Hagland asks, with East Asian societies in mind. He proposes a backward glance: 'Contemporary LGBTs in Asia and elsewhere could inscribe themselves into the textuality of their premodern cultures, asserting the "authenticity" of their identities by appropriating images of prestige in the traditional culture.'[19]

In fact, the influence is not all from the metropolis outwards. Knowledge about international engagements may return to disturb and enlarge our assumptions. Notably, many other cultures are more concerned about gender identity than about object choice. The issue in these cases is not so much whether you have sex with a man or a woman—the key factor in post-Stonewall metropolitan definitions of lesbian and gay—but whether you think of yourself as masculine or feminine. Anthropologists confirm that this is the more traditional preoccupation in many non-metropolitan contexts. In Latin America especially, Amnesty 'has documented alarming levels of abuse, including torture and ill-treatment, against transgender people' (*C.H.*, p. 25). Meanwhile current movements by transgender activists in Britain and the United States may gain strength from a knowledge of societies where roles for cross-gendered people are more developed. Knowledge of the diversity of queer subcultures in other countries may help to free up metropolitan preoccupations.[20]

My approach may be formalized through an appeal to civil rather than to human rights. For while 'civil rights' may involve an appeal to a utopian notion of the ideal *cives*, the term may more sensibly refer to the rights that citizens customarily enjoy within a given society. The rights for which lesbian and gay people struggle, then, are the same rights as everyone else in that society. To be sure, in some places nobody's rights may be very extensive or secure, but at least they will be locally acknowledged.

Working through a concept of civil rights does not produce a magic answer to ultimate questions about good and evil. In addition, as I have pointed out elsewhere, there are problems with this model. One is that it lets the sex/gender system off the hook, fostering the inference that an out-group needs concessions rather than the mainstream needing correction. Another is that it influences sexual dissidents to conceive of themselves in accord with the opportunities that the rights agenda appears to offer.[21] However, gay men and lesbians in Britain have campaigned effectively in terms of civil rights for an equal age of consent. Perhaps human rights is a necessary strategic construct, underlying our sense of ourselves *as human*, but one that should be comprehended as an abstract postulate; it may be given content and specificity in particular civil contexts, such as a religion, a constitution, a supreme court, an international campaign. Civil rights in a given country may then be regarded as a particular embodiment of human rights—one that may form a basis for contest and change.

The leading issue for lesbian and gay activists in many metropolitan countries at the present time is framed as a civil rights matter: partnership rights—the opportunity to register gay relationships such that they may attract some of the taxation and property benefits that are given to married people.[22] This campaign has also had a large measure of success. It does not mean, however, that we all want to be sucked into a sense that an approximation to conventional marriage is best for everyone. Compare, once more, *Measure for Measure*. At the start of the play, the characters are cultivating various kinds of sex lives with little regard to the state and its premium on wedlock. Angelo and Lucio are avoiding marrying women to whom they have been promised—the former because he prides himself on his chaste righteousness, the latter because he wants to play the field. The Duke is a celibate ('Believe not that the dribbling dart of love/Can pierce a complete bosom'; I.iii.2–3). Juliet and Claudio have consummated their affair without waiting for marriage. Isabella is joining an order of women. Mistress Overdone is a widow who has had her fill of marriage after doing it nine times—'Overdone by the last' (II.i.199). Only Mariana, an outcast, actually wants to get married. Only Elbow, the foolish constable, appears to be married happily.

By the end of the play, matrimony has become compulsory, on almost any terms. Angelo and Lucio are married against their wishes; how these couples are supposed to get along is not considered. Lucio names his fate in the punitive idiom of the play: 'Marrying a punk, my lord, is pressing to death,/Whipping, and hanging' (V.i.520–1). The Duke reverses the doubling device to the point where he, as the 'good' magistrate, can demand of Isabella the sexual compliance which she refused to Angelo. Overall, these marriages reaffirm the assumptions, which Angelo made initially, that the state should regulate sexual expression, by either devious or directly coercive means, and that women should make themselves available to men. On marriage, *Measure for Measure* cannot meet the criteria of the *Crimes of Hate* booklet: 'Forcing women and girls into marriage or other relationships involving repeated non-consensual sex is not only discriminatory, it can amount to torture and sexual slavery' (*C.H.*, p. 43).

The demand for marriage at the end of *Measure for Measure* is accompanied by no revocation of Angelo's initial edict that 'All houses in the suburbs of Vienna must be plucked down', except those for which 'a wise burgher put in' (I.ii.89, 92). In modern cities with an established gay scene, the corollary of compulsory marriage is the civic clean-up. As gays become more visible, affluent and central, their neighbourhoods and public spaces become potentially valuable. The civic clean-up, designed to raise property values and enhance tourist potential, becomes a persistent threat to gay subcultural resources. When a gay club in Moscow was raided in 1997, locals believed it was part of a 'cleansing' of the city in preparation for its 850th anniversary celebrations: 'Everyone who is different gets thrown into the category of people who must be removed from the city.'[23] Authorities in Rome shut down gay venues in 1998 because the intention to host EuroPride in 2000 was perceived as conflicting with the Christian jubilee (whether undercover friars were involved is not recorded).[24] Even in Amsterdam, traditional gay locations become subject to policing and closure.[25]

The most prominent recent instance is the shutting down of gay and lesbian facilities in New York by Mayor Rudolph Giuliani in the late 1990s. This, Michael Warner explains, has destroyed 'a diverse, publicly accessible sexual culture', which had enabled gay men 'to find each other, to construct a sense of a shared world, to carve out spaces of our own in a homophobic world, and, since 1983, to cultivate a collective ethos of safer sex'.[26] While gay people want the private consolations of civil partnership rights, many of them do not wish to forgo traditions of public cruising and accessible off-street cultural resources.

Gay people are subject to something like the attempts of the Duke and Angelo in *Measure for Measure* to reorient the sex/gender system of the city from above, by manipulation and compulsion. Angelo's brief encounter with dissident subcultures of the city produces the wish that they should all be whipped (II.i.135); his substitute, Escalus, adjusts the punishment (but, once again, not the system). We might look to Angelo's other double, the Duke, for an affirmation of the civil rights of Mistress Overdo and her establishment. However, they fall under the denunciation of the Duke in the guise of friar ('I have seen corruption boil and bubble/Till it o'errun the stew'; V.i.316–17).

The only person excused wedlock, finally, is Barnardine. Intriguingly, he is placed in the pastoral care of a friar: 'Friar, advise him;/I leave him to your hand' (V.i.483–4). Is this a hint for the ceremonial exit, with the characters paired off, hand in hand (including Isabella and the Duke, or not)? And what is the mode of this handling? Does the friar have Barnadine's hand twisted up behind his back, figuring a renewal of ideological control, as he works on Barnardine's 'stubborn soul' (V.i.478)? Or are their hands clasped affectionately together, like a same-sex couple, in an unexpected survival of dissident potential?

5

Crimes Unpunished:
Crimes as Punishment
Introduction to Rose George

Michèle Le Doeuff

In a hamlet of Vosges, a baby is born to a 14-year-old mother. The father is also her grandfather and great-grandfather. Three generations of teenage girls had been raped by the same male head of the family. I heard about this from the doctor to whom the baby was referred; they checked the absence of handicap while apparently turning a blind eye to what had brought the baby into this world. Society worries about genetics, not so much about how women are destroyed. And if my source is a private conversation, just as a large part of Rose George's material was collected through personal interviews, this means that awareness or a minimal knowledge of what is usually covered by some Noah's coat often begins in this way. Testimonies; dialogue.

I saw Rose George's work as 'investigative journalism' at its best and told her so. With an amused smile, she replied that 'investigative journalism' is quite a different thing. But then does the English tongue have a word to describe her efforts as a reporter to bring undisclosed criminal aspects of social life into the public eye? And where did she acquire the capacity to carry out such a survey without flinching? She read French and Italian at Somerville College, Oxford. Dealing with the most painful and shocking aspects of human life requires an impressive amount of intellectual courage; it is my belief that this may come to some individuals in an unpredictable way and develop haphazardly, and—why not?—also through reading literature. At any rate, neither in France nor in any country I know do institutions favour the idea of inserting within their various university courses this true preparation for the professional class: knowing about the wrongs women and children suffer; understanding them in order decently to address them. In a nice French town, a woman magistrate is having a nervous breakdown after just two years in office. When sitting in a lower court you see too many heart-breaking sex-related cases, even though only a modest proportion of them are reported at all. She had been brought up with the idea that sex can be a good thing, an idea my generation of feminists certainly spread when campaigning for the legalization of contraception and access to relevant information about how a body works. In law school, this young magistrate had not been prepared to encounter the fact that sex is also the site of fierce conflicts, nor to face the banality of these evils, patriarchy's extreme effects.

Gang rape, the crime which Rose George explored, is one form of sex crime among others, one aspect of patriarchy's dramatic aspects; prostitution, clitoridectomy, pornography, forced marriages are to be mentioned on a par with rapes of all kinds. The fact that incestuous rape is still breaking the lives of many dutiful daughters in villages and posh town houses just as it is in forlorn suburbs must be recalled, in order not to separate gang rape from a global context in which girls and women may helplessly be under the power of a father, then a husband, or else the easy prey of all men around them. Under the thumb of a legitimate owner, or else a *res nullius*, a thing not belonging to anyone, and hence deemed and doomed to be an object of collective consumption.[1]

Gang rape appears as mostly suburban and as having to do with immigration. And it is true that French Law relative to family *rapprochement* gives male heads of families unlimited power over the wife or wives and children: the father can put an end to the very possibility of their living in France.[2] Most immigrant households thus experience a total lack of balance in authority. There is a despot and there are dependants who seldom have a say in anything. How could such a structure fail to create a culture of acute machismo? Boys can see their fathers molesting their mothers and the whole family. Even if molested themselves, they can still identify with the tyrant: somewhere else, in a cave, in the playgrounds at school, they too can exert that absolute power which knows itself through exerting violence and destroying its object. I know of one case in the Canton of Geneva; it tallies with this and with the description Rose George provided, but we must add: the Kosovar boys who were found guilty of gang rape were much below the demands of standard schooling. Anger at seeing girls who are better integrated than themselves at school seems to be part of the picture.

Gang rape also appears to be targeting mostly young women who have managed to escape a little from the control of the patriarch heading the family. This crime could be like a punishment inflicted by male teenagers on girls who are not utterly quenched by submission to the traditional ruler. It is not just that it reinforces the power of fathers or elder brothers over girls by making the world outside the home frightfully dangerous: it amounts almost to the physical destruction of the woman who has gained some independence or is on her way to doing so. As in incestuous rape or marital rape, it is the denial that a female being is entitled to exist as an autonomous being. The young criminals stand on the side of patriarchy: if she does not obey her father, let her obey the local thugs.

Thus sex crimes can be the means through which male power, its order and disorders, can be (re)enforced. Since at least the appearance of Kate Millett's work, we have had the possibility of understanding that intercourse can be used to humiliate and to put a woman back in her place. The French translation of *Sexual Politics* has been out of print for years, by the way, though some of us keep trying to make it available again. In the recent past, lukewarm perspectives on gender have been encouraged while studies taking a critical stance against masculinism underwent various types of censorship. But this very phenomenon is patchy, uneven, not to say unpredictable, probably not typical of France as a whole and hopefully not here to stay, at least unchallenged. The best way to assess the situation is to look at what happened around a survey on violence carried out by a research team, the ENVEFF. They first published an article.[3] This was vehemently attacked by Marcela Iacub and Hervé Le Bras in a piece published in *Les Temps modernes*.[4] '*Les Temps modernes*'? And then Elisabeth Badinter took the polemic a step further, in a book expressing total contempt for feminist efforts to question violence, prostitution, pornography and so on. Feminism is taking the wrong road internationally, she claimed.[5] But a later issue of *Les Temps modernes* published a response by the ENVEFF and other feminist pieces to compensate for what had quickly come to be seen as an editorial blunder.[6] And *Nouvelles Questions Féministes* (a journal founded by Simone de Beauvoir and Christine Delphy, now edited in Lausanne) has published a volume containing several pieces on the Iacub–Le Bras–Badinter crisis. They offer the diagnosis that there is 'an upsurge of anti-feminism in Parisian drawing rooms'.[7]

Fair enough, but let us face it: those who attacked the survey (and other feminist works) are people of the Champagne socialist era. During the Jospin years, there was an attempt to muzzle voices which could hint that things were not utterly rosy for women in France. The mainstream idea was that parity (equal numbers of women and men in Parliament) was the only important and respectable goal. Even some of those who strongly disagreed with parity itself because it was grounded on the idea of sexual difference, and Elisabeth Badinder in the first place of course, seemed at least to agree with one implication of the idea: let us no longer talk about, nor hear about, the wrongs women suffer; it is disturbing for men and it could add to the government's burden; it is obsolete anyway. I do not know whether this should be called 'Parisianist and bourgeois so-called feminism' or 'downright posh anti-feminism occasionally calling itself feminism', but I really wish this form of ideology had stopped at the gates of Paris. Unfortunately, since it is a matter of class and politics, not of mere geography, you will find it in many French cities and at various universities.

In the meantime, throughout the country and particularly in forlorn suburbs, the French Movement for Family Planning (Le mouvement français pour le planning familial, MFPF) has maintained its efforts to provide contraception and access to abortion in good conditions. This did not go without shocking incidents either. In 1999, a MFPF regional centre in Villeurbanne, near Lyon, was ransacked by a gang of Far Right skinheads; they broke everything with iron bars. It was clearly (again) an act of collective retaliation against a centre working for women's emancipation. In January 2000, we held a public meeting in one of the Lyon city halls about abortion. Maintaining public speech, the sheer possibility of a calm and friendly debate about abortion, was our answer, just as initiating public speech about gang rape has recently been crucial to giving the issue a basic form of existence.

We need to do much more. I must say I see the professional class (e.g. doctors, lawyers, administrators, police officers) as the agency which ought to be properly trained so that they can have a keen sense of their social responsibility and a true knowledge of the evils they will have to deal with. How long did it take for Samira Bellil to chance on a psychotherapist who was able to help her out of the vicious spiral in which she was trapped? She had been seen by various doctors previously—standard training in psychiatry or psychotherapy seems unbelievably at variance with people's real needs.[8] Attend a trial about clitoridectomy or incest on a young girl; you may find that the behaviour, discourse, hints, body language, the dismissive not to say sarcastic tone of some barristers or public prosecutors seem to side with what the perpetrators say in their own defence. In a sense, the very structure of a 'tournante' is there too. And you will occasionally see women lawyers joining in, just as victims of gang rape are sometimes delivered to the rapists by other girls. It is a sign of social progress that women en masse now have access to the diversity of subjects you can read at university, including law and medicine. Statistically speaking, women of the professional class may be a little more attentive than their male counterparts to women who have been wronged and hurt. But it is not entirely clear, or it is chancy. Everybody, men as well as women, ought to be trained to have proper respect for those who have suffered. In January 2003, an association of women in political sciences, 'Les sciences potiches se rebellent', organized a meeting about gang rape in the Institut d'Études Politiques de Paris, giving the floor to women from the suburbs. A great step forward certainly, when public discourse and the necessary insertion of basic knowledge about patriarchy within learned institutions are still lacking. But I am not sure that many institutions emulated this initiative, which anyway took place in the margins of the Institut d'Études Politiques itself.

Intellectual feminists involved in practical issues will also have to take up the challenge. Although proud of what my generation has achieved since the early 1970s, I am convinced that the stock of ideas we created *en route* may well prove insufficient. Since the early 1970s, we have had two different approaches: one has focused on reproductive rights (along with demands for crèches and nursery schools); the other was about denunciation of crimes against women. Although united by ideas such as freedom, rights, and dignity for all women, these two approaches carried in their wakes different perceptions and values. We must now try and unify them better. Hopefully, this will be the next page of my philosophical life. All the same, if the Academy does not help the legacy and stock of ideas to pass on to the next generation and into formal education, then all we shall have to go by what we always had: associations, newspapers and books.

Share a Spliff, Share a Girl—Same Difference: The Unpleasant Reality of Gang Rape

Rose George

Gang rape, group rape, pack rape. Line-up, train, take-your-turn, party rape. If only we had as many solutions to gang rape as we have names for it. More underreported than regular sexual assaults (which are underreported enough themselves), less talked about in the press, less acknowledged in society: all reasons for Sue Lees to entitle the gang rape chapter in *Carnal Knowledge* 'the unreported crime'.[1]

In late 2001, I went to Paris to investigate an alarming rate of gang rape. I would not call it an epidemic, since I doubt that it is finite. Nor is it a 'phenomenon'. I learned instead that it is banal enough not even to be called rape. Later, while writing a research report for a documentary on rape, I learned that similar incidents were happening in the UK. That research is still in progress, so this chapter will look predominantly at the French cases, with an occasional glance to the UK.

In 2000, a feature film was released in France which caused a scandal. In a country which produced *Baise-Moi* and *Irreversible*, this is nothing unusual. But *La Squale* (the tearaway) was different. Its director, Fabrice Genestal, was once a high school teacher in the deprived Parisien *banlieue* of Sarcelles. He cast pupils from surrounding schools as his actors, and based his script on what his former pupils had told him, eventually, in after-school 'discussion workshops'. There was plenty to tell.

He had been hearing the word '*tournante*' for a while. Eventually, his pupils told him what it was: a girl is seduced by a boy, and he hands her over to his friends. They pass her round, or take their turn. The same word—*tournante*—is used for a joint. Spliff, girl, same difference.[2]

During my time in Paris, I met a friendly police officer who showed me victim depositions. He was not supposed to do this, but he was angry enough about what was happening to break the rules. The depositions contained the following stories (all names have been changed): Elodie, 14, who answered the door one day when her parents were out, and a minute later found herself facing five boys in her dining-room, and a minute after that with the first of five penises in her mouth. When she tells her story, on a video deposition, her hands never leave her face. Solange, 17, whose boyfriend held her down while his friend raped her in a stairwell, and who was on several other occasions forced to fellate four boys. When she dumped her boyfriend and got a new one, he let his friends rape her too. Nora, 14, went to a station to meet her friend Pierre, who passed her on to two of his friends, who raped her in a dingy apartment and sent her home on a train bleeding. In her deposition, she says, 'He took his trousers off. He had nothing on underneath. And he asked me to touch his . . .'. But she cannot say the word. Another girl was raped eighty-six times. Annabelle, a 21-year old student, was raped by four young men in a train near Lille. There were 200 people in the carriage.

Like their rapists, the victims in France are white, black and Arab. There are no clear ethnic lines to be drawn, unlike in London, where males of Afro-Caribbean descent statistically commit gang rape beyond demographic proportions. But the French victims still have some things in common: they are teenagers, like their rapists, and they are girls, and therefore they are targets. In the *banlieue*, or suburbs, which constitute France's deprived urban areas—with names like The Pyramids and River Valley, examples of urbanization gone wrong—being a girl means being fair game. In the words of some young women from the *banlieue*, they are either whores or submissives.

The kids who live in the *banlieue* call them 'the neighbourhoods'. Or Neuf-trois (93), Neuf-deux (92), or the other postcodes that set them apart from the 75 of the city centre, and a whole other life. Officially, they are 'difficult zones', or 'sensitive areas', both of which are accurate adjectives for these huge, grim housing estates, thrown up in the 1950s to house workers and immigrants—mostly North African, but also sub-Saharan, Antillais—for the nearby factories. But the factories closed, and the standard social spiral—unemployment, dismay, frustration—unfolded, as it unfolds in inner cities worldwide. Unemployment among young people in the *banlieue* is believed to run at 40 per cent, compared to a national average of 9 per cent. You put your 93 postcode on a job application, kids told me, and your letter goes in the bin. If your name is Arab, it goes there even faster.

France's attitude to its *banlieue* has usually been 'out of the metropolitan area, out of mind'. But occasionally the metropolis has to notice its outskirts, like in 1995, when Matthieu Kassovitz's film *La Haine* scandalized the country, with its portrayal of torched cars, violence against the police, deep-seated fury. One young student, a child of a difficult zone, tells me that this was 'positive violence, in a way'. It was a way of asking people to take notice of what had gone wrong. When the explosion failed to help, the violence turned inwards. The *banlieue* imploded, in Darwinian fashion.

The stronger minority—frustrated, furious young men—turned on the weaker: women.[3]

In 2002, I returned to France to report some more, because a young woman named Samira Bellil had published a book about her experiences, about being on the end of the implosion. She had been gang raped twice, and raped once. Yet she used her real name, in an incredible act of courage, and put her photo on the cover. She called her book 'In the hell of *tournantes*', and the title cannot have been a difficult one to choose.[4]

Her story is not untypical. When she was 14, she simply fell in love. Her boyfriend was the handsome hard man on the estate. She decided to sleep with him in a stinking basement, and when she left, his friends were waiting for her. They started kicking and beating her, and the biggest and meanest dragged her by the hair to an apartment nearby, where she spent a night being raped by three young men. The sexual torture was so revolting she still cannot describe it, fifteen years later. But it conformed, more or less, to what Rozee-Koker and Polk noted in their study of American fraternity group rapes: that degradation beyond sexual assault is more common in a group situation.[5] Fellatio, urination on the victim, use of objects are frequent, as is videotaping and text messaging. Last year, I found an anonymous testimony on a *banlieue* website which summed things up better than I could.

I sometimes think people think a gang rape is a cute orgy. They don't see the humiliation, the hours on end, the boys queuing up, the blows, the spitting, the objects, the insults, the times you faint from the pain. The 3 to 15 guys who are having a laugh, drinking, rolling joints, sending text messages to their mates telling them to come too, taking pictures, filming. And when it finishes, you know it's going to start again, in two days, a week, two weeks.[6]

Sometimes, a *tournante* is called *plan pétasse*, or slag plan, because any girl who has sex with her boyfriend is automatically labelled a slag, or *pétasse*. Sometimes it is a basement plan, because that is where it happens, as well as in garbage disposal rooms, schools, courtroom toilets. Last year, the French courts heard the case of Sabrina, 15, whose rapes occurred in all of these places. For several months she was abducted and gang raped, again and again. She reported it only when a friend noticed she smelled bad one day at school (after she had been forced to fellate two boys during morning break). Her rapists, when they finally came to court, insisted she had consented.[7]

I went one day in Paris to visit Sarcelles High School. It is twenty minutes from Notre Dame by RER train, the escape route between *banlieue* and city. It is a grim place: low school buildings encircled by housing estates. Two stops back before Sarcelles was where Nora had been raped by three boys. I had noted the address from the deposition, and tried to calculate where the apartment she had been taken to was. But I could not. When I get off at the RER station, I remember reading that this was where Samira was abducted from, the second time she was raped.

Sarcelles head teacher Jeanne Sillam has a photocopied newspaper article on her desk. It is the story of a 15-year-old girl called Samia, who was gang raped several times over a year, including in a courthouse toilet when her assailants were on trial. This school needs to keep its head teacher informed about gang rapes, because it is the kind of school where a girl wearing a miniskirt was attacked by thirty boys in the toilets.

The toilet attack was opportunistic, which made it a rarity. Everyone I spoke to—teachers, police officers, social workers—was convinced that *tournantes* are premeditated. Some even called them a hunt. (In his 1971 study of rapes and rapists in Philadelphia, Menachem Amir found that all group rapes reported to police had been planned.[8]) The tactic is simple and effective. A boy approaches a girl with his gang behind him. He might buy her a drink. He will have chosen the girl deliberately, because she does not have a big enough brother, or she is fragile or in some way vulnerable. Or because she has already broken the harsh social code of the *banlieue* by going to a party, or kissing a boy. (One teacher told me that his pupils said, 'Nightclubs are full of slags because if they're in a nightclub, they must be a slag.') The girl gives in and has sex, or intimate relations, and the boy threatens to tell unless she goes with his friends too. Occasionally there is violence involved, but usually verbal threats are enough. The violence comes later.

The trick is to isolate the victim. In the *banlieue*, where a girl's virtue is paramount, being marked as easy is a harsh sentence. No one will help her after that. Female solidarity disappeared in the *banlieue* long ago, about the time that the young men took over the streets, because they had nothing to do. They set the rules. At a family planning class, a teenage boy says, 'French girls are for fucking and Arab girls are for marrying'. The woman who told me this was shocked, not only because the boy was white and 'French', but because all the girls applauded.

In older studies on gang rapes—in American fraternity houses, for example—the use of girls to tout for other girls has not been a feature.[9] Here, it is common. Sabrina was delivered to her rapists by two girls whom she knew, who had been asked to find a 'dick-sucker'. The heroine of Genestal's film *La Squale* knew her boyfriend was involved in gang rapes, but tolerated it. The ending—where she finds female solidarity with her girlfriends—is, sadly, unrealistically optimistic.

In the *banlieue*, female solidarity has been eroded by machismo. The shame caused by any sexual assault can be crippling: both Islam and machismo prize girls' virginity. Reprisals are a real threat: apartments have been burned down; little sisters are threatened. If girls do confess, they can be sent back to the *bled*, or parents' home country, where they will probably be married off. All in all, silence is tempting.

Samira Bellil's reactions were typical. Her Algerian parents weren't easy to talk to; her father was violent. She did not report the attack, until her rapist assaulted two of her friends too. Even then, her book catalogues a litany of failure from social support systems. Her female lawyer—provided by an NGO—treated her with contempt, and neglected to tell her her court date. Social welfare organizations were no help. Street workers weren't either—there are only 3000 in the whole country, I was told. That Samira got to court at all is astonishing, not least because she lives a few streets away from her chief attacker. (He was imprisoned for two years, but is now released, and Samira still risks seeing him.) Still, she took the risk of writing a book, precisely because of the failure of anyone to help her. 'I never considered being anonymous,' she told me. 'I had to be credible. There are so many young women who have been suffering who need to open their mouths. They are so isolated. I want to give them some hope. God, they need it.'[10]

There are no firm statistics about *tournantes*. As in the UK,[11] French criminal statistics do not differentiate gang rape from any other kind.[12] There is only anecdotal evidence and guesswork. Both of these are disturbing enough. The campaigning group SOS-Viol (SOS-Rape) received seventy-three calls from juveniles between January and October 2001, or more than in the three previous years altogether. A police chief in one suburb north of Paris, with a population of 800,000, received five reports in only seven months. Social worker Richard Heyberger, who runs an emergency refuge for juveniles west of Paris, says that all the girls who come under his roof know at least one other girl who has been 'passed around'. Since her book was published, Samira Bellil has been receiving twenty to thirty letters a day, many of them from victims.

In the UK there is a similar information gap. British Crime Surveys and Home Office Research Studies (HORS 237 and 196) do not differentiate gang rape.[13] HORS 237, purporting to illuminate 'the extent and nature of the problem' of rape, dismisses 'multiple perpetrator' rape in a few lines, saying only that there were not enough reported examples for them to merit analysis.[14] It took me a couple of hours reading through newspaper reports to decide differently. February 2002: a 21-year-old is raped by six men, who form an orderly queue. March 2002: three teenage girls are raped by a group of fifteen boys, aged between 11 and 17, in Southend. In August 2003, two teenage boys raped two 15-year-old girls on Roehampton's Alton Estate, because one of the girls asked them to return the mobile phone they had just stolen from her. In September 2003, a 19-year-old man was imprisoned for six years, along with three of his friends, for raping 14- and 15-year-old girls whom they befriended in shopping centres. Sentencing him, Old Bailey judge Henry Blacksell said, 'this may be common behaviour in Ilford, but the girls still need protection'. Also in 2003, five boys aged 11 and 12 raped a girl of 10 on her way home from school. Metropolitan police detective sergeant Peter Quinn said that the boys did not realize it was an offence, and that one boy had been watching free-to-view pornography, and simply copied what he saw.[15]

The Haven, London's only sexual assault referral centre, has begun an epidemiological study of teenage group rape, but it is as yet unfinished. For now, evidence is unofficial but alarming. Out of 226 rape cases in 2000, 13 per cent involved one or more assailant, and 32 per cent of those were in the 12 to 15 age range. Among 12- to 15-year-olds who visit the centre, 23 per cent have been gang raped, compared to 14 per cent of 16- to 17-year-olds and 11 per cent in the 18 and over age group. According to one counsellor: 'If you're under 16, and you come here, you're twice as likely to have been gang raped.'

Anecdotal evidence is also the only clue to how long *tournantes* have been going on. One French student, now at college, told me that even seven years ago, boys would commonly say, 'calm down or you'll go to the basement'. That meant a gang rape. The student's sister knew about *tournantes* six years before that. In the UK, the Metropolitan police commander Andy Baker, who used to specialize in street crime, remembers often seeing groups of boys leaving a shed, and a girl leaving later. 'But you don't see those things until you're enlightened', he said.[16]

'I'd say about four in ten girls I work with have been raped', a youth worker in Hackney told me. She had been set upon by a group of boys wearing balaclavas in her college corridors, and was raped by one of the assailants two years later. 'Group rape is so common round here, girls won't talk about it. They think it's so normal, they just have to deal with it. When I bring up the subject, they just clam up. I've heard so many stories, I can't remember what happened to who.'[17]

In France, at least, the *tournantes* have hit public consciousness. But not without a fight. Fadela Amara, director of the grass-roots organization La Maison des Potes, has been working in the *banlieue* for two decades. She says the only time the public talks about *banlieue*, it's about crime, and it's about men committing crime. Women aren't even criminalized, just ignored. 'There is a law in the *banlieue*,' she says, 'but it's not the law of the French Republic.'[18]

Forged from traditional cultural prejudices about the inferiority of women, and a street power based on the law of the strongest, the law which rules the *banlieue* today is brutal, inviolable and masculine. Girls can conform to masculine norms by acting as touts or tearaways, if they pay the price of losing any solidarity with other girls. But otherwise, women are the guardians of honour, girls have to be virgins. They have to study at home, look after the men in the family, never go out. That makes them *filles biens* (good girls), and out of danger. Anyone else is a slut. If you want a 'French' life, if you want to go out, wear make-up, you get a reputation, and the reputation is irreversible.

I find this extreme. But at an after-school dance class in Sarcelles High School, I met two young teenage girls swaying to African music. Desiree, a 14-year-old Antillaise, wore tight jeans, a tightish top and a bandanna. When I asked if she could wear it in class, she looked at me incredulously. She'd get called a slut, she said. No question. A gym teacher tells me that, of the 300 girls in his school, a 'difficult zone' in Marseille, not one wears a skirt. Girls have to camouflage themselves. 'If you wear a skirt,' says one young student, 'you'd be called a slut. Immediately. You'd have hands on your ass. Whatever you wear, it has to be baggy.' Femininity has to be camouflaged.[19]

Slaps, insults, lewd comments are everyday occurrences. 'You expect it,' says another girl. If you see a girl in the *banlieue*, she's got her head down and is walking as fast as she can. 'Girls look around, see that every other girl is the same,' says Samira Bellil. 'They think that's the way it has to be. There is such fatalism.'[20]

On 4 October 2003, things changed. The boyfriend of 17-year-old Sohane Benziane had slapped another boy's girl in the face. In return, the boy set Sohane alight with lighter fuel, and his friends blocked her exit from the garbage disposal room where they were. The spot where she eventually burned to death—some scrappy grass in front of the apartment block—was two metro stops away from the ritzy Bibliothèque Nationale. Perhaps because it wasn't a rape, Sohane's case became the last straw. Fadela Amara helped to organize a national roadshow. Unusually, the roadshow members were all young women from the *banlieue*. Their slogan was memorable: '*ni putes, ni soumises*' ('neither slags nor submissives'). It was shocking, they said, but so was what was happening to them, out of sight of the French public, out of reach of all the rights that French feminism had won. 'The feminists have deserted the *banlieue*' is their campaign slogan.

I put this accusation to Julia Kristeva. Why has no one paid attention before now? She sent me back a one-page article, a year old, on 'the damage to psychic space'. A charitable interpretation of the article would have judged it irrelevant at best. 'It'll be the same thing elsewhere', says Michèle Le Doeuff, a professor of philosophy and one of the few intellectual feminists willing to dirty her hands with practical issues. 'It's frowned upon to do both practical and intellectual work.'[21]

I put the same question to film-maker Catherine Breillat. She was clear: 'There is no strong feminist movement today. Instead, there's a very strong misogyny. When the fact of the gang rapes came out, no one protested, because of fatalism.

They said "it's cultural". It's not.' Breillat—one of France's more outspoken and notorious directors—does not mince her words. She hates France, the French, being French. She blames her own culture. 'This is a macho country. It's partly Latin, partly nordic, and the result is an incredible hypocrisy. We are a country of Tartuffes. We never confront our problems, and that's why we've been disarmed by the gang rapes, because we're all complicit.'[22]

Many commentators blame this state of affairs on Islam, on patriarchal cultural attitudes that idolize male children, but do the opposite to women. 'The boys are treated like kings at home,' a local head teacher tells me, 'waited on hand and foot, then when they leave the house, they are treated like delinquents.'[23] But blaming 'tradition' is always dangerous ground to tread on, and not accurate. Young Muslim girls tell me this isn't Islam. When they go to Tunis or Rabat on holiday, they see girls of their age going out, smoking, with boyfriends. They can do none of these activities at home for fear of the consequences. They say that young people in their parents' countries are progressing, while they regress.

There are certainly cultural-religious reasons for *tournantes*, if anyone looks. At schools, boys drop out far sooner, and—as the manual labour apprenticeships have dwindled—are faced with no employment opportunities. At the same time, their access to girls (apart from their sisters and mothers) has been barred once they leave school. Sociologist Hugues Lagrange, who is an expert on youth sexuality, calls it 'the destruction of the flirt'.[24] There is neither emotional nor geographical space for youngsters to have meaningful romantic relationships.

This is not the place to discuss the causal link between pornography and sexual violence. But add together the components—no sexual access, widespread pornography—and the results are disturbing. In France, a 1998 survey by school doctor Claude Rozier found that, in a sample of eighty-five 18- to 25-year-olds, 85.9 per cent had seen a pornographic film before the age of 15.[25] DVDs circulate in high schools for a pittance, along with home-made videos of take-your-turns. 'There's no real sex education,' says a young student. 'They tell us what a spermatozoid is, but not how to treat a woman. So boys educate themselves with porn.' Not only that, but in the self-professed liberal society that is France, where mainstream feature films can show graphic sex—*Romance*, *Baise-Moi*, *Irreversible* (with its nine-minute rape scene)—and where bare breasts routinely sell yogurt. Sexual frustration in a highly sexualized society, and boys who cannot distance themselves from fictional representations of sex because their access to real relationships has been barred. It's a worrying cocktail.

In almost all the gang rape cases that have come to court in France, the fruit of this sex education is obvious. At Sabrina's court case in 2003, one boy said, with a macabre play on words, 'in our family, we're thieves (*voleurs*) not rapists (*violeurs*)'. In a northern Parisian police district, a police chief tells of a rapist who was in court for a car theft the day before the rape trial. For the car theft, he was contrite. For the gang rape, he laughed and said, 'no, she's forgotten, we did something else to her too'. Social worker Richard Heyberger, who receives juvenile criminals at his refuge, says only one boy has ever recognized what he did was a crime. He cannot think of a single boy who has actually been repentant.[26]

There is no way of telling what teenage group rapists say in British court cases, because they are never reported. Even though one court at the Old Bailey—the one with the biggest dock—is nicknamed 'the gang rape court', reporters refuse to touch these stories because they are 'too horrible'. And because, as in France, but more so, the racial component is too risky to touch.

In 1999, Channel 4 screened a documentary that followed fourteen gang rape trials through the courts.[27] All the assailants were Afro-Caribbean. The victims were mixed. There was an immediate furore, and the channel was accused of racism. Afro-Caribbean commentator Darcus Howe was a lone voice in support of the programme. Writing in the *New Statesman*,[28] he remembered his childhood in Trinidad, when he had belonged to gangs like Style-Crampers and Law-Breakers. He recounts how his next-door neighbour Betty was gang raped for hours, and how—after he spoke out in support of the Channel 4 documentary—he received anonymous phone calls saying his daughter would get gang raped too. 'My line is lean, mean and clear,' he concludes. 'I take a side in this war, the side of black women. I have four daughters whom I join in the bunker; there is nothing to discuss.'[29]

A noble statement, but not true. There is plenty to discuss. France has only begun to publicly acknowledge the sexual violence in its suburbs because one too many horrific cases came to court. Here in the UK, a half-hour documentary seems to have shut down the national consciousness for four years. Our inability to discuss teenage sexual violence is dangerous. For one thing, it breeds misconceptions. Even the term 'gang rape', which I have used, is misleading. Often, in France, the assailants are not formally linked. They could be friends or loose acquaintances. There have been reports of rapists text-messaging an ongoing rape around the area, as a kind of mass invite. Instead this is an individualistic urge—to assert masculinity, to achieve power in a powerless environment—which is manifest in a group situation. 'It is commonly believed,' wrote Sue Lees in *Carnal Knowledge*, 'that men who gang rape must be pathological bullies, fiends or maniacs, and that gang rape is far less common than individual rape. Research refutes these assumptions.'[30]

Police officers and sexual assault centre workers also balk at the idea of gang rape as a ritual. In France, of the cases I studied, there was nothing ritual about it. It was too common and too banalized to be given any formal significance. Julie Bindel of the Child and Women's Abuse Studies Unit at London Metropolitan University prefers to categorize it as a sport.[31]

Justification can easily slip into mitigation. Find a nice ethno-cultural motive, and it is easier to explain away. Group rape has traditionally been considered less perverted than solitary rape because it can be categorized as a masculinity test. Instead, it is the lack of formal ritual that shocks. The banalization of group rape in French *banlieue* is complete; here the process is ongoing. And here, other mitigating arguments—religion, tradition—fall down. Even in the sexually liberal environments of London boroughs, gang rapes are committed.

Misconceptions also spill over into the judicial environment, which already fails rape victims at all stages of the system. Gang rapes are more likely than single assailant rapes to be no-crimed, because the evidentiary burden on the victim is even more overwhelming. There have been cases of a victim facing up to twenty defence lawyers, each wanting to know where in line their client came, and what he was wearing. The threat of reprisals is intensified, because there are more perpetrators to carry it out. The shame is enhanced too: French police term gang rape victims 'ultra-raped'. Gang rape victims are more likely to commit suicide.

I was asked, when writing this chapter, to propose solutions. I have no idea where to start. Nor did the marchers on the '*Ni Putes*' roadshow, each of whom I asked for suggestions, and each of whom replied 'I have no solutions, madame'. In the UK, there are only seven sexual assault referral centres for over fifty police forces. Attrition rates are lamentable, even up to the Court of Appeal, according to as yet unpublished research by Kate Cook, who found that up to half of rape cases that reached appeal had their sentence reduced or the conviction overturned.[32] In France, the '*Ni putes, ni soumises*' campaign has met with French government ministers, and presented a five-point proposal. This includes a 'respect guide' to be handed out in schools. But the young women on the march still had to go home to a *banlieue* environment that was hostile to them for speaking up. At governmental level, the French government has instituted a law (the so-called *Loi Sarkozy*, named after former interior minister Nicolas Sarkozy) making it illegal to loiter in stairways. Good enough, but what about basements?

Others talk of education, of schools for parents. Better sex education. Less porn. Repression, not prevention. Former French interior minister Nicolas Sarkozy's law will turn juvenile detention centres into prisons. However, as Diana Scully concludes from her interviews with convicted rapists, if sexual violence is the inevitability of a patriarchal social structure, prison is fat to the flame.[33] Samira Bellil thinks repression is the last thing they need. She wants better social networks, a concrete support system that answers the phone when she calls. She wants more street educators. She wants the state to be there when she needs it. 'All I needed, after I was raped, was someone to hold out a hand to me. No one did.' It took ten years before she was introduced to the therapist who could help her, and another five years of therapy before she could write it all down. But it should not be up to rape victims to be role models. Samira Bellil has had enough. 'I can't be the spokesperson any longer,' she told me. 'I can't carry it all. There's too much violence.'[34]

France has had twenty years to addresss the *tournantes* in its midst, and has only recently set aside fifty apartments for women in crisis. Much of the blame for such tardiness should be attributed to the willingness of all parties to hide in silence. Until the '*Ni putes, ni soumises*' marchers, France's young women had no voice. They could still risk reprisals. In the UK, the victims of teenage group rapes are equally silent, as is everyone else. Back in 1971, American sociologist Menachem Amir was astonished to discover that 43 per cent of the Philadelphia police department's rape cases were committed by more than one assailant. Part of this astonishment was due to the fact, he wrote, that psychiatric literature had treated group rape 'with silence'.[35] Despite the odd academic chapter here and there,[36] things haven't much changed. And until group rape is confronted publicly, this vile sport will play on.

6

Introduction to Robert Wintemute

Christopher McCrudden

I am delighted to introduce the chapter 'Partnership Rights as Human Rights'. It is by Professor Robert Wintemute of the School of Law of King's College in the University of London.

Rob was born in the USA, grew up in Canada, and now lives in London. His undergraduate education was at the University of Alberta, where he graduated in economics in 1978. He went to Law School at McGill University, graduating first in his class in 1982. After a period of five years working for a distinguished New York law firm, he turned back to academic work, coming to Oxford to work on his doctorate, which I had the pleasure of supervising. Oxford then lost him to King's Law Faculty in London, which he joined in 1991, becoming Reader in Law in 1999, and Professor of Human Rights Law in 2003.

His academic credentials to write on the topic are unchallenged. He has published the definitive book comparing the approaches of the courts in the USA, Canada and under the European Convention on Human Rights to issues of sexual orientation discrimination and human rights law.[1] An article based on the book has recently been the centrepiece of extensive discussion in the House of Lords.[2] Although their Lordships ultimately rejected his argument, it was treated with the utmost respect.[3] He has co-edited a huge study on national, European and international legal approaches to the recognition of same-sex partnerships.[4] This was published in 2001 to wide acclaim. At the time when he gave the lecture on which this chapter is based, he had just returned from visiting the Faculties of Law at the University of Toronto and York University in Canada as Bertha Wilson Distinguished Visiting Professor of Law, where he lectured on 'Religion v. Sexual Orientation: A Clash of Human Rights?' He has previously held visiting appointments at the University of British Columbia and at Yale.

As befits an Amnesty lecturer, however, there is more to Rob than academic distinction, although there is plenty of that. He also plays an important role in the world of British and European legal affairs when issues of sexual orientation discrimination are considered. He has provided expert testimony to courts and parliamentary assemblies in the USA and Europe. He has represented the International Lesbian and Gay Association. He has been consulted by those representing the applicants in several of the most important European legal cases involving issues of sexual orientation. Indeed, in October 2001, he represented the applicant before the European Court of Human Rights in the *Fretté* case, which concerned the eligibility of a gay man to adopt a child.[5] Although ultimately unsuccessful, the Court clearly had to face important issues that otherwise would have been much less effectively put.

He brings to the topic of his chapter, therefore, immense practical legal experience on these issues, as well as academic distinction. We shall need *all* of this expertise, since the issue he is considering is one that is at the cutting edge of constitutional and human rights debates in many Western countries. It is a topic that raises strong emotions. It is a complex issue both politically and legally, involving an exploration of some very basic issues in human rights law and politics. How should we understand the concepts of discrimination and equality? What role (if any) should religious discourse play in public affairs? And what meaning should we seek to give to marriage in today's world?

I will not try to respond to, or to sum up, his chapter or the discussion that followed the lecture, but I cannot resist pointing out two issues that arise from his chapter that seem to me particularly interesting.

First, the distinction Rob draws between the symbolic and instrumental uses of anti-discrimination law seems to me to be one that repays considerable attention, since it drives us to consider in particular the links between human rights law and what has been called 'identity politics'. Is equality law the appropriate battleground on which issues of identity politics should take place? And if it is inevitable that it will take place on this ground, what are the implications of this for the future shape of the broader equality debate in Europe?

Second, what, if any, is the appropriate role of religion in today's largely secular civil and political society? Should all political argument in liberal democracies be secular? How far should identity politics encompass *religious* identity within its concerns? When does a strict separation of Church and state itself risk becoming intolerant towards the religious in everyday life?

With his usual elegance, clarity and verve, Rob requires us to think deeply about these and other issues, and we are all in his debt. He encourages us to continue to discuss the deeper issues that he has raised, and no doubt we shall.

From 'Sex Rights' to 'Love Rights': Partnership Rights as Human Rights

Robert Wintemute

Introduction

As recently as 1970, sexual activity between men was completely illegal in Scotland, Northern Ireland and the Republic of Ireland, and was stigmatized as immoral and highly undesirable by an unequal, higher age of consent in England and Wales, and in all but one of the twenty-three other countries that are now member states of the European Union.[1] Yet, in 2000, only thirty years later, the Parliament of the Netherlands passed an amendment to the Civil Code which provides that: 'A marriage can be contracted by two persons of different sex or of the same sex.'[2] In addition, as of December 2004, some form of legislation permitting same-sex couples to register their relationships, or granting them many (or very few) rights or benefits after a period of cohabitation, had been passed in at least thirteen of the twenty-five EU member states, at national or regional level, including the United Kingdom.[3] Once the Civil Partnership Act 2004 comes into force in late 2005, the UK will go beyond recognition of same-sex cohabitation and allow same-sex couples to register their relationships as 'civil partnerships'.[4]

How has this rapid legal evolution come about? What are 'partnership rights'? Who is claiming them? Where have they been granted? Why may they be considered 'human rights'?

What reasons are there for not granting them? And if partnership rights are indeed human rights, are they *universal* human rights which must eventually be respected by every country in the world?

From 'Basic Rights' to 'Sex Rights' to 'Love Rights'

At first glance, some may say that a claim by a same-sex couple to the same treatment as a different-sex couple does not look like a human rights claim. They might understand human rights violations as being about extra-judicial killing, torture and imprisonment without trial. Thus they might not view as a human rights case Lisa Grant's attempt to secure from her employer, South-West Trains, the same free rail travel benefits for her unmarried female partner, Jill Percey, as her male colleagues received for their unmarried female partners. In fact, Lisa Grant's arguments were rejected by the European Court of Justice in 1998.[5] Among the many factors influencing the Court's decision may have been its feeling that the challenged inequality was 'trivial' and did not need to be taken seriously.

This reaction to *Grant* v. *South-West Trains* is mistaken for two reasons: first, the right to be free from discrimination is itself a human right, whether or not there is any interference with physical integrity or liberty; and second, in some cases of discrimination, the symbolic value of the non-discrimination principle at stake is more important than the material benefits denied. But this reaction does reflect a practical reality: that a non-discrimination principle will be taken seriously only once it has been well established in cases where the discrimination causes substantial, tangible harm.

This progression from greater material harms to lesser

material harms to symbolic harms may be found in other areas. Legal responses to race discrimination began with the abolition of slavery and the extension of the franchise, before turning to segregation and unequal opportunities in education, employment and housing. By the time separate drinking fountains or beaches for whites and blacks in the USA and South Africa were being challenged, no one could claim that an important human rights principle was not at issue because these facilities were 'trivial'. Similarly, the law had to address the denial of contract and property rights to married women and of the vote to all women, before it could turn to the question of equal access to jobs and services. But when, in 1983, Tess Gill and Anna Coote challenged the refusal of El Vino's Wine Bar to serve them at the bar rather than at a table, it was enough for the court that they had been refused a facility on the ground of their sex.[6] No minimum threshold of detriment had to be attained.

A similar progression may be seen with regard to sexual orientation and gender identity discrimination. The first stage requires that certain 'basic rights' be respected: the right not to be killed or arrested or imprisoned without legal authority, the right not to be tortured, the right to a fair trial, and the rights to freedom of expression, assembly and association. Without these fundamental protections, it is impossible for lesbian, gay, bisexual and transgendered (LGBT) individuals to form non-governmental organizations and campaign for legal reforms, or even to meet publicly. We take these 'basic rights' for granted in industrialized democracies but, throughout much of the world, they are non-existent or only sporadically protected, as Amnesty International well knows.

Once 'basic rights' are in place, LGBT individuals can turn to the second stage, 'sex rights'. The title of this book could be read as including at least four senses of 'sex': sex as 'sexual activity'; sex as 'changing sex' or gender reassignment; sex as 'biological sex'; and sex as 'social sex role' or 'gender'. Whichever sense is used, a broad reading of 'sex rights' could capture virtually all sexual orientation and gender identity discrimination, including claims to partnership rights. However, for the sake of my argument, I will read 'sex rights' narrowly as focusing on discrimination against LGBT *individuals* because of their actual or presumed same-sex sexual activity or their undergoing gender reassignment (which discrimination ranges from criminalization of same-sex sexual activity or non-recognition of gender reassignment to the denial of employment, housing or parental rights), and as excluding the 'love rights' of same-sex *partners* (the denial of rights or benefits or recognition to any factually or legally same-sex partner an LGBT individual may have, including employment, housing and parental rights the partner derives through his or her relationship with the individual).

Defined this way, the battle for 'sex rights' for LGBT individuals in the forty-six Council of Europe countries has largely been won, at least in the realm of legal principles as opposed to the practical enforcement of these principles, and putting aside sexual freedom issues that are shared by heterosexual and LGBT individuals. In *Dudgeon* v. *United Kingdom* (1981), the European Court of Human Rights[7] held that the right to respect for private life in Article 8 of the European Convention on Human Rights does not permit blanket criminalization of same-sex sexual activity. In *B.* v. *France* (1992), the Court found that complete non-recognition of gender reassignment in public documents establishing an individual's identity violates Article 8. Since 1999, the Court has gone well beyond these minimal protections and appears effectively to have established a general principle that all discrimination by a public authority against an LGBT individual because of his or her sexual orientation (and probably also his or her gender identity) requires a strong justification, under Article 8 on its own, or under Article 14, the non-discrimination provision, combined with another Convention right.[8]

This general principle has been invoked to invalidate: (1) the exclusion of LGB members of the armed forces in *Smith & Grady* v. *UK* and *Lustig-Prean & Beckett* v. *UK* (1999); (2) the use of the sexual orientation of a biological parent as a negative factor in a child custody decision in *Salgueiro da Silva Mouta* v. *Portugal* (1999); (3) a criminal law banning group sexual activity when it is male–male but not male–female or female–female in *A.D.T.* v. *United Kingdom* (2000); and (4) unequal ages of consent to sexual activity in *L. & V.* v. *Austria* and *S.L.* v. *Austria* (2003). The Court has hesitated to apply this principle only with regard to the eligibility of an openly gay man to adopt a child as an unmarried individual, finding no violation of Articles 8 and 14 in *Fretté* v. *France* (2002). However, the Court was sharply divided, with three judges finding discrimination and a violation, three judges finding no violation for the technical reason that Article 14 was not applicable (and expressing no opinion on the justifiability of the difference in treatment), and only one judge finding no discrimination and no violation because the difference in treatment was justifiable. As for the twenty-five member states of the European Union, and every other European state aspiring to EU membership, Council Directive 2000/78/EC requires them to prohibit sexual orientation discrimination in public and private sector employment and vocational training (which covers most university ot other post-secondary education).[9]

Starting from a position in Western Europe in 1970 of enjoying 'basic rights' but limited 'sex rights', LGBT individuals have over the past three decades gradually persuaded legislatures and courts across Europe to provide much greater, if not yet complete, protection of their 'sex rights'. As a result, the new legislative and judicial battleground is what I will call partnership rights or 'love rights': legal recognition and equal treatment of the relationships between LGBT individuals and their partners. The progression from the second stage of 'sex rights' to the third stage of 'love rights' requires a society to acknowledge that there is more to the lives of LGBT individuals than a search for sexual pleasure, or a need to change their physical appearance and dress. Rather, they have the same human capacity as heterosexual and non-transsexual individuals to fall in love with another person, to establish a long-term emotional and physical relationship with them, and potentially to want to raise children with them. When they choose to do so, they will often want the same opportunities as heterosexual individuals to be treated as a 'couple', as 'spouses', as 'partners', as 'parents', as a 'family'.

Questions of LGBT 'love rights' began reaching the European Court and Commission of Human Rights in Strasbourg in the early 1980s, but it took over twenty years before the first case succeeded. The transsexual applicants in *Mark Rees* v. *UK* (1986), *Caroline Cossey* v. *UK* (1990), and *Kristina Sheffield & Rachel Horsham* v. *UK* (1998), all failed to persuade a majority of the Court that the Convention required the UK to allow them to change the legal sex on their birth certificates after gender reassignment, and to marry a person of their birth sex. Similarly, in *X., Y. & Z.* v. *UK* (1997), the Court was unwilling to require the UK to treat Mr X. (Stephen Whittle, an openly transsexual law professor at Manchester Metropolitan

University), as the legal father of the four children he and his non-transsexual female partner have had through donor insemination, even though a non-transsexual man in his position would have been treated as the legal father. But in 2002, the Court finally ran out of patience with the UK and dramatically reversed its position. By seventeen votes to nil, the Court held in *Christine Goodwin* v. *UK* and *I.* v. *UK* both that Article 8 requires the UK to amend the birth certificates of transsexual persons who have undergone gender reassignment, and that the right to marry in Article 12 (formerly confined to 'the traditional marriage between persons of opposite biological sex')[10] requires that a transsexual individual be permitted to marry a person of the sex opposite to (but not yet a person of the same sex as) their reassigned sex.

Several aspects of the Court's reasoning in *Christine Goodwin* could, at some point in the future, be extended to the right to marry a person of the same factual and legal sex (emphasis added):

98. Reviewing the situation in 2002, the Court observes that Article 12 secures the fundamental right of a man and woman to marry and to found a family. The second aspect is not however a condition of the first and the *inability of any couple to conceive or parent a child* cannot be regarded as *per se* removing their right to enjoy the first limb of this provision. . . .

100. It is true that the first sentence [of Article 12] refers in express terms to the right of a man and woman to marry. The Court is not persuaded that at the date of this case it can still be assumed that these terms must refer to a determination of gender by purely biological criteria. . . . *There have been major social changes in the institution of marriage since the adoption of the Convention* as well as dramatic changes brought about by developments in medicine and science in the field of transsexuality. . . . The Court would also note that

Article 9 of the recently adopted Charter of Fundamental Rights of the European Union departs, no doubt deliberately, from the wording of Article 12 of the Convention in removing the reference to men and women. . . .

101. . . . [I]t is *artificial to assert that post-operative transsexuals* have not been deprived of the right to marry as, according to law, they *remain able to marry a person of their former opposite sex* [cf. the ability of a gay man to marry a woman, and of a lesbian woman to marry a man]. The applicant in this case lives as a woman, is in a relationship with a man and would only wish to marry a man [her current opposite sex]. She has no possibility of doing so. In the Court's view, she may therefore claim that the very essence of her right to marry has been infringed.

At a minimum, *Christine Goodwin* requires every Council of Europe member state that has not yet done so to permit, either through judicial or legislative action, both the amendment of an individual's sex on their birth certificate (or other record of their civil status), and a marriage to a legally different-sex partner after the amendment. Nine months after the Court's judgment, the judicial House of Lords had an opportunity to make marriage immediately available to post-operative transsexual individuals in the UK, but refused to use the Human Rights Act 1998 to interpret existing legislation as allowing a post-operative transsexual woman to marry her non-transsexual male partner.[11] Instead, couples in this situation have to wait for the Gender Recognition Act 2004[12] to come into force before they can legally marry in the UK. Until then, despite their inability to marry, they are entitled to the same employment benefits as legally married couples under European Community sex discrimination law. In *KB* v. *National Health Service Pension Agency*,[13] the European Court of Justice did not follow its *Grant* v. *South-West Trains* decision, and instead held, in light of *Christine Goodwin* and *P.* v. *S.* &

Cornwall County Council,[14] that it is sex discrimination to deny a pension for surviving legal spouses of employees to the transsexual male partner of a non-transsexual female employee, who is currently unable to marry him.

Couples who are legally *and* factually of the same sex (usually two non-transsexual men or two non-transsexual women) also experienced two decades without success before the European tribunals in Luxembourg (the European Court of Justice) and Strasbourg (the European Court of Human Rights and the former European Commission of Human Rights). The European Court of Justice rejected the equality claims of same-sex couples both in *Grant* v. *South-West Trains* in 1998 (the case on free rail travel for an employee's same-sex partner discussed above) and *D. & Sweden* v. *Council* in 2001[15] (where a male employee of an EU institution argued that his male partner, with whom he had contracted a Swedish registered partnership, should be treated as though he were his legal spouse). The judgments in *Grant* and *D. & Sweden* were heavily influenced by the case law of the European Commission of Human Rights, which declared inadmissible at least seven cases brought by same-sex couples challenging discrimination in immigration or housing between 1983 and 1996.[16] Since November 1998, all cases under the European Convention on Human Rights have gone directly to the European Court of Human Rights, which is free to depart from the case law of the Commission (the former screening body).

The first properly argued[17] case to reach the Court was *Karner* v. *Austria*,[18] in which the surviving same-sex partner of a tenant was evicted after the tenant died, even though a surviving unmarried different-sex partner would have been allowed to stay in the flat. Having declared the application admissible on 11 September 2001, the Court departed from the Commission's case law and found a violation of Article 14 combined with Article 8 (respect for home) in an historic judgment of 24 July 2003 (emphasis added):

40. The Court can accept that protection of the family in the traditional sense is, in principle, a weighty and legitimate reason which might justify a difference in treatment. . . .

41. [But this] aim . . . is rather abstract and a broad variety of concrete measures may be used to implement it. In cases in which the margin of appreciation afforded to member States is narrow, as [is] the position where there is a difference in treatment based on sex or sexual orientation . . . [i]*t must also be shown that it was necessary to exclude persons living in a homosexual relationship* from the scope of application of Section 14 of the Rent Act *in order to achieve that aim* [*protection of the family in the traditional sense*]. . . .

42. . . . [T]he Court finds that the [Austrian] Government have not offered convincing and weighty reasons justifying the narrow interpretation of Section 14(3) of the Rent Act that prevented a surviving partner of a couple of the same sex from relying on that provision.

The Court's reasoning, that protection of 'the traditional family' does not require the exclusion of unmarried same-sex partners from rights or benefits made available to unmarried different-sex partners, could be extended in the future to rights or benefits that are limited to married different-sex partners, and eventually to exclusion from civil marriage itself.

Less than two weeks after the publication of *Karner*, this breakthrough at the European level was replicated at the global level in *Edward Young* v. *Australia*,[19] a challenge before the United Nations Human Rights Committee (under the Optional Protocol to the International Covenant on Civil and Political Rights) to a law granting survivor's pensions to the married and unmarried different-sex partners of war veterans,

but not to their unmarried same-sex partners. In 1994, the
Committee began to grant 'sex rights' to LGBT individuals
by holding in *Toonen* v. *Australia*[20] that the Covenant's right of
privacy prohibited Tasmanian laws banning all sexual activity
between men. In 2002, it rejected its first 'love rights' case,
Joslin v. *New Zealand*,[21] in which same-sex couples challenged
their exclusion from civil marriage, a difficult issue to present
to the Committee without a favourable European Court of
Human Rights or other international precedent to cite. But in
their concurring opinion in *Joslin*, Committee members Lallah and Scheinin noted that 'a denial of certain rights or
benefits to same-sex couples that are available to married
couples [as opposed to the right to marry itself] may amount
to discrimination prohibited under article 26 [of the Coven-
ant], unless otherwise justified on reasonable and objective
criteria'.

The Committee implicitly agreed with this observation in
Edward Young:

[I]t is clear that [Mr. Young], as a same sex partner, did not have the
possibility of entering into marriage. Neither was he recognized as a
cohabiting partner of Mr. C, for the purpose of receiving
pension benefits, because of his sex or sexual orientation. . . . [N]ot
every distinction amounts to prohibited discrimination under the
Covenant, as long as it is based on reasonable and objective criteria.
The [Australian Government] provides no arguments on how this
distinction between [unmarried] same-sex partners . . . and unmarried heterosexual partners . . . is reasonable and objective, and no
evidence which would point to the existence of factors justifying
such a distinction has been advanced. In this context, the Committee finds that the [Australian Government] has violated article 26 . . .
by denying [Mr. Young] a pension on the basis of his sex or sexual
orientation.[22]

Although the Committee did not have the opportunity to consider any justifications in *Edward Young*, because of the strange decision of the Australian government not to advance any, in future cases it will be able to invoke the reasoning of the European Court of Human Rights in *Karner*, which rejected the Austrian government's 'protection of the traditional family' justification.

A further breakthrough for 'love rights' at the global level followed in January 2004. Kofi Annan, Secretary-General of the UN, issued a bulletin stating that 'family status' for the purposes of the UN Staff Regulations would be based on 'the law of nationality of the staff member concerned'. Thus, 'a marriage recognized as valid under [that] law', or '[a] legally recognized domestic partnership contracted . . . under [that] law', would qualify the staff member 'to receive the entitlements provided for eligible family members'. However, following objections in the UN General Assembly, UN recognition of same-sex couples with a legal status under their national law was made even more discreet, by deleting references to 'family', 'marriage' and 'domestic partnership' from the bulletin.[23]

The 'What', 'Who' and 'Where' of Partnership Rights at the National Level

The 'What' and 'Who' of 'love rights' or partnership rights are closely linked, because the content of claims depends on whether they are being made by: (1) different-sex partners who are unable to marry because one partner is transsexual; (2) different-sex partners who are able to marry, but one or both of whom have chosen not to do so or both of whom have neglected to do so; or (3) same-sex partners who are unable to marry. The claims of different-sex partners with one transsexual partner are relatively simple. In the UK, once the Gender Recognition Act 2004 comes into force, finally allowing transsexual individuals to amend their birth certificates and be treated for all legal purposes as members of their reassigned sex, factually different-sex but legally same-sex couples will be transformed into legally different-sex couples able to marry.[24] They will then be able to choose to marry and, if one or both partners chooses not to do so or both partners neglect to do so, their partnership rights claims will be the same as the claims of other unmarried different-sex couples (i.e. to specific rights and obligations of married different-sex couples).

The partnership rights claims of different-sex partners who are able to marry, but have chosen not to do so or who have neglected to do so, have received increasing attention from legislatures since the 1970s. In the Netherlands, Sweden, Canada, Australia and New Zealand, for example, the trend has been to greatly reduce the differences between the rights and obligations of married different-sex couples and unmarried different-sex couples who have cohabited for a minimum period, out of a concern that the choice not to marry is often that of an economically stronger man seeking to avoid financial support obligations to an economically weaker woman. Other countries, such as the USA, provide very little recognition of unmarried different-sex couples, out of a concern that the institution of marriage will be undermined if different-sex couples are not given material incentives to join it. England and Wales lie somewhere in the middle, in that unmarried different-sex couples are recognized for the purposes of fatal accident claims, criminal injury compensation, and succession to public and private sector rented housing, but not inheritance in the absence of a will, state pensions or financial support obligations.[25]

While legislatures are often sympathetic to the partnership rights claims of unmarried different-sex couples, courts have been reluctant to hold that these couples are entitled, as a matter of constitutional or human rights law, to equal treatment with married couples. Thus, although the Supreme Court of Canada has found that 'marital status' is an 'analogous ground' of discrimination under the Canadian Charter of Rights and Freedoms (part of the Constitution of Canada),[26] the Court has also concluded that this does not require that unmarried different-sex couples be granted the same access to a property division mechanism on relationship breakdown as married couples.[27] Similarly, while the European Court of Human Rights recognizes that unmarried different-sex couples have a 'family life', it has declined to 'dictate, or even indicate' the measures to be taken with regard to such couples by European governments, who enjoy a 'margin of appreciation' in this area.[28] The Court has also said that:

marriage remains an institution that is widely accepted as conferring a particular status on those who enter it and, indeed, it is singled out for special treatment under Article 12 of the Convention. The Court considers that the promotion of marriage, by way of limited benefits for surviving spouses [denied to surviving unmarried different-sex partners], cannot be said to exceed the margin of appreciation afforded to the respondent Government.[29]

In the case of 'same-sex couples', that is, couples where both partners are legally and factually of the same sex (including transsexual individuals who are of the same legal and factual sex as their partners after their gender reassignments are recognized), partnership rights claims are more complex and fall into three categories. First, there are claims to equality with unmarried different-sex couples, as in *Grant* v. *South-West Trains, Karner* v. *Austria* and *Edward Young* v. *Australia*. These claims are politically and legally less controversial, because they do not require any changes to the institution of civil marriage, and involve same-sex couples 'piggybacking' on the existing rights and obligations of unmarried different-sex couples. The difficult decision is whether or not to create these rights and obligations in the first place. Once they exist, their extension to same-sex couples is a relatively easy step. Thus, the European Community's Council Directive 2000/78/EC, which prohibits sexual orientation discrimination with regard to 'pay' in employment, is likely to be interpreted (especially in light of *Karner* v. *Austria*) as requiring equal treatment of the unmarried different-sex and same-sex partners of employees in relation to all employment benefits, which will effectively overrule the result (but not the reasoning) in *Grant* v. *South-West Trains*.

In 1999, the Supreme Court of Canada held in *M.* v. *H.* that it was unjustifiable sexual orientation discrimination for Ontario to define 'spouse' as including an unmarried partner 'of the opposite sex', thereby precluding a financially dependent woman from claiming support from her former female partner.[30] The federal Parliament and provincial legislatures have responded by amending hundreds of laws to extend to same-sex couples the rights and obligations of unmarried different-sex couples,[31] which tend to be far more extensive in Canada than in the UK. Now, in many situations in Canada, it does not matter whether two partners are of different sexes or of the same sex, or whether or not they are married to each other. Similar legislation has been enacted in several Australian states and in New Zealand.

In England and Wales, comprehensive equalization of the limited rights of unmarried same-sex and different-sex couples is nearing completion, as a result of similar judicial application of human rights principles. In 1999 in *Fitzpatrick* v. *Sterling Housing Association*,[32] the judicial House of Lords held unanimously that the phrase 'person who was living with the original tenant as his or her wife or husband' in housing legislation could not be interpreted as including a same-sex partner (although the majority held that a same-sex partner would qualify as a 'family member'). In 2002, applying the Human Rights Act 1998 in *Ghaidan* v. *Godin-Mendoza*, the Court of Appeal reached the opposite conclusion, and the House of Lords affirmed in 2004.[33] *Karner* v. *Austria* and *Godin-Mendoza* now require equalization (but not extension) of the rights of unmarried different-sex and same-sex couples, through a combination of judicial interpretation under the Human Rights Act 1998 and legislation where this is not possible.[34]

The second category of claims by same-sex couples is to equality with married different-sex couples, without actually claiming the right to marry. This means that a same-sex couple may seek a specific right or obligation which is only granted to or imposed on married different-sex couples, and argue that they should be exempt from the marriage requirement because, unlike most unmarried different-sex couples, they are not legally able to marry. An example of this kind of claim is *National Coalition for Gay and Lesbian Equality* v. *Minister of Home Affairs*, a 1999 decision of the Constitutional Court of South Africa holding that it was combined marital status and sexual orientation discrimination to permit only the married different-sex partners of citizens to immigrate, while threatening the same-sex partners of citizens with deportation.[35]

This category of claim is easier to make in jurisdictions,

such as Canada and South Africa, where marital status discrimination is expressly or impliedly prohibited by the national constitution. In the UK, or under European Community or European Convention law, a comparable principle has yet to be established. However, same-sex couples can argue either that direct sexual orientation discrimination (inherent in the rule that prevents them from marrying) has been incorporated into the rule that denies them the right or benefit,[36] or that there is at least indirect sexual orientation discrimination: the 'facially neutral' requirement that they be married has an obviously disproportionate impact on them compared with different-sex couples, most of whom can comply with it.

Under the European Convention, the inability of same-sex couples to marry in most countries would distinguish their cases from those of unmarried different-sex couples able to marry, mentioned above,[37] and would justify an exemption from the marriage requirement.[38] Indeed, in *Joslin* v. *New Zealand*, UN Human Rights Committee members Lallah and Scheinin noted in their concurring opinion that:

when the Committee has held that certain differences in the treatment of married couples and unmarried heterosexual couples were based on reasonable and objective criteria and hence not discriminatory, the rationale of this approach was in the ability of the couples in question to choose whether to marry or not to marry. . . . No such possibility of choice exists for same-sex couples in countries where the law does not allow for same-sex marriage or other type of recognized same-sex partnership with consequences similar to or identical with those of marriage.[39]

Indirect discrimination and exemption arguments are likely to be made in a case pending before the European Court of

Human Rights,[40] and under the European Community's Council Directive 2000/78/EC (prohibiting direct and indirect sexual orientation discrimination with regard to 'pay' in employment), despite the statement in the Directive's pre-amble that 'is without prejudice to national laws on marital status and the benefits dependent thereon'.[41]

The third category of claim involves same-sex couples seeking the right of different-sex couples to contract a civil (as opposed to religious) marriage, and is therefore one of the most controversial. It should be remembered that laws prohibiting different-sex marriages between black and white individuals were the last component of legal racial segregation to be struck down by the US Supreme Court, in *Loving* v. *Virginia*[42] in 1967, thirteen years after the Court's watershed decision in *Brown* v. *Board of Education*[43] on racial segregation of state schools. As of December 2004, only two legislatures (in the Netherlands[44] in 2000 and in Belgium[45] in 2003) have been willing to open up the institution of civil marriage to same-sex couples,[46] and only four appellate courts (the highest courts of Ontario, British Columbia and Massachusetts in 2003 and Québec in 2004) have had the opportunity and courage to order governments to issue marriage licences to same-sex couples.[47] The fact that, as of July 2002, this reform had taken place only in the Netherlands explains the UN Human Rights Committee's decision in *Joslin* v. *New Zealand*. But as this reform extends to more and more countries (or states or provinces within a federal system),[48] the claim that access to civil marriage for same-sex couples is a human right will become stronger and stronger. In the USA, same-sex marriage cases are pending in many states, including California, Connecticut, New Jersey, New York and Washington. In Europe, similar cases on the right to marry (or to have a foreign marriage recognized) are pending in Austria, France, Germany, and Ireland.

It is interesting to note that, in Canada and the USA, same-sex civil marriage seems to be more controversial than joint or second-parent adoption of children by unmarried same-sex or different-sex couples, which already exists in a number of provinces and states.[49] The same is true in England and Wales, where the Adoption and Children Act 2002 will permit such adoptions (once it comes into force in September 2005),[50] even though the UK government 'has no plans' to open up civil marriage to same-sex couples. But in Continental Europe, where symbolism and intellectual elegance seem to carry more weight than in the more pragmatic common law world, joint adoption of unrelated children by same-sex couples is even more controversial than civil marriage. The idea that a child could have two legal mothers or two legal fathers is considered very disturbing. Same-sex partners can adopt each other's children only in Denmark, Germany, Iceland, the Netherlands, Norway and Sweden; can jointly adopt an unrelated child only in the Netherlands and Sweden; and can jointly adopt an unrelated child from another country only in Sweden.[51] Belgium permits same-sex couples to marry but excludes them from joint or second-parent adoption of children.[52]

Now that we know 'What' partnership rights claims are, and 'Who' is claiming them, we can ask 'Where' partnership rights have been granted and which legal form they have taken. Three levels of recognition may be observed, all three of which can exist simultaneously. The first is access to civil marriage, which (in December 2004) is found only in the Netherlands, Belgium, Canada (eight of the 13 provinces and territories, with extension to the entire country by federal legislation expected in 2005), and the United States (one of fifty states, Massachusetts). The second is an 'alternative registration system', which is intended to be a substitute for civil marriage for same-sex couples, and may provide a package of rights and duties that is: (1) equal or almost equal to civil marriage (apart from the name); or (2) substantially inferior to civil marriage.

Examples in category (1) include the 'civil union' laws in Québec or Vermont, which provide rights and obligations identical to civil marriage, and the 'registered partnership' laws in the Netherlands, Iceland, Norway, Denmark, Sweden and Finland, which include exceptions relating to adoption or donor insemination.

Examples in category (2) include the law on the *pacte civil de solidarité* or civil solidarity pact (PaCS) in France, laws in eleven out of seventeen non-African regions of Spain, and the *Lebenspartnerschaftsgesetz* or Life Partnerships Law in Germany.

It would appear that (in countries with civil marriage) no 'alternative registration system' has been created for unmarried different-sex couples only, probably because the complaint of such couples that they want to register and acquire the rights and obligations of marriage, but only if the institution is not called marriage, attracts relatively little sympathy. However, whenever such a system is being created for same-sex couples, to avoid allowing them access to civil marriage, the system will usually be extended to unmarried different-sex couples if it falls into category (2) above (substantially inferior to civil marriage) and thus does not eliminate material incentives for such couples to marry.[53] If the alternative registration system falls into category (1) (equal or almost equal to civil marriage), the majority of jurisdictions to date have confined the system to same-sex couples, so as not to create competition for marriage among different-sex couples. The UK's Civil Partnership Act 2004 follows this approach.

But the list of jurisdictions in which a category (1) law is open to all couples is growing, and currently includes the Netherlands, New Zealand, Québec and Tasmania.

The third level of recognition is what I call recognition of 'unregistered cohabitation'. The package of rights and obligations attached to unregistered cohabitation varies greatly, from the limited rights in relation to (for example) fatal accident claims, criminal injury compensation, and housing succession in England and Wales, to the substantial equality with married couples that prevails in British Columbia. But the key difference from the first two levels is that registration is neither required nor permitted. Rights and obligations are triggered once the minimum period of cohabitation, often one to three years, has been fulfilled. This means that failure to register does not leave the couple stranded without rights or obligations, but also that they cannot register if they want the rights or obligations to begin immediately (unless civil marriage or an alternative registration system is open to them).

Legislation on unregistered cohabitation generally applies to all unmarried and unregistered couples, whether same-sex or different-sex, as in (for example) Australia, Canada, New Zealand, South Africa, the Netherlands, Sweden, Portugal and Hungary. *Karner* v. *Austria* now requires this equal treatment in European Convention countries, and precludes the exclusion of same-sex couples through express legislation as in *Edward Young* v. *Australia*, or restrictive judicial interpretations, such as those of the Austrian Supreme Court in *Karner* and the House of Lords in *Fitzpatrick*. On the other hand, a neutral requirement of 'inability to marry' is sometimes used, perhaps with justification, to exclude most different-sex couples from recognition of 'unregistered cohabitation' (see examples in Table 6.1 opposite).

Table 6.1 Levels of recognition of different-sex and same-sex partnerships

Level of recognition	Different-sex partners only	Same-sex partners only (or mainly)	Different-sex and same-sex partners
(1) Civil marriage (but * = no federal recognition yet)	• all jurisdictions but those in right column	• unlikely!	• Netherlands (2000–01) • Belgium (2003) • Canada (Ontario and British Columbia in 2003, Québec, Yukon, Manitoba, Nova Scotia, Saskatchewan, Newfoundland in 2004, rest in 2005?) • USA (Mass., 17 May 2004)* • Spain (early 2005?) • South Africa (by 2006?) • Sweden (by 2007?)
(2) Alternative registration system • package of rights/duties equal or almost equal to civil marriage (but * = no federal recognition yet) (RP = registered partnership, CU = civil union, DP = domestic partnership)	• rare (if any examples exist)	• Denmark (RP) • Finland (RP) • Iceland (confirmed cohab.) • Norway (RP) • Sweden (RP) • UK (civil partnership) • USA (California)* (DP) • USA (Vermont)* (CU) *Subject to referendum:* • Switzerland (federal) (RP) (mainly same-sex)	• Australia (Tasmania)* (registered deed of relationship) • Canada (Québec) (CU) (* but broad federal recognition of unregistered cohabitation) • Netherlands (RP) • New Zealand (CU)

Table 6.1 continued

Level of recognition	Different-sex partners only	Same-sex partners only (or mainly)	Different-sex and same-sex partners
• package of rights/duties substantially inferior to civil marriage (and * = no federal recognition yet)	• rare (if any examples exist)	• Germany (almost equal package blocked by *Bundesrat*) (registered life partnership) • Switzerland (Zürich)* • USA (Hawaii)* (reciprocal beneficiaries) (mainly same-sex) • USA (New Jersey)* (DP) (mainly same-sex)	• Argentina (Buenos Aires)* • Belgium • Canada (Alberta, Manitoba, Nova Scotia) (* but broad federal recognition of unregistered cohabitation) • France (*PaCS*) • Luxembourg (*déclaration de partenariat*) • Spain (11 of 17 non-African regions) (* but limited federal recognition of unregistered cohabitation) • Switzerland (Geneva, Neuchâtel)* • USA (DC and city or county DP laws)*

(3) Unregistered cohabitation

- package of rights/duties varies greatly, but is often substantially inferior to civil marriage (no registration required, but minimum cohabitation period must be satisfied)

- exclusion of same-sex partners requires a strong justification:
  - *M. v. H.* (Sup. Ct. of Canada 1999)
  - *Karner v. Austria* (Eur. Ct. of Human Rights 2003)
  - *Edward Young v. Australia* (U.N. Human Rights Committee 2003)

examples (not comprehensive):
- UK (former rule: immigration for partners legally unable to marry) (mainly same-sex)
- USA (some public and private sector employers' benefit plans recognize unmarried same-sex partners but not unmarried different-sex partners of employees)

examples (not comprehensive):
- Australia (most states/ territories but not federal level)
- Canada (federal level and most provinces/territories)
- Croatia
- France
- Hungary
- Netherlands
- New Zealand
- Portugal
- South Africa
- Sweden
- United Kingdom

Tables 6.1 and 6.2 summarize the situation at the national level, and show where the international trend towards equal partnership rights could culminate in many countries. Table 6.1 presents the situation worldwide in December 2004.[54] Table 6.2 shows how the Netherlands and Québec, but not yet England and Wales, offer equal and varied choices of partnership rights to all couples, regardless of sexual orientation or gender identity.

Table 6.2 Equal choices for all couples?

Form of legal recognition	Different-sex couples	Same-sex couples
Civil marriage (both partners willing to marry)	Netherlands—Yes Québec—Yes England and Wales—Yes	Netherlands—Yes Québec—Yes *England and Wales—No*
Alternative registration system (both partners willing to register but not to marry)	Netherlands—registered partnerships Québec—civil unions *England and Wales—No*	Netherlands—registered partnerships Québec—civil unions England and Wales—civil partnerships
Unregistered cohabitation (one or both partners unwilling to marry or register, or both partners neglect to do so)	Netherlands—Yes Québec—Yes England and Wales—Yes (but much less recognition than in Netherlands and Québec, QC)[55]	Netherlands—Yes Québec—Yes England and Wales—Yes (but much less recognition than in Netherlands and Québec)

Why Are Partnership Rights Human Rights?

It should be clear from the examples I have mentioned above that the claims of same-sex couples to 'love rights' or partnership rights are primarily claims to (formal) equality or to freedom from (direct) discrimination. They do not usually contend that they have an independent right to inherit if their partner dies without a will, to an exemption from inheritance tax, to succeed to the tenancy of their partner's flat, to a survivor's pension, or to damages from a third party who negligently caused their partner's death. Nor do they even have to argue that they have an independent right to marry. Instead, they merely point to the fact that these rights or benefits are currently made available to married or unmarried different-sex couples, and that the institution of civil marriage exists and is open only to different-sex couples. To exclude them from these rights or benefits, or from the institution of marriage, is (direct) discrimination, based on sexual orientation or gender identity or sex, in the absence of a strong justification.

The fact that the claims of same-sex couples to partnership rights are primarily claims to (formal) equality or to freedom from (direct) discrimination makes them very powerful, because the heterosexual majority will generally not be willing to give up a right or benefit they currently enjoy, as actual or potential members of different-sex couples, merely in order to avoid extending it to same-sex couples. Thus, it is extremely unlikely that civil marriage would be abolished so as to maintain the exclusion of same-sex couples. But some 'trivial' benefits, such as the free travel in *Grant* v. *South-West Trains*, are theoretically vulnerable. In 1994, the BBC began making a £75 'honeymoon' payment, not only to employees who married, as in the past, but also to those having different-sex or same-sex commitment ceremonies. After a public outcry, it abolished the payment for all employees.[56]

The right to equality or freedom from discrimination is clearly a universal, individual, civil and political, human right found in international human rights treaties, national constitutions, and European Community or national legislation. The only question is whether discrimination based on sexual orientation or gender identity is sufficiently like discrimination based on sex, race or religion that a strong justification should be required (where a general equality provision is invoked), or that specific legislation prohibiting it should be enacted. I grappled with this question during my D.Phil. research at Wolfson College, Oxford, under the skilful and patient supervision of Professor Christopher McCrudden.[57]

There are several possibilities. One may argue that sexual orientation and gender identity should be protected as fundamental choices, like religion or political opinion, or as immutable statuses, like race, sex, age or disability. Or that they should be protected because discrimination on these grounds, properly analysed, is in fact discrimination based on sex, or because LGBT individuals form a disadvantaged group who have suffered a long history of prejudice and unequal treatment. I think I can safely conclude that there will never be agreement as to the exact reasons why sexual orientation and gender identity discrimination should be prohibited. However, legislatures and courts around the world are increasingly deciding that legal protection should be provided, either through the interpretation of general rights to respect for 'private life' or 'privacy' or to freedom from discrimination, or through the application of constitutions or legislation referring specifically to sexual orientation, gender identity or sex.

Whatever route is taken, once the general principle is established that there is a human right to be free from sexual orientation or gender identity discrimination, in the absence of a strong justification, the claims of same-sex couples require only that this general principle be applied to their specific situations, and that justifications for denying them partnership rights be carefully examined. Indeed, as mentioned above, it is only once such a principle has been adopted, and used to protect 'sex rights', that claims to 'love rights' or partnership rights will be taken seriously.

The Case Against Partnership Rights

What then are the justifications for denying 'love rights' or partnership rights to same-sex couples? The following five arguments tend to be employed by conservative individuals in relation to same-sex civil marriage, but could apply to any form of legal recognition of same-sex partnerships.[58]

First, there is tradition. 'It's always been this way.' Of course, this argument can never be conclusive, because many human rights violations, including slavery and denial of the vote to women, had long traditions before governments acted to end them. But it is true that the claims of same-sex couples do require the law and society to make sometimes uncomfortable shifts in their understandings of what is meant by 'marriage' or 'family', including when these terms appear in international human rights instruments. A few linguistic adjustments may even be required. I was very pleased that my (then) male partner's sister was in the audience on 21 February 2002 when I gave my Oxford Amnesty lecture. In the absence of same-sex marriage in the UK, was she my 'de facto sister-in-law' or my 'sister-in-law-in-fact'? And was my male partner the 'uncle', 'common-law uncle' or neither of my own sister's children? If we have managed to incorporate women into the English language by modifying our usage of 'chairman', 'policeman' and 'fireman', I think we can do the same for same-sex couples.

Second, there are religious objections. 'Not in my church/ synagogue/mosque.' It must be stressed here that we are talking about a state-celebrated civil marriage, and not about forcing any religious institution to marry a same-sex couple. As long as a separation between law and religion is observed, an assumption to which I will return below, no religious individual or institution should seek to impose their religious beliefs about the nature of marriage on others through the vehicle of the law. Nor should LGBT individuals ask the law to require religious institutions to change their internal doctrines.

Third, there is the argument that marriage is for pro-creation. 'Adam and Eve, not Adam and Steve.' This rationale is hopelessly over- and under-inclusive, to an extent that we would not tolerate for one minute in relation to discrimination based on sex, race or religion. No heterosexual couple is ever required to take a fertility test before marrying, or ever has their marriage annulled at the request of a third party because they are unable or unwilling to procreate. On the other hand, same-sex couples are able to adopt children, or to raise the genetic children of one partner, conceived during a prior different-sex relationship or through the use of reproductive technology.

Fourth, there is the slippery slope. 'What about incest and polygamy?' Although it is tempting to develop principled distinctions between same-sex marriage and incestuous or polygamous marriage, I think that a perfectly appropriate response to this question is: 'Those are separate issues.' The same-sex couples who are seeking the right to marry through legislatures and courts today are not sister and sister or brother and brother, and they are *couples*, not triples, quadruples or quintuples. If and when the movements for incestuous marriage and polygamous marriage present claims to a legislature or court, these claims may be evaluated on their merits. If the arguments that have been used for centuries in Western countries to justify prohibitions of incestuous or polygamous marriage by heterosexual individuals are sufficiently persuasive, they will prevail.

Fifth, there is the argument that same-sex marriage will devalue marriage for heterosexual individuals. 'Get your own institution.' In 1995, a conservative Canadian commentator put the argument this way:

Nothing could be better calculated to diminish marriage in people's eyes than an elite insistence on unisexing it. Gay marriage will look to much of the rest of society as a joke upon them, a campy parody of the central institution in their lives. The harm inflicted on the prestige of marriage is likely to prove very great; the last thing an already troubled institution needs.[59]

This sounds to me like members of a private whites-only or men-only club protesting that it would not be the same if blacks or women were admitted. But what is worse is that civil marriage is a *public* institution. A dominant group or majority, whether it is defined by sex, race, religion, sexual orientation or gender identity, cannot treat a public institution as its own private recreational space and exclude a subordinate group or minority, whether the public institution is a park, museum, legislature or legal regime.

On the other side of the debate, there are those who would

argue from a left or feminist perspective that same-sex couples should not be seeking access to civil marriage.[60] Instead of civil marriage, they should secure all the rights and obligations of civil marriage, or a selection of the more desirable rights and obligations, through an alternative registration system with a different name, such as 'registered partnership' or 'civil union'. But this 'separate but better' solution does not accommodate those same-sex couples who wish to have the symbolic benefits of marriage, and will feel that their relationship is stigmatized as inferior if they are confined to a separate institution. Nor does it address the problems of: (1) portability of a separate, unfamiliar institution, either internationally or internally within a federal country, and (2) exclusion from the alternative system of different-sex couples who are just as adamant about not wanting to marry.

Others would maintain that same-sex couples should not be seeking any partnership rights at all. Either marriage should be abolished and left to religious institutions, or it should be stripped of any legal consequences. Benefits should be individualized, as is the case with the National Health Service in the UK. Where resource implications make this impossible, such as in the case of a survivor's pension or sponsorship for immigration, everyone should be able to designate one beneficiary. At the very least, sexual couple relationships should cease to be privileged, and any two individuals in a non-sexual 'close personal relationship' should qualify, as the Law Commission of Canada recommended in 2002.[61]

These are all legitimate proposals, and it is possible that they could be implemented in certain situations. But it is unlikely that the institution of civil marriage will be abolished altogether, or renamed 'registered partnership' or 'civil union' for all couples. Even if all of its material benefits and burdens can be obtained through other means, net symbolic benefits will remain. Nor is it likely that the concept of a 'partner', involving a 'physically intimate personal relationship', will cease to have any legal relevance and be completely displaced by that of 'designated beneficiary' or 'close personal relationship'. As long as this is the case, same-sex couples will seek partnership rights, including access to civil marriage.

Are Partnership Rights Universal Human Rights?

Are 'love rights' or partnership rights for same-sex couples universal human rights which we can expect to see recognized one day in every country of the world? In China and India, in Egypt and Zimbabwe, in Jamaica and Paraguay? In theory, the answer must be yes. I do not subscribe to the view that local cultures can prevail over the human right to be free from discrimination. To do so would be to abandon the majority of the world's LGBT individuals and same-sex couples to their fates. But there are enormous practical obstacles to overcome.

What is the situation in the world as a whole? The rapid progress in Europe from 1970 to 2000 took LGBT individuals from 'basic rights' to increasingly well-established 'sex rights', and made current claims to 'love rights' or partnership rights possible. However, if we shift our focus from Europe to the entire world, which is the remit of Amnesty International, the progress is much less impressive. The most generous interpretation of the data, as of December 2004, is that the number of countries in which some form of legislation recognizing same-sex couples has been passed (even if the recognition is extremely limited or confined to a single region) is twenty-three: Argentina, Australia, Austria, Belgium, Canada, Croatia, Denmark, Finland, France, Germany, Hungary, Iceland, Luxembourg, the Netherlands, New Zealand, Norway, Portugal, South Africa, Spain, Sweden, Switzerland, the UK and the USA.[62] This total of twenty-three compares with the total of 191 member states of the United Nations. Clearly, with the score at twenty-three out of 191, or 12 per cent, and very limited recognition in some of these twenty-three, there is a long way to go.

The presence in the list of two 'developing' countries, Argentina and South Africa, and two formerly communist countries, Croatia and Hungary, is encouraging, but the other nineteen countries are both 'Western' (in the sense that the majority of the population is of European descent) and 'developed' (in the sense that the majority of the population has a 'developed world' standard of living). Indeed, these nineteen countries all ranked in the top twenty-four OECD countries for GDP per capita in 2003.[63] The world's two most populous countries, China and India, and the world's second largest economy, Japan, are not represented. Does this mean that the issue of legal recognition of same-sex partnerships is relevant only to countries that are 'Western' in their history, culture and values, *and* 'developed'?

I would argue that it does not. The majority of the world's potential same-sex partners (i.e. individuals who, in the absence of cultural and economic constraints, would ideally like to cohabit in a stable relationship with a same-sex partner) live in countries that are 'non-Western' or 'developing' or both. The LGBT equality movements in these countries (where individual rights are sometimes a relatively new and foreign concept, and traditional heterosexual family values may be very strong) are at an earlier stage, often still struggling to achieve social acceptance of the right of LGBT individuals to be open about their sexual orientations or gender identities, without fear of criminal prosecution or violence or police harassment, and to form associations that can work to improve their social and legal situations. Legal recognition of same-sex partnerships is therefore not a priority in most of these countries. However, as demonstrated by the attempt of two lesbian women in India to register their Hindu marriage,[64] a judicial decision in Namibia,[65] and bills in Argentina,[66] Brazil[67], Chile[68] and Colombia,[69] the issue will gradually become more important. One does not need money to fall in love.

What are the main obstacles to the extension of 'love rights' throughout the world? The first obstacle for LGBT individuals in many 'non-Western' or 'developing' countries is the absence of a functioning democracy or 'basic rights'. In 2001, Amnesty International published a report entitled *Crimes of Hate, Conspiracy of Silence: Torture and Ill-treatment Based on Sexual Identity*, which documents the extent of violations of the 'basic rights' of LGBT individuals.[70] Among the many situations Amnesty has monitored is that of over fifty men in Egypt who were prosecuted for alleged same-sex sexual activity.[71] Apart from the fact that the criminalization of their alleged sexual activity violates the International Covenant on Civil and Political Rights, as interpreted by the UN Human Rights Committee in *Toonen* v. *Australia*, the men were tortured and denied a fair trial. Until 'basic rights', the bread-and-butter of Amnesty, are respected in a country such as Egypt, it will be very difficult to establish 'sex rights' there, let alone 'love rights'.

The second obstacle for LGBT individuals is the much greater influence of religious institutions on secular law in many 'non-Western' or 'developing' countries, and the complete merger of religious and secular law in others. Religious institutions are often extremely hostile to LGBT individuals, because of their rigid view that sexual activity, procreation and the raising of children can take place only within the confines of a male–female religious marriage.[72] For example, the Roman Catholic Church, the largest denomination of Christianity, issued a report about legal recognition of unmarried different-sex couples and same-sex couples in November 2000. It says:

'de facto unions' between homosexuals are a deplorable distortion of what should be a communion of love and life between a man and a woman. . . . *The bond between two men or two women cannot constitute a real family* and much less can the right be attributed to that union to adopt children. . . . To recall . . . the grave error of recognizing or even making homosexual relations equivalent to marriage does not presume to discriminate against these persons in any way. . . . [M]*aking de facto unions equivalent to the family . . . is an evil for persons, families and societies.*[73]

The November 2000 report was followed in July 2003 by an even more focused attack on same-sex partnerships by the Vatican's Congregation for the Doctrine of the Faith:[74]

4. There are absolutely no grounds for considering homosexual unions to be in any way similar or even remotely analogous to God's plan for marriage and family. . . . 5. . . . Those who would move from tolerance to the legitimization of specific rights for cohabiting homosexual persons need to be reminded that *the approval or legalization of evil is something far different from the toleration of evil.* . . . Legal recognition of homosexual unions would obscure certain basic moral values and cause a devaluation of the institution of marriage. . . . 7. . . . *Allowing children to be adopted by persons living in* [*homosexual*] *unions would actually mean doing violence to these children,*

in the sense that their condition of dependency would be used to place them in an environment that is not conducive to their full human development. *This is gravely immoral.* . . . 10. If it is true that all Catholics are obliged to oppose the legal recognition of homosexual unions, Catholic politicians are obliged to do so in a particular way. . . . When legislation in favour of the recognition of homosexual unions is proposed for the first time in a legislative assembly, the Catholic law-maker has a moral duty to express his opposition clearly and publicly and to vote against it. To vote in favour of a law so harmful to the common good is gravely immoral. . . . 11. . . . *Legal recognition of homosexual unions* or placing them on the same level as marriage *would mean . . . the approval of deviant behaviour*, with the consequence of making it a model in present-day society.

In some Islamic countries, the situation is even worse. Although Islam, like Christianity and Judaism, accommodates a wide range of beliefs and doctrines, its extremist elements have succeeded in imposing Islamic Shari'a law in some countries. Certain provisions of Shari'a law are clear violations of international human rights standards, but those on same-sex sexual activity are among the most severe. Iranian criminal law provides for the death penalty for a first conviction of male–male anal intercourse, and for a fourth conviction of female–female sexual activity.[75] In Saudi Arabia, three men were beheaded on New Year's Day 2002 for engaging in 'acts of homosexuality'.[76] As for Afghanistan under the Taliban, men convicted of anal intercourse were placed next to walls which were bulldozed so as to collapse on them.[77]

I would argue that, even if every religion in the world agrees that LGBT individuals should be boiled in oil, and cites ancient texts requiring this penalty, religious doctrines must be deemed absolutely irrelevant in determining the content of secular laws and human rights. Although it may be observed with varying degrees of strictness, a separation between law and religion is a defining principle of every liberal democracy. Without such a principle there can be no freedom of conscience and religion, for the beliefs of the religious majority will be imposed on others through the vehicle of the law, and the direct translation of religious authority into legal authority is itself incompatible with democracy. The religious majority may seek to have their beliefs reflected in secular laws, but they must do so through reasoned secular arguments. Religious texts or doctrines must be excluded from legislative and judicial debates because, unlike secular laws, they rely on an inaccessible, extra-democratic source of authority which cannot be challenged and overturned by reasoned arguments, other than in the very long term.

The fundamental character of the separation between law and religion was affirmed on 13 February 2003 by the European Court of Human Rights. In *Refah Partisi (Welfare Party)* v. *Turkey*, a unanimous seventeen-judge Grand Chamber of the Court held that, while Turkey must tolerate its communist and socialist political parties, it could justifiably ban an Islamic political party without violating the right to freedom of association:

90. . . . [The Court] reiterates that, as protected by Article 9, freedom of thought, conscience and religion is one of the foundations of a 'democratic society' within the meaning of the Convention. It is, in its religious dimension, one of the most vital elements that go to make up the identity of believers and their conception of life, but it is also a precious asset for atheists, agnostics, sceptics and the unconcerned. The pluralism indissociable from a democratic society, which has been dearly won over the centuries, depends on it. That freedom entails, *inter alia*, freedom to hold or not to hold religious beliefs and to practise or not to practise a religion. . . .

91. . . . The Court has frequently emphasised the State's role as the neutral and impartial organiser of the exercise of various religions, faiths and beliefs, and stated that this role is conducive to public order, religious harmony and tolerance in a democratic society.

Applying these principles, the majority held that Islamic Shari'a law 'is incompatible with the fundamental principles of democracy', that there was sufficient evidence that the Welfare Party intended to impose it, and that Turkey was not obliged to wait until the Welfare Party attempted to do so:[78]

123. . . . It is difficult to declare one's respect for democracy and human rights while at the same time supporting a regime based on sharia, which clearly diverges from Convention values, particularly with regard to its criminal law and criminal procedure, its rules on the legal status of women and the way it intervenes in all spheres of private and public life in accordance with religious precepts. . . . In the Court's view, a political party whose actions seem to be aimed at introducing sharia in a State party to the Convention can hardly be regarded as an association complying with the democratic ideal that underlies the whole of the Convention.

I am confident that people around the world will gradually be persuaded of the correctness of the ideals of liberal democracy, as expressed by the European Court of Human Rights, and that political, social and economic conditions will eventually permit the adoption of these ideals. This means that, one day, there will be a separation of law and religion not only in Turkey but also in Saudi Arabia, and that LGBT individuals and same-sex couples there will achieve 'basic rights', 'sex rights' and 'love rights', including access to civil marriage.

Conclusion

Maintaining and improving human rights protection around the world requires constant vigilance and infinite patience. Despite all the legal instruments against race and sex discrimination, genocide and ethnic cleansing continues to occur, and some women still do not have the vote, let alone equal opportunities in education and employment. Given all the obstacles, it is possible that, by the close of the twenty-first century, the majority of countries in the world will still refuse to accept that the partnership rights of same-sex couples are human rights. However, thanks to the hard work of Amnesty International, Human Rights Watch, the International Lesbian and Gay Association, the International Gay and Lesbian Human Rights Commission, ARC International and other non-governmental organizations,[79] as well as the generosity of their supporters, we will convince them in the end.

7

Introduction to Marina Warner

Roy Foster

The last time Marina Warner spoke at Oxford it was to give the Clarendon Lectures under the title 'Fantastic Metamorphoses': this is apt, since her work is fantastic on many levels and undergoes metamorphoses all the time. As her long list of honours and recognitions indicates, she occupies a unique position as a cultural historian: this has been so since the tremendous impact of her study of the Virgin Mary, *Alone of All Her Sex*, more than a quarter of a century ago. *Joan of Arc* and *Monuments and Maidens* confirmed her as a pioneer in deconstructing the manipulation of feminine myth and mystique. With *No Go the Bogeyman*, *From the Beast to the Blonde* and *Managing Monsters* (her Reith Lectures) she proceeded to deconstruct myth, folklore and fairytales with equal originality, fluency and erudition. And she has also written brilliantly about photography and psychical research.

But that is far from all. Her justly acclaimed novels *In a Dark Wood*, *The Skating Party*, *The Lost Father* and *Indigo* have won prizes, and been widely translated; they constitute a considerable *oeuvre* in themselves. Her fiction shares the strengths of her cultural histories: at once nuanced, challenging and passionate. Above all, the following chapter may be read as a kind of coda to her haunting last novel *The Leto Bundle*. In that book, dealing with the life of a symbolic woman refugee and her children, travelling across the ages, Warner explored repetitions, injustice, the transmission of historical experience, the possibility of expiation and reconciliation, and the uses of truth. Weaving an ingenious fictional web, these complex questions were masterfully placed in apposition and incisively interrogated. Much in the following chapter similarly explores the psychology and philosophical associations of apologizing for terrible historical actions, which so often has more to do with the 'self-fashioning' of the apologizer than any real restitution of dignity and moral standing to those wronged. This is most often the case, it seems, when the wronged are numbered among the far-distant dead, such as Irish Famine victims, expropriated Maoris, or the Muslim victims of the Crusades—all of whom have received ritual apologies in recent years.

How meaningful can these gestures be to the supposed descendants of such victims, and what moral right have the political actors of our own day to assume this mantle? Historians often concentrate on the problematic aspects, but Marina Warner rightly probes the practice of apology culture to reveal the psychoanalaytic presumptions behind it: highly relevant, since the kind of 'history of memory' pioneered by Pierre Nora and others constructed the historical approach that validates retrospective apologizing. This approach has allowed a new kind of time-continuum, as well as a radically relativist approach to evidence—crystallized in the South African Truth and Reconciliation Committee's several definitions of 'factual or objective truth', 'social or dialogue truth', 'narrative truth' and 'healing truth', penetratingly dissected in this chapter.

Apology, as Warner puts it, has become 'a secularized ritual'. In South Africa or Northern Ireland this has shown potential signs of becoming a valuable process, though the traumatic divisions and wounds remain; the day when the process is introduced to the Middle East seems far away, and the events of the past two years have brought it no nearer. This chapter looks back as much as forward, tracing how apology intersects with public confession, in foundational texts such as St Augustine's *Confessions*. Above all, she illuminates what the process has meant for women as victims of history's juggernaut—*The Leto Bundle* again. But she ends with another novel, Gillian Slovo's *Red Dust*, and shows how public apology in South Africa has been scrutinized and used by the daughters of the murdered activist Ruth First. Thus she returns to that problematic question of truth and resolution, noting how the separate discourses of justice and apologetics are 'hyphenated' in the South African process by eliminating the issue of retribution.

There are other queries. The process of empathy with victimhood can be exploitative in itself, 'adapting a feminine form of self-presentation to exculpate acts undertaken with socially recognized authority'. The developing trend to measure out retrospective justice and guilt in terms of economic compensation diverts resources from more immediately suffering victims in the traumatic present. The commodification and exploitation of past wrongs, presented with a combination of narcissism and public relations spin, has entered the political lexicon, complicating the ancient impulse to heal wounds through a formalized and collusive demonstration of contrition. These are not easy questions, but Marina Warner's work has never taken refuge in easy answers: an approach demonstrated in this chapter with all her characteristic imagination, authority and panache.

Who's Sorry Now? Personal Stories, Public Apologies

Marina Warner[1]

Introduction

Apology is a kind of language, as well as an area of *mentalité* and of sensibility embodied in discourse and in writings of different kinds, and today I am going to probe the apologetic state and the feelings associated with apology, in order to throw light, if possible, on the meaning of public apology in the many distempered areas of the past and the present where human rights are violated. As we go, we shall meet beckoning figures, as if on travelling on some allegorical map of a pilgrim's progress: Vindication, Confession, Regret, Remorse, Recognition, Exculpation, Retraction, Responsibility, Repentance, and then towards the end of the journey, Expiation/Atonement, Placation, Reconciliation—flanked by two pairs of strong twins, Reform and Redress, Reparation and Restitution, with the angel of Redemption hovering overhead. The prefix that recurs so frequently in these words denotes that these states of mind arise in response to something that has occurred; they respond to a prior act or event and are made in relation to an object, which then bears back on the subject—an apology is in this sense an agreement, a compact between different parties, not a lone initiative. I will be coming back later to this recursive recombining and mutual self-fashioning.

I will look at four scenes in literature which illuminate states that seem to me to follow upon one another in the act of apology:

- First, the existence of an injustice, testified by the sufferer: for this I am going to take Aeschylus' magnificent study in suffering, *Prometheus Bound*, and focus on Io, the young woman who has been changed into a cow and rushes on stage; perpetually stung by a gadfly and driven on in her mad flight, she wails and cries out against her wrongs.

- Second, the apologist, the one who accepts responsibility—or takes the blame—and speaks of regret and—it is implied—pledges reform and redress. Here my principal subject will be the St Augustine who speaks through his *Confessions*.

- Third, the response of the apologee: the person to whom the avowal of guilt is made; and here I will look at *The Marriage of Figaro*, and at the exquisite harmonies of forgiveness and reconciliation in the final act.

- My fourth and final scene, looking at what the future may hold, will come from Gillian Slovo's most recent novel *Red Dust*, a popular, accessible page-turner and bestseller that vividly explores the issues raised by the Truth and Reconciliation Commission (TRC) in South Africa. As you know, the TRC asked people to tell their stories. It proposed—and reached—a revolutionary form of trying to achieve some kind of peace or *modus vivendi* in a country that had been torn by internal strife by offering amnesty to all crimes committed in pursuit of political ends, provided they were admitted, with the significant exception of rape. Slovo's book also constitutes a challenge to J.M. Coetzee's bitter pessimism, in his allegory of post-apartheid retributive and redistributive justice, the Booker prize-winning, controversial novel *Disgrace*: by contrast, in its own ironical way, *Red Dust* explores the circuitous paths to healing and a new future.

The Present State of Apology

Before I turn to these four scenes, I will offer a quick overview of the present state of apology.

The Pope has apologized on nearly a hundred different occasions, and at a special Mass for the Millennium he bundled up 2000 years of Church injustice into one comprehensive plea for forgiveness and purification. He invoked crimes against Jews, women, minorities in general, and some historical episodes in particular, such as the Crusades and the Inquisition. After invoking each category, what he actually said was, 'We forgive and ask forgiveness.' He did not mention the complicity of the Vatican with fascism, in both Italy and Germany, and he left out all allusion to homosexuality. Thus while his acknowledgement of the Church's guilt and his repentance were convincing and warmly welcomed for some, they did not go far enough for others.

In 1970 Willy Brandt went down on his knees at Auschwitz, in a founding act of atonement through apology, to acknowledge the evil of the Third Reich and its murder of Jews and others whom it considered undesirables. President De Klerk has apologized to the victims of apartheid, and Swiss bankers for their part in safeguarding Nazi gold. Bill Clinton apologized to many groups, including the ex-prisoners who were used in human experiments over syphilis; he also apologized to the victims of the civil conflict in Rwanda (which he could have done something to prevent). The Queen formally apologized to the Maoris for the treaty that dispossessed them of their lands; and in India for the massacre of Amritsar in 1919. Tony Blair has followed suit with regard to the Irish Famine.

In terms of responsibility for the sufferings at issue, there is a clear difference between all these sayers of sorry.

Public apologies made by leaders of world affairs cast them in priestly roles: Tony Blair is not *directly* implicated in every case in the acts for which he has apologized, nor is Clinton. Indeed, they show themselves rather more reluctant to do so when they are directly involved. Their verbal retractions are magical, sacramental acts, designed to ease and soothe and purge hatred and grudge, as religious rituals exorcize demons. These apologies differ from public statements of responsibility and regret from persons who are involved: the police in the Stephen Lawrence case, for example.

Apology is a new political enthusiasm, especially when it concerns the sins of the past; it unites two different forms of speech, both of them deeply intertwined with ideas about self-examination and self-disclosure, with, in short, ways of remembering oneself: a theological and sacramental language of repentance and atonement, on the one hand, and on the other, the psychoanalytic practice of the 'talking cure', and the psychotherapy group meeting to help relieve bereavement, mental distress and the victims of abuse. The French have even introduced a new word, *répentance*, to describe these contemporary acts of apology and atonement.

Neither of these discourses is properly speaking juridical or political: in this regard, presidential politics has become less presidential than priestly. However, as Roy L. Brooks writes in *When Sorry Isn't Enough*, 'What is happening [in the age of apology] is more complex than "contrition chic" or the canonization of sentimentality.'[2] In the wake of the Second World War, the possibility of healing grief and easing social conflicts through speech acts, through rites of mourning and expiation, through an evolved, secular verbal magic has passed into the public arena all over the world.

Many tributaries, very tricky to navigate, flow from this main current of public avowals and disavowals: not least, must an apology lead to reparation to be meaningful at all? That is, without a subsequent act of reparation or restitution, can it be fully constituted as an apology? Or is it a performative speech act that changes something of itself? Is it the soft answer that turneth away wrath? Is the recognition of wrongdoing that it embodies efficacious of itself? In other words, as Wole Soyinka asked, 'Is knowledge on its own of lasting effect?'[3]

Or again, is an apology in and of itself a plea for forgiveness which reaches completion only if and when that pardon is granted? The sacrament of penance in Catholic rite sets out three stages: contrition, which if sincere will be granted absolution; but the confessor sets a penance, to be performed in order to make the absolution take, like finishing the course of antibiotics even once you are better. In several languages, the word *apology* does not exist independently of the word for forgiveness: 'je vous demande pardon', the French phrase, and likewise the Italian, 'mi scusi', differ from the English 'I'm sorry' (French has 'je suis desolée'), so the nuanced degrees in English between the formal, 'I apologize' and the personal, 'Forgive me', do not operate. (However, 'pardon' contains the admission of fault, while the weaker phrase for regret, 'je m'excuse', includes a hint of a reason for the act—an excuse.) One might reverse the French and say instead, 'Qui s'accuse s'excuse' (to accuse oneself is to excuse oneself); English appears to be unusual in its range of differently inflected terms: the formula for apology in Ibo, for example, one of the languages spoken in Nigeria, also turns on pardon: 'biko gbaghala mm' means 'Please forgive me.'

Among the many bitter issues, past and present, in which victims, survivors or their descendants are demanding apology, are some very serious, large questions of the historical past: in Australia, the government has refused to apologize to the Aborigines for their oppression during the colonial era, though it has done so to those called 'the stolen generation', who were forcibly separated in infancy from their parents to be brought up in white homes. In Japan, the comfort women conscripted during the Second World War have not accepted the conditional apology so far on offer. Most burningly of all, a campaign in America calls for an apology for slavery. This almost destroyed the UN conference in Durban in 2003, when Britain, alone among EU countries, refused to agree to apologize, and argued for—and eventually negotiated—a strong statement of regret and repudiation instead.

Fear of the consequences that would follow a public apology—demands for reparation, for monetary damages along the model of an insurance claim—is the most patent reason for official reluctance to apologize. But there are other reasons which I hope will emerge in the course of this chapter.

The Gender of 'Sorry'

Hard questions are raised by the rise in official statements of responsibility, framed in the language of apology, and by the growing demand that they be forthcoming for different actions in history, and they are related to issues of sex and gender in the first place not simply because women are frequently the subjects of the wrongs—not least the victims of rape in wartime. The issue of slavery, and the calls for an apology from European nations and the USA on account of their slave-trading and slave-owning pasts, of course concern women, and the reparation that the demand entails would have to include the female descendants of slaves.

For this chapter in a series on 'Sex, Gender and Human Rights', I want to look at the gender of sorry, and focus on the gendered inflection of apology as a form of speech, at the utterance's relationship to female character and expected roles, and what this implies for the practice in the political arena. When I asked a friend of mine, the writer Jonathan Keates, who is also an English teacher (at a central London boys' secondary school), if he ever asked his pupils to apologize to one another, he told me that he had done so on some occasions, and it cost boys dearly to do so, because, as he put it, 'it's a girly thing'. This is also my impression—and I think the scenes I am going to explore will help us understand why, and also other aspects of apologetic public behaviour.

At the anecdotal level, the word 'Sorry' is almost my way of saying 'Hello'. It is probably the word I habitually use most often—sometimes as a way of hailing a waiter, or even, I am not beyond saying it, when someone treads on *my* foot. There may be a class aspect to this, of a certain upbringing and a liberal conscience, but nevertheless, saying sorry can be a way of life. Rather more seriously, I want to give my support to acts—verbal utterances—which represent revulsion against wrongdoing, to accept that to forgive and forget is the better part and to acknowledge the enchanting power of language to bring about changes in the air—aery nothings, however insubstantial, are aery somethings too, as Hippolita says in *A Midsummer Night's Dream*, a story made up of immaterial words can make a permanent impression, can 'grow[s] to something of great constancy'.

But, but, but. I am still very uneasy about the currents carrying the spate of apology today. The personal is political, yes, but perhaps that is the problem—the feminist slogan has won an extraordinary, moral victory, namely that different groups want their sorrows recognized in a language of compassion and, at the same time, the Lords of Creation want to show adherence to it, by accepting a vicarious guilt and expressing their sorrow for it. As Meursault comments wryly to himself in *The Outsider* by Albert Camus, 'In any case, you're always partly to blame.' Nevertheless, this self-inculpation for events in the past is a deep irony, for should politics be personalized to this extent? Should an existential model of subjectivity encompass the structure of human rights? I feel I am getting in very deep here, but I wanted to find out why I laughed a hollow laugh when I arrived in San Francisco on the day that the Archbishop of California was apologizing to all those who had been abused as children by nuns and priests. The thought of Blair shucking off the inconvenient complications of the colonial past in Ireland by saying he was sorry also made me snort; and I want to shake the Pope, frail as he is, when he says he forgives and asks for forgiveness—from God—for 2000 years of sins of the Church against women, and cry out, 'Yes, well, what are you doing about us now?'

It is significant that the Catholic sacrament, if all the conditions are met, shrives the penitent of the sins that have been confessed and lifts guilt from the wrongdoer; Puritan or Protestant guilt by contrast cannot be shed by mere contrition or even subsequent acts of penance: this may underpin the difference between the Pope's acts of apology, and the consequences of apology in the USA and in Anglican Britain—also of course the birthplace of making gains through the insurance market.

Scene One: Io

So to my first scene: Aeschylus' *Prometheus Bound*. The play opens with the heroic Titan brutally tied and staked to a rock by the figures of Strength and Violence; he justifies the acts that have roused the god's anger against him, his outrage taking the form of passionate accusation of Zeus and the new, *arriviste* gods on Olympus and an equally impassioned self-justification for his acts in stealing fire and other exploits that defy the Gods. This tragic, archetypal figure of human heroic suffering will not bend his will or retract his action. The God of the Sea, Oceanus, rising out of the chasm roaring around the rock where Prometheus struggles against his bonds, chides him, saying:

> Have you not learnt, Prometheus, anger's a disease
> Which words can heal?

But Prometheus holds to his sense of right, and does not offer a soft answer. He broods instead on revenge. At this point Io erupts on to the stage—Io, one of the many young women who has had the misfortune to catch Zeus' roving eye, has been changed into a heifer by his wife and is being driven without rest, bitten continually by a gadfly. Io cries out against the stings as she rushes on; Prometheus recognizes her, and, in his prophetic role as the one who sees ahead, tells her he can see her future destiny—but the chorus interrupt and ask to hear Io's story from her own mouth. Prometheus takes up their call; he says:

Tears and lamenting find their due reward when those
Who listen are ready too with tears of sympathy.

Io speaks: she describes Zeus' desire, the divine decrees that she and her parents obeyed, and the terrible penalty that fell upon her as a consequence.

Io is one of the many victims in Greek tragedy and myths who tell of 'the heavenly crimes' of the gods, as Ovid puts it in *The Metamorphoses*; she is only one of a host of girls or nymphs who are raped by the Olympians and then condemned for this pollution to terrible punishments, sometimes to banishment, to pariah status, to social exclusion, to transmutation into animal or plant or watery form. Callisto becomes a bear after Zeus makes her pregnant; Leto is assaulted by peasants who refuse to let her use their water supply after she has given birth and needs to wash herself. They prefigure, it seems to me, all the women with bundles, the scattered, fleeing figures on the roads of Europe and of Asia and of Africa. But what is odd, unexpected and important is that these female heroines of ancient mythology speak of their sufferings, and that they figure, crucially in the imaginary past of humanity: they are the founders of culture.

Io closes her testament to her own plight with the words:

'That is my story . . .
                              do not out of pity comfort me
With lies. I count false words the foulest plague of all.[4]

Prometheus then informs her, gleefully, what lies ahead, and he modifies Io's tale of woe into a promise of revenge: she will be the ancestor, after thirteen generations of the Greeks, including that most Dorian of heroes, Heracles himself. So Io, the flyblown cow, becomes the foremother of civilization. Writing about Io's wanderings, Julia Kristeva, in her essay on being a foreigner, sees her case embodying the existential contingency of women: 'The fact remains,' she writes, 'that in Greece the bride was thought of as a foreigner, a suppliant. . . . The wedding ritual stipulated that the bride was to be treated neither as a prey nor as a slave but as a "suppliant, placed under the protection of the hearth, and taken by the hand to her new abode".'[5]

In Aeschylus' vision, history itself is grounded in personal trials and tribulations (in legal terminology, this is called the Victim Impact Statement); his tragedy tells the story of a male inaugurator, Prometheus, bringing useful gifts to Earth—fire, knowledge—while the woman, Io, acts as the biological mother of the race. In this language of sexual polarity, Prometheus defies the chorus of women when he proclaims:

> Never persuade yourself that I, through fear of what
> Zeus may intend, will show a woman's mind, or kneel
> To my detested enemy, with womanish hands
> Outspread in supplication for release. No, never!

Io personifies this abjectness, she exercises no power, no authority, and as the gadfly bites her again, and she interrupts Prometheus in terrible pain, and cries out terribly, makes her exit with the lines:

> I can't govern my tongue; words rush out at random.

Excess of language, spilling out beyond control, beyond organization, under pressure of a genuine state of suffering, here marks the extreme agony of persecution in Io's case; this index of suffering will recur in convincing testimony from those who are wronged. Indeed, the very word 'wronged' sounds the closing note of the whole play, as the heavens fall in and the ocean rises up to engulf Prometheus, still chained, in a cataclysm.

The wronged, like Io, do not however want the consolation of 'false words' in response to their genuine cries of woe. But the call she makes—and tragic figures like her make—stirs our pity and fear, in Aristotle's famous definition; it makes us sorry for her, and through her, for the plight of sufferers like her.

The move from empathetic sorrow to public apology is of course unthinkable within the order of Greek fate; its appearance today, as a response to tragic injustice, results from the growth of our ever deeper investment in concepts such as responsibility, blame, accountability, which search out individual human agents, actors, perpetrators. Apology, a secularized ritual, grows out of identity politics, and its particular, Ionic aspect of victimhood. Victim politics have a long reach into the past, but they have acquired a new salience.

History may be lost to view when it is personified in a suffering subject: and this is where the work that I do, the writing I am committed to, converges with the issue, and turns it into a bristling and jagged, intractable problem. Since the 1980s, women writers in particular have been recomposing the 'the book of memory' in order to give muted subjects their voice: novelists such as Keri Hulme in New Zealand, Natalie Gordimer in South Africa, Toni Morrison and Maxine Hong Kingston in the USA, and Margaret Atwood in Canada, have been actively engaged in reconstituting, through empathy and imagination, lost histories and lost strands of courage and invention; they have summoned reserves of 'negative capability' in order to engage passionately with the past. Adrienne Rich, the American poet, has been credited with coining the term 're-visioning', with reference to the political enterprise, within feminism, of recasting the past, of reascribing value, of working against the grain of received opinion and received stories. If history is an agreed fable, as Voltaire said ('l'histoire est une fable convenue'), then any initiative to change things must begin with stories. Adrienne Rich's vision of the writer's engagement includes a dark and mordant perspective on Memory, in *An Atlas of the Difficult World*, a fine and complex series of meditations on contemporary issues. One poem begins, 'Memory says Want to do right?: Don't count on me', and then, as Memory speaks, she remembers the twentieth century, and using the first person and the present tense offers us harrowing images:

> I am a canal in Europe where bodies are floating
> I'm a mass grave . . .
> I'm accused of child-death of drinking blood . . .,
> there is spit on my sleeve there are phone calls in the night.'[6]

She continues, taking us through more of the atrocities and horrors of the recent past. Elsewhere, Rich asks, 'What does it mean to say *I have survived*?'[7] With fierce irony, she is calling for a newly imagined, reactivated history, a new storehouse of stories that will reconfigure Memory, for a way of speaking that will force the silence to open up its secrets.

The embassies of campaigners for apologies belong to this same enterprise, and their popularity reflects the unexpected success, it strikes me, of the fictional revisionist mode since the 1980s. The reason that fiction and women figure in the forefront of this development is that such storytelling has been concerned explicitly with the sufferings of the silenced, invisible, oppressed and unchronicled past: with anonymous, marginal and disappeared peoples. Toni Morrison, in her novel *Jazz*, writes, in the narrator's voice, about the black male protagonist: 'I want to be the language that wishes him well.'[8]

In the field of apology, it can likewise work as language that wishes someone well.

Her fictions, like *Beloved*, embody voices of the voiceless: drawing on first-person accounts such as the autobiography of Mary Prince, the first woman to write about a life in slavery,[9] Morrison turned the lens of history around to look, not at the victorious—or defeated—generals of the civil war, but at its consequences for ordinary individuals. Through this act of imaginary identification, a writer like Morrison follows in the footsteps of the abolitionists who supported historical women like Mary Prince to stand witness; she is pressing literature into the service of liberty and justice. As Jacqueline Rose has succinctly summed up the relation between such acts of writing and the struggle for rights, 'Accountability halts at the barrier of identification. As does atrocity. All the evidence suggests that people do not kill if they can imagine themselves in the other person's shoes.'[10]

An economy of virtue flourishes around claims of injustice; like pilgrims kissing the wounds of the crucified Christ, contemporary political subjects seek to touch these springs of sympathy, and apologists—by consenting and yielding and admitting wrong—strive to reach the same condition of pathos, and consequently partake in the currency of merit.

Roy Foster, who introduced me when I delivered this chapter as a lecture in the Sheldonian Theatre, Oxford, has pointed to the problem and shown, with a dose of sharp scepticism and withering wit, how wishful, imaginary narratives, not historical inquiry, have impinged upon and shaped political allegiances and even policy in his collection of essays, *The Irish Story: Telling Tales and Making it Up in Ireland*.[11] This new coin of sympathy risks turning into a black market in competitive injury, an inflationary spiral of self-pitying self-justification.

How did we reach this point? How has tragic pathos, such as Aeschylus communicates, or the polyphony of a Toni Morrison novel stirringly aroused, become instrumentalized to deepen conflict, and not the intended opposite? How has grief become grievance, to echo Seamus Heaney once more?

In order to supply some light on this question, and see how strongly it bears on the issue of apology, we need to take a detour through the contradictory somersaults of the word in its long history.

Apology's first meaning is vindication, as in the term, *Apologia pro vita sua*, used by John Henry Newman as the title for his great testimonial to his own conversion; but, slanted through the idea of vindication as an avowal, a confession, apology has acquired its present, widespread meaning as a formal statement of culpability.

Plato calls Socrates' defence at his trial 'The Apology'; pleading for his life, against charges of corrupting Athenian youth, Socrates emphatically does not apologize.

How did the concept—and the practice—shift from this righteous reasoning in self-defence to the abject, self-abasing petition of apologizing as we understand it today? From the Promethean stand of heroic defiance to the adoption of the Ionic suppliant?

So to the second scene in literature, which I hope will illuminate the issue: St Augustine's *Confessions*.

Scene Two: St Augustine's *Confessions*

In the *Confessions*, the Bishop of Hippo invokes the god he loves, calling him unceasingly in the vocative: Tu—Thou or You. Augustine searches his heart, his conscience, his mind; he inaugurates self-portraiture in fiction.

Apologies take place in dialogue: they must be made in the presence of someone, the letter must be sent, the message delivered, the speech made to an audience, there must be an addressee. They share this character with confession, and in Augustine's accents, the effect is 'unusually intimate', a personal heart-to-heart, which 'break[s] down the boundary', the historian Peter Brown writes in his recent introduction to the *Confessions*, 'between prayer and literature'.[12] Echoing with the pleading, praise-singing, breast-beating and lyric laments of the Psalms, Augustine analyses his self, his life and character up to the year 397 when he is speaking to God through these words (with 'his back turned to us').

Like Io, he cries out of wrongs done—*but in this case by himself*, the particular individual with an individual case history, but also Augustine, a man like any other, he writes. He does not begin with his own memories, but with the ordinary first experiences of any baby just as he has observed in others. He addresses God with insistent, plangent intensity: 'my confession, O my God, in Your sight is made silently, and yet not silently, for it makes no sound, yet it cries aloud in my heart'. Through the deep-digging psychic archaeology of the book, Augustine commands our interest—and our admiration—today because his probing is so unrelenting and often breathtaking in its penetration, because he shows us someone scrutinizing feelings for their value, their honesty, their depths—their truth. In so doing, in writing this way and making this canonical text, Augustine also inaugurates the utterance of the I or ego as a major, if not *the* major point of origin for truth-telling. This is where Augustine holds up a model of the apologist: he makes a reckoning of his inner being, he begs for God's love and understanding for his faults—and for forgiveness in exchange for his sincerity. The *Confessions* admit some small, particular crimes—stealing pears when a young lad—and grieve over a general predicament of human sinfulness, evidenced in himself especially as carnal lust. The act of avowal leads to acknowledgement of wrongdoing, and thence to renunciation. This text institutes, it could be said, the high virtue of putting oneself in the wrong.

Or, to express the same thought differently, Augustine's *Confessions* enact the way an offender, seeing the offending part and plucking it out, as it were, anneals and refines and lightens his being. Augustine is too subtle, too eloquent, too persuasively anguished to be self-serving; but his example presents a warning of what supplicating self-scrutiny can profitably achieve for the confessor.

Peter Brooks' recent book, *Troubling Confessions*, tackles the relationship between law and literature, legal confession and autobiography, and he has shown lucidly and with great sensitivity how the urge to confess in order to feel better can propel an accused subject to admit to crimes he or she never committed: the psychological hunger to gain the approval that confessing itself confers overcomes even the instinct for survival, and innocent men and women consent to incriminate themselves.[13]

In this personal story which Augustine tells, he not only expresses his sorrow at his own transgressions; in doing so he presents himself to God stripped of all his worldly achievements and authority; he abases himself, never dwelling on his position as a powerful bishop in a city in the largest province of the Roman Empire at a moment when the Church embodied authority (after all, Augustine was presiding in Court dispensing justice on a daily basis). But he allows little of this to show: his *cris de coeur* shed layer after layer, not only of the psychic defences of self-love, but also deny the world's returning gaze and its esteem; the narcissism here takes the form of pressing himself on God the beloved: Augustine, having parted from a long-cherished sexual companion, and renounced all sexual activity at great cost to his own nature, adopts God as his lover instead:

It is with doubtful knowledge, Lord, but with utter certainty that I love You. You have stricken my heart with Your word and I have loved You. And indeed heaven and earth and all that is in them tell me wherever I look that I should love You. . . . But what is it that I love when I love You? . . . in a sense I do love light and melody and fragrance and food and embrace when I love my God—the light and the voice and the fragrance and food and embrace in the soul . . . I breathe that fragrance which no wind scatters, I eat the food which is not lessened by eating, and I lie in the embrace which satiety never comes to sunder.[14]

The founding document of auto-biography, the model for the two great Catholic Saint Theresas (Teresa of Avila and Thérèse of Lisieux) and their monumental works of auto-biography, a forerunner of Freud's talking cure and of Proust's fiction, the *Confessions* grounds subjectivity in affect, and within that category of consciousness, in emotional, needy, supplicating lovingness. I think you will catch the drift of what I am saying: that the subjectivity in Augustine's literary self-portrait wagers all its sincerity, its powers of persuasion in his humbling himself, by speaking as a woman to his beloved Lord God. Who else cries out in his book as he does? His mother, Monica. In the fourth-century Roman Empire, his representation of himself in this abject and powerless, Ionic state was even more startling—there really was nothing to compare with Augustine's *Confessions* before he wrote them, probably because no man would have thought of showing himself in such a demeaning light—with such womanish weakness.

I am not saying, by the way, that women *are* weak: but that womanly weakness, as exemplified by Io, could be co-opted as a persuasive form of speech, and its representations confer unexpected authority on a non-female speaker.

The public apologies issued by statesmen and by the Pope on behalf of past transgressors live under the sign of Augustinian thought, it seems to me. For the Pope, humbling himself, and with him the whole Church in order to beseech God for forgiveness and purification for all the 2000 years of wrongdoing, echoes the great confessing saint's accents.

The Queen is head of a Church, and her apologies, issued in her capacity as Head of the Commonwealth, have rubbed off some of the chrism of her ecclesiastical office. As for Bill Clinton and Tony Blair, their apologies—their confessions—seek to heal and cleanse as vicars, by proxy, standing in for agents to whom they do not stand in apostolic succession. Whom are they speaking for? In politics this is a false genealogy of power, it seems to me.

There are several more problems here: not least the violence done to history, to imagine it can be parcelled up and put away, that it can be *ended*. But, you might rejoinder, what if the actions do good, if they calm the trouble, ease the pain, or, in the language of conflict resolution, recognize the wrong, and in so doing manage to give right to the victims?

If these are the consequences, then apology, as in Augustine's *Confessions*, can possibly add to the sum of justice in the world through a ceasing of hostilities, a negotiated peace (a resolution of conflict). Apologies are not made however by the apologist alone. They cannot work unilaterally, but only in dialogic exchange. St Augustine and the Pope, no doubt with his great confessing forebear in mind, depend on a listening God who relents towards them in order to reach the shriving they desire. Similarly, the Jewish prayer, recited on Yom Kippur, the day of atonement, implies that God will incline his ear and grant what the petitioners implore as they inculpate themselves in strong language:

> We have abused and betrayed. We are cruel
> We have destroyed and embittered other people's lives . . .
> We have been both violent and weak . . .
> We have yielded to wrong desires, our zeal was misplaced. . . .
> Nothing escapes you, nothing is hidden from your gaze. Our God and God of Our Fathers, have mercy on us and pardon all our sins; grant atonement of all our iniquities, forgiveness for all our transgressions.

God can perhaps be relied on in ways that individuals or groups cannot, and apology turns into atonement and cleanses the apologist only when it meets and merges with the consent of the respondent(s). It is by agreeing to the spell, by the one who grants pardon, that the spell takes hold.

So to my third scene, an ideal, perhaps, in which an apology is given and accepted, and forgiveness ensues.

Scene Three: *The Marriage of Figaro*

We skip on several centuries again: from Augustine in what is present-day Algeria to Lorenzo Da Ponte and Mozart in Vienna in 1786, and *The Marriage of Figaro*. And on, to the last act: and the complex masquerade that gradually sheds its masks as the imbroglio turns from conflict to harmony, mirrored in the music.

The Countess, disguised as the servant Susanna, is going to the assignation which her husband, the Count, has been scheming to set up with Susanna all along; Susanna, disguised as the Countess, is looking on as they meet in the dark in the garden; so is Figaro, who thinks it really is Susanna yielding to the Count's seduction. But he soon realizes his mistake. Then, knowing the Count is watching, Figaro makes love to the false Countess and enrages the Count, who steps out and cries foul, calling for the guards—this is the opening of the final scene.

The Count rages at Figaro, and at the supposed Countess, until everyone, still in disguise, and of course in the know, begs 'Perdono'.

But with defiant masculine pride, he refuses. This is a feudal aristocrat who has been angling for his *droit de seigneur* with Susanna and lives by a double standard as if by divine right.

The musical exchanges repeat his grandiloquent rejections of their pleas, his 'no' tolling to their entreaties.

Finally, the real Countess issues from her hiding place and sheds her disguise; she asks for perdono on behalf of all. The Count, and his supporters, seeing his mistake asks her, in a lovely, slow phrase that is marked in the libretto 'in a supplicatory tone', to forgive *him*.

Then there is a pause, the action suspended, and a silence in the music—will *she* accept *his* request for pardon, *his* apology? Or will she, following his patrician lead, refuse?

With ineffable grace, she accepts his plea for forgiveness (and this is, as I said before, the equivalent of an apology in Italian).

She sings, 'Più docile sono, e dico di sì.'

(I am more amenable—[kinder]—and I say I will.)

And the moment of horror and quarrelling, betrayal and

dishonour is lifted up and away by the music of unity, serenity and pleasure, ending on the word 'festeggiar'—feasting.

Here the peacemaking power of the apology granted appears in all its beauty and promise of reconciliation.

It is striking that the Countess, of all the dramatis personae in the opera, reflects most intensely and inwardly on her state, her feelings and—her sufferings; she is the most poignant and by far the least comical person in the plot. Her blessing, healing forgiveness, arising from her love for her philandering and tyrannical husband and her wronged state, unites and delivers them all from strife; the librettist Da Ponte's sharing out of the emotions definitely consigns this 'docility' to the female social role—in a comedic outcome that presents an absolute test case for ideas of feminine virtue.

The original play by Beaumarchais notoriously stirred up a furore and was banned by the King, on account of the valet Figaro's insubordination, and the plot's critique of aristocratic privilege. The denouement of the drama is therefore ironical: the Countess has in the end allowed her husband, her master, to carry on as before. Mozart's music puts a soothing patch over this bad cluster, but it may be that the rousing call to feasting with which the whole opera ends sings against that defeat. Few expect the Count to change his spots; he is clearly unregenerate: perhaps this is what Jacques Derrida means when he writes, apropos of Abraham killing Isaac, 'One only ever asks forgiveness for something unforgivable. One never has to forgive the forgivable, there's the aporia of the impossibility of pardon.'[15]

Now to my fourth scene.

Scene Four: Gillian Slovo, *Red Dust*

Gillian Slovo's *Red Dust* dramatizes an emblematic case of amnesty for the murder of a prisoner, heard before the Truth and Reconciliation Commission in a small, imaginary town in the dusty wilderness of the South African interior. Clearly and cleverly plotted, *Red Dust* dramatizes several characters in a small town twisting and shifting around the act of owning up.

In 1985, two policemen tortured a suspected ANC fighter, the local schoolmaster's son Steve Sizela, and killed him; quite early in the book one of them, Dirk Hendricks, admits, 'Ja. . . . In hindsight: it was wrong. I am truly sorry for the hurt I caused.' This is the only unmistakeable apology in the story; and it proves hollow. His fellow torturer Muller, on the other hand, is not inclined to recant or repent; he even engineers his own death in order to avoid appearing before the commission to give evidence and admit his guilt. The novel plays with many different permutations on honesty and dishonesty, on deception and self-deception, on loyalty and disloyalty, on lies and conflict, in the public quest for truth and reconciliation. It is a cynical, ironical fiction in the spy thriller mode, but shot through with a kind of fervour of hope that arises from its unique historical origins.

The TRC did not require an apology as such, but disclosure; as I said at the beginning, if the crime were committed to political ends, disclosure was deemed sufficient. Above all, it did not follow up any crime, however heinous, with penalties if the perpetrator co-operated. By implication, the witnesses combined the two opposing historical discourses of apologia and apology: by explaining what and how they had done what they did, they were somehow divested of it; by fully acknowledging their guilty participation in evils, they contributed to the purification of the nation's memory.

The philosophy of the Commission, developed under the sign of Christian penance, was also inspired by a Zulu concept of peacemaking called *ubuntu*, meaning compassion, empathy, the recognition of the humanity of the other.[16] Archbishop Desmond Tutu, one of the principal architects of the Commission, calls his autobiography *No Truth without Forgiveness*, and, as so many women appeared to testify to the disappearance and sufferings of victims—they were the widows, orphans, mothers of those who had been killed—they had to do plenty of the work of forgiving; and were thereby also cast in the Countess's role.[17] They stood most to lose by the terms of the Commission, which amnestied murderers— Gillian Slovo and her sister Sean Slovo attended the hearing of the man who killed their mother, Ruth First, and they have both written, in different ways, about this ordeal. Of the 7,128 applications for amnesty, only fifty-six were from females who had committed crimes themselves.

From the point of view of personal storytelling, the Truth and Reconciliation Commission in South Africa worked with a radical form of relativism in respect of historical narrative. As Anthea Jeffery points out in her book on the TRC, the Commission invoked four different types of truth as basic principles, partly conceived by the formerly imprisoned activist, now judge, Albie Sachs.[18] The first kind of truth was 'factual and objective truth'—what actually took place. This is the equivalent of Freud's 'material truth'.

The second truth was 'social or dialogue truth', which, according to the document, was established through interaction, discussion and debate. The devisers then added something we can recognize very strongly from today's world, 'narrative truth', which was victims' recitations, including 'perceptions, stories and myths': witnesses or participants talking of 'their own . . . perceptions . . . how they saw events, both subjectively and in accordance with the collective memory of the group'. This corresponds to Freudian psychoanalytic confession. These truths were seen not in synthesis but in apposition.

Most interestingly of all, I think, in terms of what the work of repair or work of words can achieve, how the work of reconstituting the self through speech and storytelling can develop, was the fourth kind of truth, 'healing truth'—'the kind . . . that places facts and what they mean within the context of human relationships'. This implies that 'healing truth' might even diverge from narrative truth, testimony and objective truth, that these things may actually be in conflict or in opposition. Severe critics of the TRC's procedures, such as R.W. Johnson in the *London Review of Books*, expressed disquiet at the indifference this pursuit of healing truth showed in establishing the actual sequence and character of events as they had occurred and pointed to the Commission's equal disregard of rules of evidence in a court of law.[19] Another political commentator, Ian Buruma, more anxiously than angrily, wrote, 'the steady substitutions of political argument in public life with the soothing rhetoric of healing is disturbing. . . . Memory is not the same as history, and memorialising is different from writing history.'[20]

These critics might agree with Isabel Hilton's description of what she found in Chile, which she reported to the other participants in the OpenDemocracy.net discussion of the process against General Pinochet:

There was a truth commission in Chile. But now the truth has come out in the case against Pinochet to a degree that simply didn't happen before. And it was the impetus of justice—the impetus of the judge who has called for the stories to be told and the evidence to be collected—which has enabled the people to say, 'That was how history was.' . . . Until the record is straightened by an act of justice of a fundamental kind, which acknowledges the history and the rights of the people who died and their survivors . . . language remains corrupted. To restore such values as justice, a real act must take place. Pinochet has to be called a criminal. He has to be indicted and tried.[21]

But the model followed in South Africa was not primarily a legal tribunal. However much it may have resembled one in formalities, it was ritualistic and therapeutic. Jacqueline Rose uses the language of psychoanalysis to indicate the problem in relation to justice: that justice belongs in the realm of the superego, whereas apologetics—speaking bitterness, narratives of wrongdoing, personal cries of anguish—arise from the unconscious, and these utterances can be fantasies, as we know. In the Freudian perspective they are truth to self, whether or not they took place in actuality. The two discourses are incommensurate, though the TRC attempted to hyphenate them, by eliminating the retributive character of justice, its meting out of penalties.[22]

Gillian Slovo has written that attending the amnesty hearing for her mother's murderers filled her with fury that there would be no justice in the form of punishment, and she has since commented widely on her misgivings about 'restorative' as opposed to 'retributive justice', and she notes perceptively the shift from activity to confession within the movement for a new South Africa: 'The defiant rallying cry of "Don't Mourn, Mobilise" was succeeded by a new slogan: "Revealing is Healing." This is what the TRC said about itself and these were the words that were spread on banners and hung around the public halls that were home to most of the TRC victims' hearings.'[23] At the same time, Gillian

Slovo recognizes the political necessity her father Joe Slovo and his co-revolutionaries faced, so she draws a distinction between the personal impact of the TRC on herself and her family and its political purposes, and she believes that through the hearing she learned the truth about her mother's death, 'not because the murderers told the truth—I am convinced they lied throughout—but because the process forced me to understand their mind-set and who they were. . . . I do in the end believe that it is better to know the truth, no matter how painful. In that, I think the hearing did bring me some kind of peace', as the creators of the TRC so ardently intended.[24]

Her own novel *Red Dust* explores the painful contradictions in her experience, since the healing that takes place in the book only happens deep down in the inner psyches of those who have suffered from the crimes of the past, beneath layers and layers of deception and intrigue, political bargaining and expediency, egotistical jockeying for survival and reputation that constitute the hearing in the small town at the centre of her book. *Red Dust* ironizes the TRC's good intentions and undermines the sincerity of apology. It dramatizes a theatre of male simulation, contest and performance, but, and it is an important but, it shows that forgiveness—the Countess's mercy—helps the victims, even while the perpetrators remain unredeemed. We are back with Derrida's perception of the impasse around pardon: that only the unforgivable asks for forgiveness.

It is one of the principal ironies of the TRC that women's voices, telling the story of violence done to themselves, rather than speaking of crimes they witnessed, were few: a special Gender Commission was convened to encourage women to come forward, with mixed results. Antjie Krog, the poet and rapporteur for the TRC, and author of the remarkable report *Country of My Skull*, diagnoses the problem in a chapter actually called 'Truth is a Woman'. The problem is circular: rape did not fall under the amnesty provision because it was not considered political. Thus rapists could not confess with impunity. But, as the harrowing stories she reports reveal, political crimes committed against activist women almost invariably involved rape or other sexualized brutality. And the victims of these crimes did not want to speak of them: this particular atrocity escaped the bounds of language—of the talking cure, of the healing truth—and fell outside the remit of apology, in the form practised by the TRC.[25] Even the limited speech of the poor cow, Io, was withdrawn—with the best possible intentions—from the range of possibilities of women in the South African conflict. Cynthia Ngewu, one of the mothers who testified before the TRC, called for 'the real-real story [that] nobody knows'.[26]

So, a kind of discourse patterned on the exclusion and humility of the suffering subject, coded feminine, was not ultimately available to women themselves. Or rather it was available, but when they adopted it, they did not command the same possibilities of release or authority or reparation as the men. In *Red Dust*, Gillian Slovo has written herself out of this impasse by refusing emotive language, lament, confession and autobiographical modes in general, and created an *alter ego* who is a smart, shrewd, unattached and childless Manhattan-based human rights lawyer.

As Bob Marley sang, 'No Woman No Cry.'

Conclusion

I first gave this paper on 14 February 2002. St Valentine's Day offers couples the chance to celebrate, but those without a beloved feel the lack more acutely on this day, however much they tell themselves it is a profiteering manoeuvre at a slack time of year on the high street, that it is another tawdry example of the commodification of everything that lives that's holy. The current swell in apologies draws up into its energies many causes and griefs. Since I began my research, I have noted offers of—and demands for—apologies everywhere: the Belgian government has apologized for the murder of Patrice Lumumba (though it was carefully phrased not to admit direct guilt) while here, in this country, the father whose premature baby's body was found in a hospital laundry refused the hospital's apology. Every day brings a fresh report of similar statements, some attempting to put right trivial mistakes, other to redress calamities.

Like lovers on Valentine's Day, apologies are also now more conspicuous than ever by their absence. An apology has become a very powerful instrument of recognition, and retention or refusal to give one withholds that recognition with new sharpness. In Australia, the Prime Minister who refused to apologize to the Aborigines found himself facing a hall in which the audience turned their backs to him and stood like that throughout his speech to return the deep insult he had inflicted. This fresh stimulus to anger has sharpened in turn the potentially placatory use of apology. When one is rejected, the attempt to placate is shown up as an empty gesture: it is not enough to say you're sorry. Elazar Barkan, author of the fine study *The Guilt of Nations*, discusses in some detail how the debate around the issue may be applied at best to finding a way forward, and the demand for apologies, its acceptance and even its refusal constitute the first moves in the difficult journey towards reconciliation.[27]

In conclusion: apologizing has come to seem the necessary ground in which new values can take root and grow into social and human rights for groups that identify themselves as wronged. It is a form of communication, in which the subjective self is implicated, and which, when made in public, stresses the display of humility, the loss of authority of the apologist; it adopts a language of passionate and personal sincerity identified with degraded, weak suppliants, with victims like Io, with sinners like Augustine, and so its expressions of empathy help redeem the perpetrator of the wrong by association with the object of the apology. It adapts a feminine form of self-presentation to exculpate acts undertaken with socially recognized authority—kings and bishops, prime ministers and popes love to assume its inflections.

Apologizing represents a bid for virtue and can even imply an excuse not to do anything more about the injustice in question. Encurled inside it may well be the earlier meaning of 'vindication'. Thus it can offer hypocrites a main chance. It can also, as in the case of the priestly self-fashioning of some political leaders, make a claim on their own behalf of some sacred, legitimate authority.

Apologies consent to the story told by the wronged victim or victims in question, and contribute, today, to the revisioning of national history and the shaping of group identities. But whereas writers struggle with the complexity of meanings, these 'agreed fables' often exacerbate grudge and grievance.

When sought by such an aggrieved community, an apology *can* restore dignity and spread forgiveness, by recognizing, as in *ubuntu*, the dignity and presence of the oppressed. It seems that the dignity restored by the apology can make the wronged feel eased. In this way the fully compacted apology works as a spell, a verbal formula that effects change. The redemption lies not with the one who apologizes but in the mercy that the one who accepts shows.

But again this fails to redress the trouble, to institute reforms. It represents retrospective avenging rather than prospective action. At its harshest, it may even maintain the parties in their disequilibrium: the Count still getting away with it, the Countess still wronged. In South Africa, the circumstances were exceptional, and the TRC offered an exceptional remedy; but its religious and ritual confessional and expiatory processes should not be followed, in my view, in other contexts, for example, the Balkans. Of course, Slobodan Milosevic would be no more likely to make a clean breast of things in return for amnesty at a TRC hearing than he is going to collaborate with the Court in The Hague. But is it thinkable that an apology could ever be acceptable in such a case?

Then, on another twist of this writhing problem, do restitution and reparation require apology, the admission of wrong, before they can begin? Should they? Again this surely represents a failure of the law, which should be able to institute human rights on first principles, not only in response to a personal story. Apart from the almost intractable inequities in tracing lineal descendants of, say, famine victims or of slaves, justice through economic compensation diverts resources from measures that would strengthen human rights, here and now. I am with Paul Gilroy, author of *The Black Atlantic*, and he commented to the *Guardian* on the campaign in the USA for slavery compensation: 'This is what consumer culture does, makes financial transactions and commodities out of injustices. It'll be, "There's your money, now shut up." '[28]

In summary, it seems to me that the closer the two parties stand to the events at issue, the more genuine—and even effective—an apology can be, if it is followed by reform of the circumstances in which the act took place: it was entirely proper for the Chief Constable to apologize to the Lawrence family for the conduct of the police, because the police were also giving a solemn undertaking to change their ways. This of course still has a very long way to go. Concomitantly, the further the apologist and apologee stand from the events in question, the more symbolic, religious, diversionary and obstructive and even false the exchange seems to me to be. Writers indeed have their work cut out in the quest for justice, the theme Aeschylus so intensely explored.

We must still say, with Io:

> do not out of pity comfort me
> With lies. I count false words the foulest plague of all.

Endnotes

Introduction

1. Under Article 14 of the European Convention on Human Rights in Europe (see also Article 13 of the EC Treaty), and under section 15(1) of the Canadian Charter of Rights and Freedoms. It is also prohibited in South Africa under both the interim and final versions of the post-apartheid Constitution. Readings include: *Salgueiro da Silva Mouta* v. *Portugal* (2001) 31 EHRR 47 (European Convention on Human Rights); *Egan* v. *Canada* [1995] 2 SCR 513 (Canadian Charter); *National Coalition for Lesbian and Gay Equality* v. *Minister for Home Affairs (No.1)* (1999) 1 SA 6 (South African Interim Constitution); *Toonen* v. *Australia* (1994) 1–3 IHRR 97 (ICCPR). At domestic level within the UK, sex- and sexual orientation-based discrimination is expressly prohibited in employment and related areas, while statutes—and, to a considerable extent, the common law—must, due to the Human Rights Act 1998, be read as far as it is possible to do so in the light of the European Convention case law which prohibits discrimination on either ground.

2. *Craig* v. *Boren* (1976) 429 US 290; for a possibly stricter standard, see *US* v. *Virginia* (1996) 518 US 515.

3. *Lawrence* v. *Texas* (2003) 123 S Ct 1406; *Romer* v. *Evans* (1996) 517 US 620.

4. References in this Introduction are to the online version of the Report. This is available via the 'library' link at http://www.amnesty.org, by citing the Amnesty library reference ACT 40/016/2001. This Report follows on from Amnesty International United Kingdom's 1996 Report entitled *Breaking the Silence: Human Rights Violations Based on Sexual Orientation*.

5. References in this Introduction are to the online version of the Report. This is again available via the 'library' link at http://www.amnesty.org, by citing the Amnesty library reference ACT 40/001/2001.

6. References in this Introduction are to the online version of the Report. This is again available via the 'library' link at http://www.amnesty.org, by citing the Amnesty library reference ACT 77/001/2004.

7. *Crimes of Hate*, pp. 5–6.

8. Ibid., p. 15.

9. Ibid., p. 16.

10. *Broken Bodies*, p. 1.

11. Ibid., p. 6.

12. Ibid., p. 11.

13. *It's In Our Hands*, p. 1.

14. *Broken Bodies*, p. 10; see also p. 55.

15. *It's In Our Hands*, p. 6. But see also the broader statement—'one of the key aspects of every culture'—at p. 29.

16. *Broken Bodies*, p. 15; see also p. 19 and the discussion at p. 51 of unaccompanied women being viewed as 'common sexual property'. For examples from *It's In Our Hands*, see pp. 17, 19–20, 30.

17. *It's In Our Hands*, p. 17.

18. *Crimes of Hate*, p. 7.

19. As Robert Wintemute points out (in Chapter 6), the distinguishability of legal claims based on sex and sexual orientation discrimination has occupied courts and theorists to a considerable extent. In relation only to legal claims (as opposed to social categorizations) the formulation adopted in the text is intended to be neutral. For further legal analyses, see the decisions in Case C-249/96, *Grant* v. *South-West Trains* [1998] ECR I-621 and *Macdonald* v. *Attorney General for Scotland* and *Pearce* v. *Governing Body of Mayfield School* [2003] UKHL 34, and the arguments made in David Pannick, *Sex Discrimination Law*

(Oxford: Clarendon Press, 1985), pp. 201–3; Cass Sunstein, 'Homosexuality and the Constitution' (1994) 70 *Indiana LJ* 1; Andrew Koppelman, 'Why Discrimination Against Lesbians and Gay Men is Sex Discrimination' (1994) 69 *NYULRev* 197, *Antidiscrimination Law and Social Equality* (New Haven, CT: Yale University Press, 1996), ch. 4; Robert Wintemute, 'Recognising New Kinds of Direct Sex Discrimination: Transsexualism, Sexual Orientation and Dress Codes' (1997) 60 *MLR* 334; John Gardner, 'On the Ground of Her Sex(uality)' (1998) 18 *OJLS* 167, 179–183; and Nicholas Bamforth, 'Sexual Orientation Discrimination after *Grant* v. *South-West Trains*' (2000) 63 *MLR* 694.

20. Cited in *Crimes of Hate*, p. 31.
21. *Broken Bodies*, p. 47; see also pp. 48–49 and *It's In Our Hands*, pp. 23–24, 50–51.
22. *It's In Our Hands*, p. 22.
23. *Broken Bodies*, p. 42.
24. *Crimes of Hate*, p. 25.
25. Ibid., p. 19.
26. Ibid., p. 30.
27. Ibid., p. 23.
28. Ibid., p. 20.
29. Ibid., p. 19.
30. Ibid., p. 18.
31. Ibid., p. 6.
32. *It's In Our Hands*, p. 20. See also the example at p. 93.
33. *Broken Bodies*, p. 2 (emphasis added); see also *It's In Our Hands*, p. 39.
34. *Broken Bodies*, pp. 24–25. For examples, see pp. 37–40.
35. Ibid., p. 38.
36. *Crimes of Hate*, p. 7.
37. *It's In Our Hands*, p. 35. See also Susan Moller Okin's chapter, discussed below.
38. *Crimes of Hate*, p. 8.

39. *Crimes of Hate*, p. 14; see, more generally, pp. 13–18.

40. Ibid., p. 15.

41. *Broken Bodies*, pp. 26–30.

42. *It's In Our Hands*, p. 87. See also pp. 88–92.

43. *Broken Bodies*, pp. 30–36; see also *Crimes of Hate*, p. 29.

44. Ibid., pp. 9–15; *Crimes of Hate*, pp. 8–10; *It's In Our Hands*, pp. 10–11, 72, 74–75.

45. *It's In Our Hands*, ch. 8.

46. *Broken Bodies*, p. 5; see further Andrew Clapham, *Human Rights in the Private Sphere* (Oxford: Clarendon Press, 1993).

47. *Crimes of Hate*, pp. 9–10.

48. Ibid., p. 10.

49. For attempts to do so, see Nicholas Bamforth, *Sexuality, Morals and Justice* (London: Cassell, 1997), and David A.J. Richards, *Women, Gays, and the Constitution* (Chicago, IL: University of Chicago Press, 1998), and *Identity and the Case for Gay Rights* (Chicago, IL: University of Chicago Press, 1999).

50. *Crimes of Hate*, p. 7.

51. Id.

52. Id.

53. (2000) 29 EHRR 493; Article 13 (the right to an effective remedy) was also found to have been violated in this case.

54. It should be stressed that rights other than non-discrimination—for example, relating to autonomy/dignity or arguably privacy—could also be involved in such claims (see further Nicholas Bamforth, 'Same-Sex Partnerships and Arguments of Justice', in Robert Wintemute and Mads Andenaes (eds), *Legal Recognition of Same-Sex Partnerships* (Oxford: Hart, 2001)).

55. The word 'purported' is used given the wide array of views which exist concerning the efficacy or otherwise of law as a device of social regulation.

56. See *It's In Our Hands*, p. 35, discussed in the text to n.37 above.

57. For discussion, see S.B. Ortner and H. Whitehead (eds), *Sexual Meanings: The Cultural Construction of Gender and Sexuality*

(Cambridge: Cambridge University Press, 1981), esp. ch. 1; Edward Stein (ed.), *Forms of Desire: Sexual Orientation and the Social Constructionist Controversy* (New York: Garland, 1990); Michael Warner (ed.), *Fear of a Queer Planet: Queer Politics and Social Theory* (Minneapolis, MN: University of Minnesota Press, 1993); Diana Fuss, *Essentially Speaking: Feminism, Nature and Difference* (New York: Routledge, 1990); Elizabeth Frazer and Nicola Lacey, *The Politics of Community: A Feminist Critique of the Liberal-Communitarian Debate* (Hemel Hempstead: Harvester Wheatsheaf, 1993); Jeffrey Weeks, *Against Nature: Essays on History, Sexuality and Identity* (London: Rivers Oram, 1991).

58. For a picture of the 'Neither Whores Nor Submissives' protests which resulted (discussed in George's essay), see *It's In Our Hands*, p. 16.

59. Robert Wintemute, 'Sexual Orientation Discrimination', ch. 15, in Christopher McCrudden and Gerald Chambers (eds), *Individual Rights and the Law in Britain* (Oxford: Oxford University Press, 1994).

60. At a more philosophical level, see John Rawls' rejection of arguments based upon fundamentalist religious doctrine (as opposed to arguments which relate to a religious comprehensive doctrine but which are prepared to engage with the requirements of public reason): *Political Liberalism* (New York: Columbia University Press, 1993), Lecture VI, and 'The Requirement of Public Reason Revisited', in Rawls' *Collected Papers*, ed. Samuel Freeman (Cambridge, MA: Harvard University Press, 1999).

61. For examples of such arguments in play, see *Grant v. South-West Trains*, n.15 above; *Egan v. Canada*, n.1 above.

Notes to Chapter 1

1. Michel Foucault, 'What is Critique?' in *The Politics of Truth*, ed. Sylvère Lotringer and Lysa Hochroth (New York: Semiotext(e), 1997), transcript by Monique Emery, revised by Suzanne

Delorme *et al.*, translated into English by Lysa Hochroth. This essay was originally a lecture given at the French Society of Philosophy on 27 May 1978, subsequently published in *Bulletin de la Société française de la philosophie* 84:2 (1990), p. 50. This essay is reprinted with an essay by myself entitled 'Critique as Virtue' in David Ingram, *The Political* (London: Basil Blackwell, 2002).

2. Ibid., p. 52.
3. Ibid., pp. 52–3.
4. Ibid., p. 53.
5. See www.iglhrc.org for more information on the mission and accomplishments of this organization.
6. See Adriana Cavarrero, *Relating Narratives* (London: Routledge, 1997).
7. See Giorgio Agamben, *Homo Sacer: Sovereign Power and Bare Life*, trans. Daniel Heller-Roazen (Palo Alto, CA: Stanford University Press, 1998), pp. 1–12.

Notes to Chapter 2

1. For fuller accounts of the movement than I am able to give here, see e.g. Charlotte Bunch, 'Women's rights as human rights: toward a re-vision of human rights', *Human Rights Quarterly* 12 (1990), pp. 486–98; Charlotte Bunch and Niamh Reilly, *The Global Campaign and Vienna Tribunal for Women's Human Rights* (New Brunswick, NJ: The Center for Women's Global Leadership, 1994); Elisabeth Friedman, 'Women's human rights: the emergence of a movement', in Julie Peters and Andrea Wolpers (eds), *Women's Rights, Human Rights: Feminist Perspectives* (New York: Routledge, 1995); Margaret Keck and Kathryn Sikkink, *Activists Beyond Borders: Advocacy Networks in International Politics* (Ithaca, NY: Cornell University Press, 1998). For a more theoretical account of the movement than I can give here, see Brooke Ackerly and Susan Moller Okin, 'Feminist social criticism and the international movement

for women's rights as human rights', in Ian Shapiro and Casiano Hacker-Cordon (eds), *Democracy's Edges* (Cambridge: Cambridge University Press, 1999), pp. 134–62.

2. Bunch and Reilly, *The Global Campaign*, p. 131.

3. International Declaration of Human Rights, adopted 19 December 1948, Article 12.

4. *Covenant for the New Millennium: The Beijing Declaration and Platform for Action* (Santa Rosa, CA: Free Hand Books, 1996), p. 20.

5. For confirmation of these views, see Deepa Narayan (ed.), *Can Anyone Hear Us?*, and Deepa Narayan, Robert Chambers, Meera Kaul Shah and Patti Petesch (eds), *Crying Out for Change*, vols 1 and 2 of *Voices of the Poor* (New York: Oxford University Press, 2000). See also the discussion of evidence from both sources in Okin, 'Poverty, wellbeing and gender: what counts? Who's heard?' (2003) 22 *Philosophy and Public Affairs* 281.

6. *Beijing Declaration*, p. 82.

7. Ibid., pp. 11–13.

8. Ibid., pp. 13–14.

9. Hilary Charlesworth, 'What are "international women's human rights"?', in Rebecca Cook (ed.), *Human Rights of Women: National and International Perspectives* (Philadelphia, PA: University of Pennsylvania Press, 1994), p. 75.

10. Hilary Charlesworth and Christine Chinkin, *The Boundaries of International Law: A Feminist Analysis* (Manchester: Manchester University Press, 2000), p. 162.

11. *Beijing Declaration*, pp. 9–10.

12. *New York Times*, 16 September 1995, p. A7.

13. See e.g. Susan Moller Okin, 'Feminism and multiculturalism: some tensions' (1998) 108 *Ethics* 661; Ayelet Shachar, *Multicultural Jurisdictions: Cultural Differences and Women's Rights* (Cambridge: Cambridge University Press, 2001).

14. See e.g. Aziza Y. Al-Hibri, 'Is Western patriarchal feminism good for Third World/minority women?', in Susan Moller

Okin, *Is Multiculturalism Bad for Women?* (Princeton, NJ: Princeton University Press, 1999); Chandra Mohanty, 'Under Western eyes', in *Third World Women and the Politics of Feminism* (Bloomington, IN: Indiana University Press, 1991); Ann Norton, 'Review essay on Euben, Okin, and Nussbaum' (2001) 29 *Political Theory* 736.

15. Joel Richard Paul, 'Cultural resistance to global governance' (2002) 22 *Michigan Journal of International Law* 84.

16. Martha C. Nussbaum, 'Religion and women's human rights', in her *Sex and Social Justice* (Oxford: Oxford University Press, 1999).

17. For a clear account of this case, see Kirti Singh, 'Obstacles to women's rights in India', in Rebecca Cook (ed.), *Human Rights of Women* (Philadelphia, PA: University of Pennsylvania Press, 1994).

18. Albert O. Hirschman, *Exit, Voice and Loyalty: Responses to Decline in Firms, Organizations, and States* (Cambridge, MA: Harvard University Press, 1970).

19. Martha Fineman, *The Illusion of Equality: The Rhetoric and Reality of Divorce Reform* (Chicago, IL: The University of Chicago Press, 1991); Susan Moller Okin, *Justice, Gender, and the Family* (Princeton, NJ: Princeton University Press, 1989), esp. ch. 7.

20. Partha Dasgupta, *An Inquiry into Well-being and Destitution* (Oxford: The Clarendon Press, 1993), esp. chs 11 and 12; Amartya Sen, 'Gender and co-operative conflicts', in Irene Tinker (ed.), *Persistent Inequalities: Women in World Development* (New York: Oxford University Press, 1991).

21. Mary Wollstonecraft, *A Vindication of the Rights of Woman* (1792); John Stuart Mill, *The Subjection of Women* (1869).

22. Monique Deveaux has recently argued that such issues of sex (in)equality within cultural or religious groups are rightly matters for deliberative democratic decision-making within each group, with the full participation of women: Deveaux, 'A deliberative approach to conflicts of culture', in Avigail Eisenberg and Jeff Spinner-Halev (eds), *Minorities within*

Minorities (Cambridge: Cambridge University Press, 2005). While very sympathetic to this view in circumstances in which a recently and seriously oppressed group is first articulating its customs and law to be fully recognized by the wider society in which it lives, I argue that in some other circumstances, at least within liberal states, the liberal requirement that women and men be treated equally is justified: Okin, 'Multiculturalism and feminism: no simple question, no simple answers', in Eisenberg and Spinner-Halev, *Minorities within Minorities*.

23. Charlesworth and Chinkin, *The Boundaries of International Law: A Feminist Analysis* (New York: Juris Publishing, 2000), p. 239.

24. Acceptance of this was based on near-religious belief among economists of the 'Kuznets' curve'—a model claiming that growth, though likely in the short run to lead to increased economic inequality, in the long run leads to the reduction of inequality. Despite Kuznets' own statement that his model was highly speculative, and despite a large-scale empirical study in the early 1970s that refuted it, the curve remained tenacious among economists until very recently.

25. See Marilyn Waring, *If Women Counted: A New Feminist Economics* (San Francisco, CA: Harper Collins, 1988), for a brilliant pioneering feminist critique of the misleading assumptions discussed here, especially this one. For a more recent and more sophisticated critique, see Naila Kabeer, *Reversed Realities: Gender Hierarchies in Development Thought* (London: Verso Press, 1994).

26. This example is summarized from Kabeer, *Reversed Realities*, pp. 175–7.

27. See e.g. Nancy Folbre, 'The black four of hearts: toward a new paradigm of household economics', in Judith Bruce and Daisy Dwyer (eds), *A Home Divided: Women and Income in the Third World* (Stanford, CA: Stanford University Press, 1988): see also Folbre, *The Economics of the Family* (Brookfield: Edward Elgar, 1996).

28. Gary Becker, *A Treatise on the Family* (Cambridge, MA: Harvard University Press, 1981).

29. This account of the programmes is derived from Kabeer, *Reversed Realities*, pp. 165–6.

30. For a succinct account of this see William Avery, 'The origins of debt accumulation among LDCs in the world political economy' (1990) *Journal of Developing Areas* 503.

31. John Williamson, 'What Washington means by policy reform', in Williamson (ed.), *Latin American Adjustment: How Much has Happened?* (Washington, DC: Institute for International Economics, 1991).

32. Gita Sen and Caren Grown, *Development Crises and Alternative Visions: Third World Women's Perspectives* (New York: Monthly Review Press, 1987); see also Diane Elson, 'Male bias in structural adjustment', in Haleh Afshar and Carolyne Dennis (eds), *Women and Adjustment Policies in the Third World* (New York: St Martin's Press, 1991).

33. For a fairly recent summary of the evidence for this, see K. Subbarao and Laura Raney, 'Social gains from female education: a cross-national study' (1995) 44 *Economic Development and Cultural Change* 105.

34. William Easterly, *The Elusive Quest for Growth: Economists Adventures and Misadventures in the Tropics* (Cambridge, MA: MIT Press, 2001).

Notes to Chapter 3

1. Acknowledgements: I have benefited greatly from Anupama Rao's incisive comments and constructive suggestions on an earlier draft of this chapter; Steven Pierce and Kaushik Sunder Rajan provided valuable input at various points; Nicholas Bamforth gave gentle and helpful editorial guidance; Mallarika Sinha Roy's research assistance was timely and efficient: my grateful thanks to all of them for their expertise and generosity in helping out. Queen Elizabeth House, University of Oxford, provided funding towards research assistance, which is gratefully acknowledged.

2. This formulation invokes Gayatri Spivak's description of the predicament of the *sati* (the Hindu woman burned on the funeral pyre of her husband) in colonial India who was faced by the 'dialectically interlocking sentences that are constructible as "White men are saving brown women from brown men" and "The woman wanted to die" ', pronounced by colonial rulers and indigenous patriarchy, respectively. See Gayatri Chakravorty Spivak, *A Critique of Postcolonial Reason: Towards a History of the Vanishing Present* (Harvard, MA: Harvard University Press, 1999), p. 287.

3. You-me Park, 'Comforting the Nation: "Comfort Women", the Politics of Apology and the Workings of Gender', special issue on 'Righting Wrongs, Rewriting History', ed. Homi K. Bhabha and Rajeswari Sunder Rajan (2000) 2.2 *Interventions* pp. 199–211

4. Chandra Talpade Mohanty, 'Under Western Eyes: Feminist Scholarship and Colonial Discourses', in Chandra Talpade Mohanty, Ann Russo and Lourdes Torres (eds) *Third World Women and the Politics of Feminism* (Bloomington, IN: Indiana University Press, 1991), pp. 51–79.

5. Radhika Coomaraswamy, *Integration of the Human Rights of Women and the Gender Perspective: Violence Against Women; Developments in the Area of Violence Against Women* (Report of the Special Rapporteur on violence against women, its causes and consequences, submitted in accordance with Commission on Human Rights resolution 2002/52). Commission on Human Rights, UN Economic and Social Council, E/CN.4/2003/75, 6 January 2003.

6. The Human Development Index (HDI) on women's wellbeing and equality is a composite index measuring male–female sex ratios, and women's life expectancy, participation in parliaments and legislative assemblies, access to education, work burden and economic activity. For details see Human Development Report 2003. In the Gender Development Index

(which is not always consistent with the HDI) some of the lowest ranking countries are Pakistan (120), Nepal (119), Kenya (115), Chad (135) and Zambia (133). See http://www.undp.org/hdr2003/indicator/indic_196_1_1.html.

7. Ruth Vanita and Saleem Kidwai (eds), *Same Sex Love in India: Readings from Literature and History* (London: Macmillan, 2000), p. 194.

8. This point is made by Ruth Vanita, 'Thinking Beyond Gender in India', in Nivedita Menon (ed.), *Gender and Politics in India* (New Delhi: Oxford University Press, 1999), pp. 531–2.

9. It was only in 1994 that the threat of HIV/AIDS led to the formation of a NGO, the AIDS Bhedhav Virodhi Andolan (AIDS Anti-discrimination Movement), which has begun to agitate for the removal of an outdated law, joined by other gay–lesbian groups.

10. The Mathura rape in 1980 is the most well known of such cases in India. Mathura was a young tribal woman raped in custody by police in Maharashtra. As a result of an open letter written by four prominent lawyers to protest the acquittal of the policemen in court, women's groups all over the country came together to demand a retrial and also major reforms in rape laws.

11. M. Jacqui Alexander, 'Redrafting Morality: The Postcolonial State and the Sexual Offences Bill of Trinidad and Tobago', in Chandra Talpade Mohanty, Ann Russo and Lourdes Torres (eds), *Third World Women and the Politics of Feminism* (Bloomington, IN: Indiana University Press, 1991), pp. 133–52, esp. p. 147.

12. For an extensive discussion of issues of sexuality and violence tackled by the Indian women's movement, see Kalpana and Vasanth Kannabiran, *De-eroticizing Assault: Essays on Modesty, Honour and Power* (Calcutta: STREE, 2002).

13. Rosalind Petchesky offers a critical survey of the different United Nation summits on women's issues. In the 1994 Cairo

conference, the emphasis was on women's reproductive and sexual rights. Following this, women's health rights began to feature prominently at the conferences in Copenhagen (World Summit for Social Development, March 1995), and the Fourth World Conference on Women (Beijing, September 1995) which consolidated the agenda for the women's reproductive health rights movement The decisive shift towards freedom of 'sexual orientation' and 'sexual expression' was in the direction of defining 'sexual right'. The Beijing *Platform*, para. 96, says, 'The human rights of women include their rights to have control over and decide freely and responsibly on matters related to their sexuality, including sexual and reproductive health, free of coercion, discrimination and violence.' See Rosalind Petchesky, *Reproductive and Sexual Rights: Charting the Course of Transnational Women's NGOs* (Geneva: United Nations Research Institute for Social Development, 2000, Occasional Paper 8), esp. p. 16.

14. The National Population Policy document was produced in 2000. See http://www.mohfw.nic.in/. See Upendra Baxi, *Gender and Reproductive Rights in India: Problems and Prospects for the New Millennium* (New Delhi: United Nations Population Fund, ND), p. 21 (emphasis in original).

15. Spivak, *A Critique of Postcolonial Reason* (Harvard, MA: Harvard University Press, 1999), p. 419 and elsewhere.

16. See e.g. Gale Summerfield and Nahid Aslanbeigui, 'The Impact of Structural Adjustment Programmes and Economic Reforms on Women', and Maria Mies, 'World Economy, Patriarchy, and Accumulation', in Nelly P. Stromquist (ed.), *Women in Third World: An Encyclopedia of Contemporary Issues* (New York and London: Garland Publishing, 1998).

17. See e.g. Rhacel Salazar Parrenas, 'At The Cost of Women: The Family and the Modernization-building Project of the Philippines in Globalization', which examines the Philippine state's efforts to maintain a patriarchal 'moral disciplining of

women' amidst an increasing outflow of women migrants.
(2003) 5.1 *Interventions* pp. 29–44.

18. Examples would include women workers in the informal
sector who organized themselves as SEWA (Self-Employed
Women's Association) in India—SEWA has become a global
model for such initiatives. Sex workers' movements are also
becoming increasingly global in their linkages. The threat of
HIV/AIDS has had an unlikely fall-out, the emergence of
sex workers as an empowered collective engaged in actively
preventing the spread of the disease and in opposing child
prostitution. See e.g. Nandini Gooptu, *Sex Workers in Calcutta
and the Dynamics of Collective Action: Political Activism, Community
Identity and Group Behaviour* (Helsinki: United Nations University, World Institute for Development Economics Research,
2000, Working Paper No. 185).

19. In an interview Gayatri Chakravorty Spivak describes recent
tribal rights activism in India that has started to deploy human
rights language in this instrumental fashion: 'the people began
to be aware that there was this initiative here that could help
them'. See 'Gayatri Chakravorty Spivak in conversation with
Anupama Rao', (1999) 1.4 *Interventions* pp. 594–9, esp. p. 596.

20. In the interview cited above, Spivak explained that while it was
local human rights institutions in the first place that tribal
groups invoked, there is also a requirement that each of these
cases [of violation of rights] should also be reported to the
United Nations Commission for Human Rights. In response to
a question about the politics of internationalizing such local
issues, she reiterates her conviction that 'India has enough of a
human rights mechanism' and expresses reservations about UN
involvement (about inviting the UN 'into what is basically our
business'), but she also defends petitions to the UN since they
perform the useful function of informing 'an uneducated inter-
ested party', a 'non-academic international [Western] audience'
about local human rights violations.

21. The Nigerian human rights group BAOBAB for Women's Human Rights, responding to the host of petitions and letter-writing campaigns about Amina Lawal (sentenced to stoning to death for adultery in August 2002), called for international supporters of human rights to refrain from 'counterproductive and uninformed campaigns undertaken without consulting local groups'. They pointed to the harm caused by inaccurate reports, the volatility of the political situation in Nigeria, the danger of backlash, the need to avoid circulating negative stereotypes of Islam, and the desirability of working within local shari'a courts to win this and similar cases. For the full statement, see http://www.africaaction.org/docs03/wom0305.htm.

22. One of the most famous of such examples in India is the story of Kamala, a poor woman, who was 'bought and sold three times in a week' in 1981, in Madhya Pradesh. Three journalists from the national newspaper, *The Indian Express*, bought her the third time, and ran her story prominently in their newspaper, while the editor took her case up to the Supreme Court. The Supreme Court ordered her to be placed in a destitute women's home in Delhi, but she disappeared and has not been heard of since. Her story was adapted into a Marathi play and later a film version was also made. Upendra Baxi is critical of such a 'commodification' of the plight of poor women. See his 'From Human Rights to the Right To Be a Woman', in Amita Dhanda and Archana Parashar (eds), *Engendering Law: Essays in Honour of Lotika Sarkar* (Lucknow: Eastern Book Company, 1999).

23. But see e.g. Spivak in *A Critique of Postcolonial Reason*, on the US boycott of garments produced by child labour in Bangladesh, when the GATT agreement of 1994 threatened to swamp Northern markets with garments manufactured in the South. Spivak clarifies that she is not opposing the eradication of child labour: 'the children certainly do not present their working conditions favorably. . . . But in the absence of any redress or

infrastructural support, they find the remote American decision to take their jobs away altogether confusing' (pp. 417–18).
Her concern is 'about making human rights a trade-related
investment issue. It is about the easy goodwill of boycott politics. It is about the lazy cruelty of moral imperialism. It is about
doing deals with local entrepreneurs, themselves bound by
their own greed and the greed of global trade resulting in
no labor laws. It is about finding in this a justification for a
permanent involvement in a country's affairs through foreign
aid' (p. 415).

24. Mary John has pointed out that the emphasis on women's efficiency in the new economic regime of India simultaneously
accentuates the incapability and irresponsibility of their men,
especially if they be poor Muslims or dalits. Further, the World
Bank's emphasis on understanding gender in terms of an inside/
outside dichotomy misleadingly associates (all) women with the
'private' world and (all) men with the 'public'. As she points
out, vast numbers of poor women have to work; and men from
lower castes or minority groups often do not have access to the
'outside' power available to upper-caste Hindu men. See Mary
E. John, 'Gender, Development and the Women's Movement:
Problems for a History of the Present', in Rajeswari Sunder Rajan
(ed.), *Signposts: Gender Issues in Post-independence India* (New
Brunswick, NJ: Rutgers University Press, 2001), pp. 117–19.

25. Dalit (formerly 'untouchable') women have begun to insist on
their 'difference' of identity and experiences within the mainstream Indian women's movement. The specific forms of violence suffered by dalit women emerge from the case studies
presented in *Broken People: Caste Violence Against India's
'Untouchables'* (New York: Human Rights Watch, 1999). Dalit
women suffer from an unsympathetic legal system, a brutal
police force and casteist patriarchal landlords. See also Anupama
Rao, 'Understanding Sirasgaon: Notes towards Conceptualizing
the Role of Law, Caste and Gender in a Case of "Atrocity" ',

in Rajeswari Sunder Rajan (ed.), *Signposts: Gender Issues in Post-independence India* (New Delhi: Kali for Women, 1999).

26. For example, Susan Moller Okin, 'Feminism and Multiculturalism', (1998) 108 *Ethics* pp. 661–84; and Martha Nussbaum, *Sex and Social Justice* (New York: Oxford University Press, 1999).

27. Partha Chatterjee, 'Secularism and Tolerance', in Rajiv Bhargava (ed.), *Secularism and Its Critics* (Delhi: Oxford University Press, 1998).

28. Avigail Eisenberg, 'Diversity and Equality: Three Approaches to Cultural and Sexual Difference', in Constitutionalism Webpapers, ConWEB, No. 1/2001, http://www.les1.man.ac.uk/conweb/.

29. Page 14, emphasis mine.

30. Page 19.

31. Razia Ismael, 'The Girl Child: India's Forgotten Priority, a Policy Consultation at the Close of the SAARC Decade'. Lecture delivered at SAARC Girl Child Day celebration, India International Centre, New Delhi, 2000.

32. See Rajeswari Sunder Rajan, *The Scandal of the State: Women, Law, and Citizenship in Postcolonial India* (Durham, NC, and London: Duke University Press, 2003), p. 249.

Notes to Chapter 4

1. William Shakespeare, *Measure for Measure*, ed. J.W. Lever (London: Methuen, 1965).

2. Amnesty International, *Crimes of Hate, Conspiracy of Silence* (London: Amnesty International, 2001, Amnesty library reference ACT 40/016/2001). Referred to hereafter in the text as '*C.H.*'.

3. Rosemary Curb and Nancy Manahan (eds), *Breaking Silence* (London: Columbus Books, 1985), p. xx.

4. See Moisés Kaufman, *The Laramie Project* (New York: Vintage Books, 2001).

5. Jonathan Dollimore, *Sexual Dissidence* (Oxford: Clarendon Press, 1991), p. 33.

6. Leo Bersani, 'Is the Rectum a Grave?' in Douglas Crimp (ed.), *AIDS: Cultural Analysis, Cultural Activism* (Cambridge, MA: MIT Press, 1988), pp. 208–9.

7. *Measure for Measure*, ed. Lever, pp. xxxv–lv.

8. Ibid., p. xxxix.

9. William Shakespeare, *Othello*, ed. M.R. Ridley (London: Methuen, 1962), V.ii.369–70.

10. See Michael J. Redmond, '*Measure for Measure* and the Politics of the Italianate Disguised Duke Play', in Michele Marrapodi (ed.), *Shakespeare and Intertextuality* (Rome: Bulzoni, 2000).

11. Kiernan Ryan, *Shakespeare* (3rd edn) (London: Palgrave, 2002), p. 140.

12. Pierre Macherey, *A Theory of Literary Production*, trans. Geoffrey Wall (London: Routledge, 1978).

13. Cf. Kathleen McLuskie, 'The Patriarchal Bard: Feminist Criticism and Shakespeare: *King Lear* and *Measure for Measure*', in Jonathan Dollimore and Alan Sinfield (eds), *Political Shakespeare* (2nd edn) (Manchester: Manchester University Press, 1994), p. 97.

14. *Mendoza* v. *Ghaidan* [2002] EWCA Civ. 1533; [2002] 4 All ER 1162. See further *Gay Times*, April 2001, p. 54; Stonewall, *Equal as Citizens* (London: Stonewall, 2001), pp. 15–17. The Court of Appeal's decision has since been affirmed by the House of Lords: *Ghaidan* v. *Godin-Mendoza* [2004] UKHL 30.

15. Jeffrey Weeks, *Invented Moralities* (Cambridge: Polity Press, 1995), p. 119.

16. Douglas Crimp with Adam Rolston (eds), *Aids DemoGraphics* (Seattle, WA: Bay Press, 1990), p. 138.

17. *Gay Times*, May 2001, p. 62.

18. Quoted in William J. Spurlin, 'Broadening Postcolonial Studies/Decolonizing Queer Studies', in John C. Hawley (ed.),

Postcolonial Queer (Albany, NY: State University of New York Press, 2001), p. 196.

19. Paul EeNam Park Hagland, 'International Theory and LGBT Politics: Testing the Limits of a Human Rights-based Strategy', (1997) 3 *Gay and Lesbian Quarterly* pp. 357–84, esp, pp. 371, 375.

20. See Alan Sinfield, 'Transgender and Les/bi/gay Identities', in David Alderson and Linda Anderson (eds), *Territories of Desire in Queer Culture* (Manchester: Manchester University Press, 2000).

21. See Alan Sinfield, *Gay and After* (London: Serpent's Tail, 1998), pp. 18–26.

22. Stonewall, *Equal as Citizens* (London: Stonewall, 2001), pp. 22–3.

23. *Gay Times*, October 1997, p. 58.

24. *Gay Times*, April 1998, p. 61. For comparable incidents in Bulgaria, China and Egypt, see *Gay Times*, September 1996, p. 58; May 1997, p. 61; July 2001, p. 69.

25. Gert Hekma, 'The Disappearance of Sexual Radicalism in The Netherlands', in Gert Hekma (ed.), *Past and Present of Radical Sexual Politics: Working Papers* (Amsterdam: The Mosse Foundation, 2004), pp. 158–64.

26. Michael Warner, 'Zones of Privacy', in Judith Butler, John Guillory and Kendall Thomas (eds), *What's Left of Theory?* (New York: Routledge, 2000), p. 90.

Notes to Introduction to Chapter 5

1. Wine at ancient banquets was called *res nullius*, a thing to be consumed in common (contrast with the classical use of the term in Roman Law as meaning a new thing, capable of acquisition by anyone).

2. I have mentioned this point as often as possible. See my essay 'Each man in his cave', in Alison Jeffries (ed.), *Women's Voices, Women's Rights, Oxford Amnesty Lectures 1996* (Westview Press, 1999), p. 102 and *Women's Philosophy Review* 30 (2002), pp. 34–35. Although the real answer (which would be to grant immigrant

women an autonomous status) has not yet been considered, at least a small step in the right direction has recently been made. Minister Sarkosy promised that foreign women who came to France to join a husband and were later divorced would not be deported out of the country.

3. Maryse Jaspard and the ENVEFF team, 'Nommer et compter les violences envers les femmes: une première enquête nationale en France', in (2001) 364 *Population et sociétés*; the complete survey is now published as a book, *Les Violences envers les femmes, une enquête nationale* (La Documentation française, 2003).

4. No. 623, February/April 2003.

5. Elisabeth Badinter, *Fausse Route* (éditions Odile Jacob, 2003).

6. No. 624, May/June/July 2003.

7. *Nouvelles Questions Féministes* 22, 3 (November 2003) (Editions Antipodes, Lausanne) [from table of contents: Equipe Enveff: Violences vecues, fantasmes et simulacres. Comment analyser les violences envers les femmes. Patrizia Romito: Les attaques contre les enquetes sur les violences envers les femmes, Magdalena Rosende, Celine Perrin, Patricia Roux, Lucienne Gillioz: Sursaut antiféministe dans les salons parisiens].

8. Samira Bellil, *Dans l'enfer des tournantes* (Denoël, Paris, 2002).

Notes to Chapter 5

1. Sue Lees, *Carnal Knowledge: Rape on Trial* (London: The Women's Press, 1992), esp. pp. 37–65.

2. Interview with the author, November 2001.

3. For contemporary news reports, see: Claire Chartier, 'Cités, L'humiliation des files', *L'Express*, 21 June 2001; Frederic Chambon, 'Les viols collectifs revelent le misere affective et sexuelle des cités', *Le Monde*, 24 April 2001; Émilie Lanez, 'Viol collectif: La grande peur des cités', *Le Point*, 1 December 2000. For more general literature concerning *banlieues*, see A. Begag and C. Delorme, *Quartiers sensibles* (Paris: Seuil, 1994); A. Jazouli,

Une Saison en banlieue (Paris: Plon, 1995); P. Merlin, *Les Banlieues* (Paris: Presses Universitaires de France, 1999); J. Menanteau, *Les Banlieues* (Paris: Le Monde-Editions, 1994); H. Rey, *La Peur des banlieues* (Paris: Presses des Science Po, 1996); J-M. Stébé, *La Crise des banlieues* (Paris: Presses Universitaires de France, 1999); H. Vieillard-Baron, *Les Banlieues* (Paris: Flammarion, 1996).

4. Samira Bellil, *Dans L'enfer des Tournantes* (Paris: Gallimard, 2003).

5. Robin Warshaw, *I Never Called it Rape* (New York: Harper Perennial, 1994), ch. 7.

6. http://www.macite.net.

7. *Le Parisien*, 24 October 2001, p. 14.

8. *Patterns in Forcible Rape* (Chicago, IL: University of Chicago Press, 1971).

9. See e.g. Susan Brownmiller, *Against Our Will* (London: Secker & Warberg, 1975); Robin Warshaw, *I Never Called it Rape*, n.5 above.

10. Interview with the author, April 2003.

11. See e.g. *British Crime Survey*, 2000.

12. Hugues Lagrange, interviews with the author, November 2001 and April 2003.

13. Jessica Harris and Sharon Grace, *Home Office Research Report 196: A Question of Evidence? Investigating and Prosecuting Rape in the 1990s* (1999); Andy Myhill and Jonathan Allen, *Home Office Research Report 237, Rape and Sexual Assault of Women: The Extent and Nature of the Problem* (March 2002).

14. HORS 237, p. 86.

15. 'Twenty four hours with rape squad', *Sun*, 24 March 2003.

16. Interview with the author, June 2003.

17. Id.

18. This statement was made at a press conference held in April 2003.

19. Interview with the author, November 2001.

20. Interview with the author, April 2003.

21. Id.
22. Id.
23. Interview with the author, November 2001.
24. Interviews with the author, November 2001 and April 2003; see further Hugues Lagrange, *Les adolescents, le sexe, l'amour* (Paris: Syros, 1999).
25. *Liberation*, 23 May 2002; *Nouvel Observateur*, 25 July 2002.
26. Interview with the author, April 2003.
27. *Dispatches*, November 1999, Laurel Productions.
28. 25 June 2001 and 23 August 1999.
29. *New Statesman*, 25 June 2001, p. 22.
30. N.1 above, p. 37.
31. Interviews with the author, 2002 and 2003.
32. Kate Cook, *Rape Appeals Study: Some Summary Finding* (Manchester Metropolitan University, unpublished).
33. Diana Scully, *Understanding Sexual Violence* (London: Unwin Hyman, 1990), p. 166.
34. Interview with the author, April 2003.
35. N.8 above, p. 200.
36. See e.g. Susan Brownmiller, *Against Our Will*, n.9 above; Robin Warshaw, *I Never Called it Rape*, n.5 above; Susan Lees, *Carnal Knowledge*, n.1 above.

Notes to Introduction to Chapter 6

1. Robert Wintemute, *Sexual Orientation and Human Rights: The United States Constitution, the European Convention and the Canadian Charter* (Oxford: Oxford University Press, 1997).
2. Robert Wintemute, 'Recognising New Kinds of Direct Sex Discrimination: Transsexualism, Sexual Orientation and Dress Codes' (1997) 60 *Modern Law Review* 334.
3. *Macdonald* v. *Advocate General for Scotland; Pearce* v. *Governing Body of Mayfield School* [2003] UKHL 34 (House of Lords).

4. Robert Wintemute and Mads Andenaes (eds), *Legal Recognition of Same-sex Partnerships: A Study of National, European and International Law* (Oxford: Hart Publishing, 2001).

5. *Fretté* v. *France* [2002] 2 FEC 39 (European Court of Human Rights).

Notes to Chapter 6

1. The exception was Italy. See Kees Waaldijk, 'Towards the Recognition of Same-sex Partners in European Union Law: Expectations Based on Trends in National Law', in Robert Wintemute (ed.) and Mads Andenaes (hon. co-ed.), *Legal Recognition of Same-sex Partnerships: A Study of National, European and International Law* (Oxford, Hart Publishing, 2001), pp. 649–50, 651 n.60.

2. Civil Code, Book 1, Article 30(1), as amended by the Act on the Opening Up of Marriage of 21 December 2000, in force on 1 April 2001.

3. See Wintemute, *supra* n.1, at pp. 775–9, and updated version at http://www.ilga.org (World Legal Survey, Laws Recognizing Same-Sex Partnerships). The thirteen EU member states are: Austria, Belgium, Denmark, Finland, France, Germany, Hungary, Luxembourg, the Netherlands, Portugal, Spain, Sweden, and the UK. In Austria, recognition of same-sex partners has so far been limited to criminal law (e.g. the right not to testify).

4. See Department of Trade and Industry, Women and Equality Unit, 'Civil Partnership: A Framework for the Legal Recognition of Same-sex Couples', http://www.womenandequality unit.gov.uk/research/pubn 2003.htm (30 June 2003); Civil Partnership Act 2004, http://www.hmso.gov.uk/acts.htm (royal assent on 18 November 2004).

5. Case C-249/96, *Grant* v. *South-West Trains* [1998] ECR I-621.

6. See *Gill* v. *El Vino Co Ltd.* [1983] QB 425 (CA).

7. All judgments and admissibility decisions of the European Court of Human Rights are available at http://www.echr.coe. int (HUDOC, Case Title = name of applicant; tick 'Decisions' at left if applicable).

8. See *Van Kück* v. *Germany* (12 June 2003) (German courts' failure to require private insurance company to reimburse cost of gender reassignment violated Article 8; not necessary to consider Article 14) (4–3 judgment). See also Robert Wintemute, ' "Within the Ambit": How Big *Is* the "Gap" in Article 14 European Convention on Human Rights?' [2004] *European Human Rights Law Review* 366; 'Filling the Article 14 "Gap": Government Ratification and Judicial Control of Protocol No. 12 ECHR', [2004] *European Human Rights Law Review* 484.

9. See http://europa.eu.int/eur-lex/en/search/search_lif.html (Year = 2000, No. = 78).

10. See *Sheffield & Horsham* v. *UK*, para. 66.

11. See *Bellinger* v. *Bellinger* [2003] 2 All ER 593. Cf. *A.* v. *Chief Constable of West Yorkshire Police*, [2004] 3 All ER 145 (a transsexual woman is legally female when searching another person as a police officer, but legally male if she seeks to marry a man).

12. See http://www.lcd.gov.uk/constitution/transsex/index.htm.

13. Case C-117/01, [2004] IRLR 240.

14. Case C-13/94, [1996] ECR I-2143.

15. Joined Cases C-122/99 P, C-125/99 P, [2001] ECR I-4319.

16. See Robert Wintemute, 'Strasbourg to the Rescue? Same-sex Partners and Parents Under the European Convention', in Wintemute, *supra* n.1, at pp. 714–18.

17. One of the main reasons for the Court's declaring *Mata Estevez* v. *Spain* (Application No. 56501/00) inadmissible on 10 May 2001 would seem to be that the applicant was not represented by a lawyer, and therefore could not present the arguments for departing from the Commission's case law.

18. Application No. 40016/98.

19. Communication No. 941/2000, 18 September 2003 (views adopted on 6 August 2003), http://www.unhchr.ch/tbs/doc.nsf (Search the Database, 'Edward Young').

20. Communication No. 488/1992, 4 April 1994 (views adopted on 31 March 1994), http://www. unhchr.ch/tbs/doc.nsf (Search the Database, 'Toonen').

21. Communication No. 902/1999, 30 July 2002 (views adopted on 17 July 2002), http://www. unhchr.ch/tbs/doc.nsf (Search the Database, 'Joslin').

22. Views of the Committee, para. 10.4.

23. UN Secretariat, 'Secretary-General's bulletin: Family Status for Purposes of United Nations Entitlements', ST/SGB/2004/4, 20 January 2004; replaced by 'Secretary-General's bulletin: Personal Status for Purposes of United Nations Entitlements', ST/SGB/2004/13, 24 September 2004. See also *Jean-Christophe Adrian* v. *Secretary-General*, 30 September 2004 (judgment adopted on 23 July 2004), Case No. 1276, Judgment No. 1183, http://www.ficsa.org/news/news.asp?NewsID=133 (Administrative Tribunal of the United Nations) (French *PaCS* of UN staff member with his male partner gives rise to spousal rights).

24. The Act provides (in ss. 4–5) that married couples who, after the gender reassignment of one partner, are factually same-sex but legally different-sex must divorce before the gender reassignment can be legally recognized. After legal recognition, they become factually and legally same-sex and unable to marry.

25. See Anne Barlow, *Cohabitants and the Law*, 3rd edn (London, Butterworths, 2001).

26. *Miron* v. *Trudel* [1995] 2 SCR 418.

27. *Nova Scotia (Attorney General)* v. *Walsh* [2002] 4 SCR 325.

28. See *Saucedo Gómez* v. *Spain* (Application No. 37784/97) (26 January 1999) (inadmissible) (rights upon relationship breakdown).

29. See *Shackell* v. *UK* (Application No. 45851/99) (27 April 2000) (inadmissible) (entitlement to widow's social security benefits).

30. [1999] 2 SCR 3.

31. See Robert Wintemute, 'Sexual Orientation and the Charter: The Achievement of Formal Legal Equality (1985–2005) and Its Limits', (2004) 49 *McGill LJ* 1143, 1156 n.58.

32. [1999] 4 All ER 705.

33. [2002] 4 All ER 1162 (CA), [2004] 3 All ER 401 (HL).

34. See Robert Wintemute, 'Same-sex Partners, "Living as Husband and Wife", and Section 3 of the Human Rights Act 1998', [2003] *Public Law* 621; Robert Wintemute, 'Sexual Orientation and Gender Identity', in Colin Harvey (ed.), *Human Rights in the Community* (Oxford, Hart Publishing, 2005). The Civil Partnership Act 2004 makes many of the necessary changes.

35. The Court has followed *National Coalition* in *Satchwell* (25 July 2002, 17 March 2003), *Du Toit* (10 September 2002), and *J. & B.* (28 March 2003). Judgments of the Court are available at http://www.concourt.org.za.

36. Cf. *James* v. *Eastleigh Borough Council*, [1990] 2 All ER 607 (House of Lords) (direct sex discrimination where a 'facially neutral' rule, all pensioners swim for free, incorporated the direct sex discrimination inherent in the different retirement ages for women and men).

37. See *Saucedo Gómez* and *Shackell, supra* nn.28–29.

38. Cf. *Thlimmenos* v. *Greece* (2000) (Articles 14 and 9 of the Convention required an exemption, for a Jehovah's Witness unable to perform military service for religious reasons, from a neutral rule barring persons convicted of felonies from the profession of chartered accountant).

39. See *supra* n.21.

40. *M.W.* v. *UK*, Application No. 11313/02 (denial to same-sex partner of bereavement benefits provided only to legal spouse of deceased). See *Liberty Newsletter* (Summer 2002, Case

Notes), http://www.liberty-human-rights.org.uk/resources/
newsletters/pdf-docs/summer-02.pdf. Cf. *Shackell, supra* n.29;
Mata Estevez, supra n.17.

41. Recital 22. Arguments of direct and indirect discrimination
were rejected in *R. v. Secretary of State for Trade and Industry, ex
parte Amicus*, [2004] IRLR 430 (QB Div, Admin Ct). Yet in
2004, the EC legislature provided an exemption from marriage
requirements for the same-sex partners of EC staff members,
effectively reversing the outcome in *D. & Sweden v. Council*. See
Staff Regulations, Article 1d(1), as amended by Council Regulation 723/2004/EC, Official Journal, 27 April 2004, L 124, p. 5:
'non-marital partnerships shall be treated as marriage provided
that [the couple produces a legal document recognised as such
by a Member State, acknowledging their status as non-marital
partners, and the couple has no access to legal marriage in a
Member State]'.

42. 388 US 1 (1967).

43. 347 US 483 (1954).

44. See *supra* n.2.

45. Law of 13 February 2003 opening up marriage to persons of
the same sex and modifying certain provisions of the Civil
Code, *Moniteur belge*, 28 February 2003, p. 9880 (in force on
1 June 2003).

46. The next two could be Spain (where the government approved
a *proyecto de ley* or bill on 30 December 2004), and Sweden
(where the legal differences between civil marriage and registered partnership will soon be eliminated, and Parliament has
asked the government to appoint a commission of inquiry on
gender-neutral marriage legislation).

47. See *Halpern v. Canada (Attorney General)* (10 June 2003), 65 OR
(3rd) 161, http://www.ontariocourts.on.ca/decisions/2003/
june/halpernC39172.htm (Ont. CA) (ordering immediate
issuance of marriage licences); *EGALE Canada Inc. v. Canada
(Attorney General)* (indexed by court as *Barbeau v. British*

Columbia (Attorney General)) (1 May 2003), 225 DLR (4th) 472, http://www.courts.gov.bc.ca/../../../../jdb-txt/ca/03/02/ 2003BCCA0251.htm (BCCA) (suspending judgment until 12 July 2004), (8 July 2003), 228 DLR (4th) 416, http://www.courts. gov.bc.ca/Jdb-txt/CA/03/04/2003BCCA0406.htm (BCCA) (ordering immediate issuance of marriage licences); *Goodridge* v. *Department of Public Health*, 798 NE2d 941 (Mass., 18 November 2003) (4–3) (Massachusetts Constitution requires equal access to civil marriage for same-sex couples from 17 May 2004); *In re the Opinions of the Justices to the Senate*, 802 NE2d 605 (Mass., 3 February 2004) (4–3) (a separate law establishing 'civil unions' for same-sex couples only is not sufficient); *Ligue catholique pour les droits de l'homme* v. *Hendricks* (19 March 2004), http:// www.jugements.qc.ca/primeur/documents/liguecatholique-19032004.doc (Qué. CA) (ordering immediate issuance of marriage licenses, subject to twenty-day statutory waiting period). See also *Fourie* v. *Minister of Home Affairs* (30 November 2004), http://www.server.law.wits.ac.za/sca/index.php (Supreme Court of Appeal of South Africa) (developing the common law concept of marriage to embrace same-sex partners, but leaving in place statutory obstacles not challenged in the case).

48. In Canada, the federal government decided not to appeal the decisions of the Ontario and BC courts. Instead, it asked the Supreme Court of Canada to approve a draft bill opening up civil marriage to same-sex couples in every province and territory of Canada. The Court did so on 9 December 2004. See *Reference re Same-Sex Marriage*, 2004 SCC 79, http://www.lexum.umontreal.ca/csc-scc/en/index.html. The federal government plans to introduce the bill in the federal House of Commons early in 2005.

49. It is authorized by express legislation or a decision of the highest court in British Columbia, Manitoba, Newfoundland, Northwest Territories, Ontario, Québec, Saskatchewan, California,

Connecticut, District of Columbia, Massachusetts, Illinois, New Jersey, New York, Pennsylvania and Vermont.

50. See ss. 50(1), 51(2), 144(4).

51. Legislation on joint adoption by de facto couples in the Navarra, Basque Country and Aragon regions of Spain would appear to be as broad as Sweden's. The Spanish government's proposed legislation allowing same-sex couples to marry would also cover joint adoption.

52. Bills that would end this exclusion are pending in the Belgian Parliament.

53. Exceptions include the laws in Germany, which would be in category (1) but for the opposition of the *Bundesrat*, and in several US states, where there is great concern that full inclusion of different-sex couples even in a category (2) law would undermine the attractiveness of marriage to such couples. They are included in Hawaii, only if they are legally unable to marry, and in New Jersey (and California in category (1)), only if they are aged 62 or over and would lose social security benefits if they married.

54. For citations for most of the laws in Table 6.1, see Wintemute, *supra* n.3.

55. See Law Society of England and Wales, 'Cohabitation: The Case for Clear Law: Proposals for Reform' (19 July 2002), http://www.lawsociety.org.uk/influencinglaw/policyin response/view=article.law?DOCUMENTID=207751.

56. 'BBC puts end to "honeymoon cash" for gays', *Independent* (24 May 1994), p. 2.

57. See Robert Wintemute, *Sexual Orientation and Human Rights: The United States Constitution, the European Convention, and the Canadian Charter* (Oxford, Oxford University Press, 1995, 1997); 'Recognising New Kinds of Direct Sex Discrimination: Transsexualism, Sexual Orientation and Dress Codes' (1997) 60 *Modern Law Review* 334: 'Sex Discrimination in *MacDonald* and *Pearce*; Why the Law Lords Chose the

Wrong Comparators', (2003) 14 *King's College Law Journal* 267.

58. See Nicholas Bamforth, 'Same-sex Partnerships and Arguments of Justice', in Wintemute, *supra* n.1, pp. 46–53 (on 'new natural law').

59. David Frum, 'Any serious attempt to promote marriage as an institution excludes nearly every item on the gay-rights agenda', *Saturday Night* (Canada) (December 1995), p. 67.

60. See Janet Halley, 'Recognition, Rights, Regulation, Normalization: Rhetorics of Justification in the Same-Sex Marriage Debate', and William N. Eskridge, Jr., 'The Ideological Structure of the Same-Sex Marriage Debate (And Some Postmodern Arguments for Same-Sex Marriage)', in Wintemute, *supra* n.1.

61. See 'Beyond Conjugality: Recognizing and Supporting Close Personal Adult Relationships' (21 December 2001), http://www.lcc.gc.ca/en/themes/pr/cpra/report.asp.

62. See *supra* n.3.

63. See http://www.oecd.org/dataoecd/48/5/2371372.pdf (purchasing power parity).

64. See http://news.bbc.co.uk/1/low/world/south_asia/1357249. stm (29 May 2001 report on marriage of Jaya Verma and Tanuja Chauhan in Ambikapur, Chattisgarh State).

65. *Chairperson of the Immigration Selection Board* v. *Frank*, Case No. SA 8/99 (Supreme Court of Namibia, 5 March 2001) (reversing trial decision ordering that German female partner of Namibian woman be granted permanent residence).

66. *Proyecto de ley de Unión Civil para parejas del mismo sexo 'parteneriato'*, *Diputada* Laura C. Musa, *Cámara de Diputados*, 11 December 1998, No. 7816-D-98, http://www.sigla.org.ar (*Derechos Civiles*).

67. *Projeto de Lei No. 1151 de 1995, Disciplina a parceria civil registrada entre pessoas do mesmo sexo e dá outras providências*, http://www. arco-iris.org.br/ prt/leis/c leis 1151.htm.

68. See *Proyecto de Ley de Fomento de la no Discriminación y Contrato de Unión Civil entre Personas del Mismo Sexo*, http://www.movilh. org/modules.php?name=News&file=article&sid=148 (2 June 2003).

69. See *Proyecto de ley No. 43 de 2002 por la cual se reconocen las uniones de parejas del mismo sexo, sus efectos patrimoniales y otros derechos*, http://www.piedadcordoba.net/ipw-web/portal/cms/ modules.php/name=News&file=article&sid=76.

70. See http://web.amnesty.org/shop/index/ISBN 0862103029. See also Vanessa Baird, *Sex, Love and Homophobia: Lesbian, gay, bisexual and transgendeer lives* (Amnesty International UK, July 2004), http://www.amnesty.org.uk/lgbt/books/.

71. See http://www.amnesty.org/library/index/ ENGMDE120092003 (13 March 2003). See also Scott Long, *In a Time of Torture: The Assault on Justice in Egypt's Crackdown on Homosexual Conduct* (Human Rights Watch, 2004), http:// hrw.org/reports/2004/egypt0304.

72. For a longer discussion, see Robert Wintemute, 'Religion vs. Sexual Orientation: A Clash of Human Rights?' (University of Toronto), *Journal of Law and Equality* (2002) 1, p. 125. http:// www.jle.ca/files/vln2/JLEvln2art1.pdf.

73. 'Family, Marriage and "De Facto" Unions' (Pontifical Council for the Family, dated 26 July 2000, published on 21 November 2000), http://www.vatican.va/roman curia/ pontifical councils/family, paras. 23, 47 (emphasis added).

74. 'Considerations Regarding Proposals to Give Legal Recognition to Unions Between Homosexual Persons' (approved by Pope John Paul II on 28 March 2003, dated 3 June 2003, published on 31 July 2003), http://www.vatican.va/roman curia/ congregations/cfaith/documents/rc con cfaith doc 20030731 homosexual-unions en.html. (emphasis added).

75. See Islamic Penal Law approved by the Islamic Consultancy Parliament on 30 July 1991, ch. 1, Articles 110, 131.

76. See http://www.iglhrc.org/php/section.php?id=5&detail=88

(but it is not clear whether sexual activity involved minors who did not consent or could not legally consent).

77. See http://www.iglhrc.org/php/section.php?id=5&detail=309.

78. On 3 November 2002, the Adalet ve Kalkinma Partisi (Justice and Development Party), a moderate descendant of the Welfare Party that does not advocate the imposition of shari'a law, won a majority in the Turkish Parliament.

79. See http://www.amnesty.org.uk, http://www.hrw.org, http://www.ilga.org, http://www.ilga–europe.org, http://www.iglhrc.org, http://www.arc-international.net.

Notes to Chapter 7

1. Acknowledgements: I would like to thank Gillian Slovo for her most helpful and generous comments and response; David Edgar, whose play *The Prisoner's Dilemma* helped me think about these issues; Jacqueline Rose for inspiring my interest in the first place; Hermione Lee, Kenneth Gross, Megan Vaughan, Timberlake Wertenbaker, Lisa Appignanesi, Eileen Wanquet, Jonathan Keates, Roy Foster, Susan Rubin Suleiman, Ian Buruma, Elleke Boehmer, Alberto Manguel and Wes Williams for offering many helpful suggestions; Imogen Cornwall-Jones for research help, and Anthony Barnett, Susan Mary Richards, Isobel Hilton, David Hayes and Rosemary Bechler at open-Democracy.net for their work on the web version.

2. Roy L. Brooks, 'Introduction', in Roy L. Brooks (ed.), *When Sorry Isn't Enough: The Controversy over Apologies and Reparations for Human Injustice* (New York: New York University Press, 1999), p. 3.

3. Wole Soyinka, *The Burden of Memory; The Muse of Forgiveness* (New York: Oxford University Press, 1999), p. 9, quoted in Jacqueline Rose, 'Apathy and Accountability: The Challenge of South Africa's Truth and Reconciliation Commission to the

Intellectual in the Modern World', in Helen Small (ed.), *The Public Intellectual* (Oxford: Blackwell, 2002).

4. Aeschylus, *Prometheus Bound*, trans. Philip Vellacott (Harmondsworth: Penguin, 1961), p. 40.

5. Julia Kristeva, *Strangers to Ourselves*, trans. Leon S. Roudiez (New York: Columbia University Press, 1991), p. 46, quoting Marcel Detienne, *Ecriture d'Orphée*.

6. Adrienne Rich, 'Eastern War Time', in *An Atlas of the Difficult World: Poems 1988–1991* (New York: Norton, 1991), p. 46.

7. Rich, 'Through Corralitos under Rolls of Cloud', op cit., p. 48.

8. Toni Morrison, *Jazz* (London: Chatto & Windus, 1992), p. 161.

9. *The History of Mary Prince A West Indian Slave Related By Herself* [1831], ed. Moira Ferguson (London, 1987).

10. Jacqueline Rose, 'Apathy and Accountability . . .', in Helen Small (ed.), *The Public Intellectual* (Oxford: Blackwell, 2002), p. 175.

11. R.F. Foster, *The Irish Story: Telling Tales and Making it Up in Ireland* (Oxford: Oxford University Press, 2001).

12. Augustine, *Confessions: Books I–XIII*, trans. F.J. Sheed [1942–43], Introduction by Peter Brown (Indianapolis, IN and Cambridge: Hackett, 1993), Book X, II, p. 173.

13. Peter Brooks, *Troubling Confessions: Speaking Guilt in Law and Literature* (Chicago, IL: Chicago University Press, 2001).

14. Ibid., X, VI, pp. 176–177.

15. Jacques Derrida, 'La Littérature du secret', in Chantal Zabus (ed.), *Le Secret: motif et moteur de la littérature* (Louvain-la-Neuve: Recueil de Travaux, 1999), pp. 1–34, esp. p. 7.

16. Jacqueline Rose, 'Aux marges du littéraire: Justice, Verité, Réconciliation', in Julia Kristeva and Evelyne Grossman (eds), *Actes du colloque: Où en est-on avec la théorie littéraire?* (Paris VII, 1999), *Textuel* 37, April 2000, pp. 99–107.

17. See Jacqueline Rose, 'Apathy and Accountability . . .', in Helen

Small (ed.), *The Public Intellectual* (Oxford: Blackwell, 2002), p. 163.

18. Anthea Jeffery, *The Truth about the Truth Commission* (London, 1999).

19. R.W. Johnson, 'Why There Is No Easy Way to Dispose of Painful History', *London Review of Books*, 14 October 1999, pp. 9–11.

20. Ian Buruma, 'The Joys and Perils of Victimhood', *New York Review of Books*, 8 April 1999.

21. Justice in the World's Light, a discussion between Juan Garces, Geoffrey Bindman, Isabel Hilton and Anthony Barnett, www.openDemocracy.net, 15 June 2001.

22. Rose, 'Aux marges du littéraire'.

23. Gillian Slovo, from the 'Sorry! The politics of apology' debate, posted on www.openDemocracy.net, 5 December 2002.

24. Ibid.

25. Antjie Krog, *Country of My Skull: Guilt, Sorrow and the Limits of Forgiveness in the New South Africa*, ed. Luke Mitchell (London: Vintage, 1999), pp. 269–290; see also Carli Coetzee, ' "They Never Wept, the Men of my Race": Antjie Krog's *Country of My Skull* and the White South African Signature' (2001) 27 *Journal of Southern African Studies*, pp. 685–696.

26. Ibid., p. 292.

27. Elazar Barkan, *The Guilt of Nations: Restitution and Negotiating Historical Injustices* (Baltimore, MD, and London: Johns Hopkins University Press, 2000).

28. Ed Vuilliamy, 'Black Leaders Divided Over Reparations for Slavery', *Guardian*, 26 August 2001.

Index